Battlefields
of the
Civil War

A Guide for Travellers

Battlefields
of the
Civil War

A Guide for Travellers

Blair Howard

HUNTER
PUBLISHING INC

Hunter Publishing, Inc.
130 Campus Drive, Edison NJ 08818
732 225 1900, 800 255 0343, Fax 732 417 0482
e-mail: hunterpub@emi.net

In Canada
1220 Nicholson Rd., Newmarket, Ontario
Canada L3Y 7V1, 800 399 6858, Fax 800 363 2665

In the UK
Windsor Books International
The Boundary, Wheatley Road, Garsington
Oxford, OX44 9EJ England
01865-361122, Fax 01865-361133

ISBN 1-55650-847-6

Second Edition © 1998 Blair Howard

Maps by Joyce Huber, PhotoGraphics

Cover photograph by Frederica Georgia/*Photo Network*

For complete information about the hundreds of other travel
guides offered by Hunter Publishing, visit our Web site at:
www.hunterpublishing.com

4 3 2 1

Contents

Foreword

To the casual visitor the "National Military Park" is just another nice place to visit, to spend a quiet day out with kids. It is the mission of this book to change that; by telling the story, in as simple terms as possible, of the action as it took place; by bringing back to life a few of the principle characters and the deeds they performed while under the greatest stress imaginable. The National Parks, these special portions of our heritage, should mean more to us than a simple picnic on a sunny afternoon in some pleasant spot that has little more significance than any other weekend getaway spot. If we can help you to understand a little of what occurred, and why – and if when you visit one of these great fields of battle you are able to follow the action via the ship of your imagination – then you will surely become at least a little richer for the experience.

Please, take the time to read each story as you tour your chosen "Field of Dreams." Take the time to ponder the great events that took place upon them; events that changed the face of our nation, at once, and forever.

Chapter 1

An Introduction

During the years 1861 to 1865 the nation was involved in a great civil war. It was a vicious war – a war where combatants that once might have lived next door to one another engaged in such blood-letting as the world had never seen before. Men who once stood side by side in church on Sunday fought one against the other for causes that could and would change the course of the nation for ever.

In the early days, as the first shots were being fired, it was a war almost romantic in its concept. Men of both sides, each with great ideals, donned heroic uniforms and sallied forth laughing and boasting of the great deeds they would do. By the time the war ended it had cost the nation dearly. More than 600,000 young men had given their lives for one cause or the other.

The situation at the start in January 1861 was as follows: The North consisted of 23 states, seven territories and a population in excess of 20 million people; the South numbered eleven states and a population of only nine million, more than three million of whom were slaves. The economy of the North was, for the most-part, an industrial one; the South had an agrarian economy and essentially only one crop – cotton. The North raised more food and its manufacturing capacity was at least five times greater than that of the South. More than 70% of the nation's railroads were in the North, and most of the nation's money was on deposit in Northern banks.

Although the North had some four million men eligible for military duty against a little more than one million in the South, it was not felt at the time that the South, should the situation deteriorate into war, would be at any great military disadvantage. After all, even the most casual observer had to agree that military leadership would be the most crucial element, and in this the South was by far superior. An extraordinary number of West Point graduates came from the South, almost all of whom, including Robert E. Lee, defected to answer the Confederate call to arms. Many officers in the United States Navy did the same, returning to their homeland and forming the nucleus of the Confederate Navy.

The beginnings of the conflict can be traced back to the arrival of the first slaves in Jamestown in 1619, and certainly to Thomas Jefferson's Declaration of Independence of 1776 that declares as self-evident truth that all men are created equal. During the years that followed the Declaration a number of incidents that built eventually into a tidal wave of public opinion against slavery pushed the nation inevitably toward civil war. By 1800 several Northern states had passed laws abolishing slavery, and by January 1808 the importation of slaves into the United States had ended. This, however, did not end the breeding and buying and selling of slaves already within the country. In May 1824 and again in April 1828 Congress passed Protected Tariff Laws that discriminated against the slave states of the South, causing the president of South Carolina College in Columbia to ask, "*Is it worthwhile to continue this Union of States, where the North demands to be our masters and we are required to be their tributaries?*"

In January 1831 William Lloyd Garrison began publishing *The Liberator,* a newspaper dedicated to the abolition of slavery, and in November 1832 South Carolina nullified the Tariff Acts of 1824 and 1828, declaring itself prepared to secede from the Union if the government decided to use force.

By 1856 events were rapidly approaching boiling point and the situation was made even worse when Senator Charles Sumner of Massachusetts rose in the Senate and delivered a blistering attack on the South in general, and on Senator Andrew P. Butler in particular. The situation deteriorated even further when representatives from South Carolina walked into the Senate and beat Sumner into unconsciousness.

Things came to a head on October 16th, 1859, when abolitionist

John Brown together with a group of five blacks and sixteen whites, including his own sons, launched an attack on the Federal arsenal at Harper's Ferry in Virginia. The force of United States Marines that was sent to put down the insurrection was led by a man who within just a couple of years was to become legend: Colonel Robert E. Lee.

Finally, on December 20, 1860, the following was published in the *Charleston Mercury*:

"Passed unanimously at 1.15 o'clock, p.m. December 20th, 1860. An Ordinance. To dissolve the Union between the State of South Carolina and other states united with her under the compact entitled "The Constitution of the United States of America." We, the people of the State of South Carolina, in Convention assembled, do declare and ordain, and it is hereby declared and ordained, that the ordinance adopted by us in Convention, on the twenty third day of May, in the year of our Lord one thousand seven hundred and eighty eight, whereby the Constitution of the United States of America was ratified and also, all acts and parts of Acts of the general Assembly of this State, ratifying amendments of the said Constitution, are hereby repealed; and that the union now subsisting between South Carolina and other States, under the name of "United States of America," is hereby dissolved. THE UNION IS DISSOLVED."

As the cold days of 1860 ended the new year began in a blaze of rhetoric. On January 21 Jefferson Davis, the senior Senator from Mississippi, rose from his seat in the Senate to address the assembly.

"I rise, Mr. President, for the purpose of announcing to the Senate that I have satisfactory evidence that the State of Mississippi, by a solemn ordinance of her people in convention assembled, has declared her separation from the United States." On February 20th, 1861, in Montgomery, Alabama, Jefferson Davis took the oath as the first President of the Confederate States of America. And so it began.

The opening shots of the war were fired almost in a holiday

atmosphere. Fort Sumter in South Carolina fell to the Confederacy on April 13. Two days later President Lincoln issued a proclamation that called into service 75,000 militia for three years and did in effect declare war on the Confederacy.

The Civil War of 1861 to 1865 has, over a century and a half, taken on a new appeal. The stories of individual heroism, desperate battles, and great men have passed into legend. Tales of Lee, Jackson, Stuart, Thomas, Sherman, and Grant now compete on equal terms with those of Agamemnon, Ulysses, Paris and Achilles. The names of the great battles of the Civil War: Shiloh, Antietam, Gettysburg, and Chancellorsville have gone down in history alongside those of Troy, Crecy, and Agincourt.

Today, all that remains to remind us of the dreadful days of the Civil War are a handful of National Military Parks dedicated to the memory of those that died there. Most are quiet places; places where one can be alone, close to history, close to the men whose names ring out as clearly as they did in the throes of fearful conflict. They are places where one can sit and think, reflect perhaps upon the legacy of those desperate times. They are places where one cannot fail to be moved by the presence of something very intense, though not easily described, that remains locked within the trees and stones of these great fields of war.

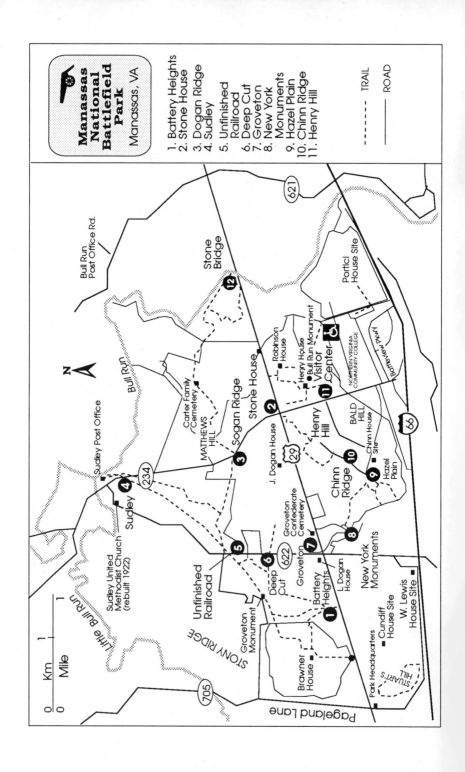

Chapter 2

1st Manassas

July, 1861

The Manassas National Military Park is located 26 miles south of Washington DC near the intersection of I-66 and VA 234 at 12521 Lee Highway, Manassas, VA 22110. The phone number is 703-754-1861. The Visitor Center is open daily except Christmas.

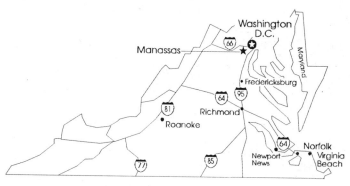

By the evening of July 21st, 1861, after the sounds of the first shots of the Civil War proper had died away and the smoke of battle had cleared, those two names would be echoing across the nation. It was the real beginning of a conflict that would have a momentous effect on the American continent. It signaled the end of an era, the end of an age of style and elegance. After Sunday, July 21st 1861, nothing would ever be quite the same.

After the fall of Fort Sumter on April 14th, 1861, there seemed to be a lull in the progress of the war. The two capitol cities of Washington and Richmond lay only 120 miles apart with four rivers separating them: the James, the York, the Rappahannock, and the Potomac. With the two capitol cities so close, it was only natural that each would seem a desirable military objective for the other. During the months following Fort Sumter and preceding Bull Run the two presidents, Lincoln and Davis, both came under pressure to advance upon the other's capitol. With the cry *"On to Richmond"* on their lips, the United States Congress had met in extraordinary session on July 4th; and on July 16th 35,000 men in a merry assortment of uniforms, none of which gave any indication of allegiance, marched out of Washington under the command of General Irvin McDowell.

Gen. Robert E. Lee.

Meanwhile, in Richmond, a man whose name was soon to become synonymous with Confederacy, Robert E. Lee, was making plans of his own. Lee, having examined his conscience and found that his heart and allegiance lay with his native Virginia, was newly retired from the United States Army and was serving as military adviser to Confederate President Jefferson Davis. Lee had already determined the importance of Manassas as a railroad junction and, because it was located only 30 miles or so from Washington, as a possible jumping-off point for an attack on the Union capital.

On May the 8th Confederate Brigadier General Philip St. George Cocke was stationed at Manassas Junction with four companies of infantry. By the end of the month he had been joined by Brigadier General M.L. Bonham with a full brigade, and on June 1st they were joined by General Pierre Gustave Toutant Beauregard, the victor of Fort Sumter, now in command of all Confederate forces in Northern Virginia.

Beauregard, too, was making plans to attack the Union capital. These involved General Joseph Eggleston Johnston and his army of 12,000 men who were, at this point, facing Union Brigadier General Robert Patterson's army of 18,000 in the Shenandoah Valley.

Beauregard's plan, as it was presented to Richmond on July 14th, was that Johnston should leave one fourth of his army guarding the passes to the Blue Ridge Mountains, moving the rest of his army to join Beauregard at Manassas Gap. They would then advance on Fairfax Courthouse and position themselves to attack the Union forces at Falls Church and Alexandria, thus driving them into the Potomac River. This done they would together smash Patterson's army at Winchester, then advance from two sides on Washington itself.

Gen. P.G.T. Beauregard.

It was a bold plan, but one that never got off the ground. On July 16th General McDowell's army of five divisions marched out of Washington. By the evening of the 17th they had reached Fairfax Court House, 20 miles out of Washington, and were beginning to run into Confederate skirmishers. They chased these off and then celebrated the action by parading through the town with flags flying and the band playing. That evening General Beauregard made history by sending the first ever war-time telegraph to Richmond. It read: *"The enemy has assaulted my outposts in force. I have fallen back on the Bull Run,*

Gen. Joseph E. Johnston.

and will make a stand at Mitchell's Ford. If his force is overwhelming I shall retire to the Rappahannock Railroad Bridge, saving my command for defense there and future operations. Please inform Johnston of this, via Staunton, and also Holmes. Send forward any reinforcements at the earliest possible instant and to every possible means."

On the morning of July 18th General Johnston received the following telegram from Richmond, *"General Beauregard is attacked. To strike the enemy a decisive blow a junction of all your effective force will be needed. If practicable make the movement, sending your sick and baggage to Culpepper Court House either by railroad or by Warrenton. In all arrangements exercise your discretion."*

So, Johnston made his move. Rather than try to defeat Patterson, he decided his best course of action was simply to slip away from the area unnoticed, and he did. Meanwhile, General McDowell was marching happily on toward Centerville. Centerville was a sleepy little place, a stagecoach stop along the route from Washington to Winchester. By July the 20th, however, the community had taken on a new look. Most of McDowell's force was encamped there almost within range of the Confederate artillery across the Bull Run River to the west. Clearly, a major confrontation was imminent.

There was something of a holiday atmosphere about the encampment. All through the 19th and 20th the Union army received visitors from Washington. Many of them were local dignitaries, Senators, Congressmen and their ladies. All moved freely about the encampment as they wished. They came on horseback and in carriages with picnic baskets and their finest clothes ready for the festivities and the dancing to begin when the battle was over and the Rebels had been driven back to Richmond.

Meanwhile, at Manassas on the 20th of July, the first elements on General

Gen. Irwin McDowell.

Johnston's army were beginning to arrive by railroad from the Shenandoah Valley. These included a Virginia brigade under the command of General Thomas J. Jackson – a man who was within hours to become an American legend. Johnston himself arrived at noon in the company of General Bee and troops from Alabama and Mississippi. Beauregard's army now numbered close to 30,000.

That evening General McDowell gave orders that during the early morning hours of the next day, the 21st of July, his army was to move out across the Bull Run. At this stage in the war, however, there was little urgency in the movement of the troops, and although the Union artillery was ready to move at the appointed time the infantry was not. Tyler's division started down the turnpike toward Stone Bridge and the Bull Run; they were nearly an hour late. The divisions of Generals Hunter and

The 30-pounder Parrott fires the first shot at Bull Run.

Heintzelman's were to make for and cross Sudley Ford by no later than 7 a.m. It was a long, slow march of about six miles and, as dawn broke, the marching Union soldiers, choked by the dust of the road, took frequent breaks to pick blackberries and to fill their canteens.

The first shot of the battle was fired sometime after daylight. As the Union force was still moving slowly into position a deafening report rang out across the battlefield. It had been fired with some pomp and ceremony by artillery Captain Carlyle from a 30-pounder Parrott rifle, a huge cannon brought along especially for the occasion. The battle of 1st Manassas had begun.

The main tour of the 1st Manassas battlefield is a short one, a walk of about one mile, with side trails, around most of the main points of interest. You can follow the tour markers and listen to the taped descriptions to be found at each stop, or you can wander around this small portion as you will, arriving at each stop however it might suit you best. If you decide to do it that way you might like to go first to the Jackson equestrian monument just to the east of, and behind, the Visitor Center on Henry Hill.

Henry Hill:
It is close to this position that General Jackson earned his famous nickname. As soon as he arrived on the field he was able to see that Henry Hill would be a deciding factor in the battle. He deployed his brigade of Virginians here on the hill and waited for the advancing Union army as it approached from the across the Warrenton road pushing the brigades of Bartow, Evans, and Bee in front of them in one great disorganized and retreating mob. General Bee, spotting Jackson and his brigade on the hill in front of him, waved his sword and shouted, *"Look! There stands Jackson like a stone wall! Rally behind the Virginians!"* And, for the most-part, they did, and General Thomas J. Jackson had gained a nickname that would make him immortal. General Bee was fatally wounded only moments later. You will find his memorial about100 feet away from here to the south.

> From the Jackson memorial you might like to walk over to the row of cannon just to the south of the rebuilt Henry House.

Sometime around the middle of the afternoon General McDowell ordered an assault on Henry Hill. To support the action he sent two batteries of artillery under the commands of Captains Charles Griffin and James Ricketts to this position just 300 yards from the Confederate artillery position of some 26 guns, marked by the row of cannon close to the Jackson monument. Griffin and Ricketts opened fire on the Confederates with devastating effect but soon came under rifle fire from the Henry House. Immediately they turned several of their guns on the house causing severe damage to it, and the death of the Widow Judith Henry, for whom the hill was named. Before long, however, Griffin and Ricketts found themselves to be in a dangerously exposed position. Their infantry support had been scattered to the four winds in a superb cavalry action by Col. J.E.B. (Jeb) Stuart. And then, just when all seemed lost, they saw what they believed to be help on the way. A blue-coated regiment of infantry was moving quickly toward them. Believing them to be Union soldiers they held their fire until it was too late. The 33rd Virginia infantry delivered a devastating volley of fire that put both of the Union batteries out of action and

The Stone House at Manassas.

captured the guns for the Confederacy. Quickly a Federal counter attack was mounted and the guns were recaptured. And so it went on, one counter attack after another. The guns changed hands repeatedly and eventually were of no further use in the battle to either side.

At this early point in the war there was much confusion on the battle-field because of the similarities of uniforms. Some Union regiments wore gray and some Confederate units wore blue. Even the two national flags were similar enough to cause confusion. In fact it was at 1st Manassas that General Beauregard redesigned the Confederate battle flag, creating the Stars and Bars.

When you are ready to continue your tour it's just a short walk from Henry Hill to the top of Buck Hill located to the rear of the Stone House. There you will have a good view of Matthews Hill and the Stone House itself.

Matthews Hill:
This was the scene of the first major exchange in the first battle of Manassas. It was there, at about nine o'clock that morning, that Union Colonel Ambrose E. Burnside's brigade (he was the man with the famous whiskers) ran into Colonel Nathan Evans' Confederates, who had just moved into position after realizing that the Federals were crossing the Bull Run river at Sudley Ford. For awhile the Confederate force was able to hold its ground, but, as Burnside received reinforcements, they were slowly forced back toward the Warrenton Road. It was only the arrival of Confederate reinforcements in the form of General Bee and Colonel Bartow that saved them from a complete rout.

But further Union reinforcement forced the Confederates into retreat once again, across the Warrenton Road and up Henry Hill toward the Robinson House to the southeast.

The Stone House you see at the bottom of this hill was built in the early 1800s and was opened as a tavern. It was used a hospital during the war.

The Stone Bridge is where Confederate Colonel Nathan Evans was posted at dawn on the morning of the battle. It was General McDowell's plan to make the Confederates believe that he intended to cross the Bull Run here; his real intention, however, was to cross the river by way of Sudley Ford. Colonel Evans' brigade was deployed in line of battle on both sides of the road, behind the crest of the hills just to the west. In the early light of the dawn Evans' observers could see the clouds of dust kicked up by the marching feet of the approaching Union troops of General Tyler's division about a mile away in the distance. Immediately they prepared for action and by full daylight the Union force could be seen drawn up in line of battle some distance away in front of them. At about 5:30 a.m., echoing

The Stone Bridge.

across the fields, came the sound of the single shot fired from the huge Federal 30-pounder Parrott rifle of Captain Carlyle's battery, and the battle had begun.

For about an hour, at odd intervals, the two sides at the Stone Bridge exchanged musket and cannon fire. But, as time wore on, Evans began to realize that nothing was happening and he began to feel the Union force in front of him was nothing more than a diversion. It was about an hour after the start of action that Evans learned the main body of the Federal army was moving to the north, and that the real attack would come in the form of an assault on his left flank.

Leaving a small force to guard the Stone Bridge, Evans marched the remainder of his brigade, about 1,200 men and two 6-pounder cannon, upstream and across the valley of the Young's Branch tributary of the Bull Run to the high ground on Matthews Hill above the Stone House. He placed his force in line of battle so they could take advantage of a wide field of fire over the open fields across which he knew the Federals must come.

Chinn Ridge:
It was here at Chinn Ridge that the Confederates were able to rout the main Federal force and so bring about the end of the first battle of Manassas.

All day long the tide of battle had swung this way and that, and by mid afternoon the outcome still lay in the balance. At about 3 p.m. Confederate General Kirby Smith arrived with the last reinforcements from the Shenandoah Valley. He had not been long on the field when he was severely wounded and the command of his men fell to Colonel Arnold Elzey. Elzey and his men were rushed to the aid of the left flank of the main Confederate force just to the east of here. Colonel Jubal Early's brigade was thrown into the fight here on Chinn Ridge. At four o'clock that afternoon General Beauregard, sensing that he might have the advantage, whipped his army into a frenzy of excitement and enthusiasm. The Confederate army surged forward and, for the first time during the war, screamed the rebel yell, rending the air and filling the waiting Federal troops with terror. It was too

Edmund Ruffin, who fired the final shot.

much. The Federal line broke under the first onslaught of the screaming Southerners. The vast majority of the Union force panicked, abandoned their weapons and equipment, and ran headlong from the field. The rout was total. Men cut the harnesses of the wagon horses and rode them bareback from the field leaving their artillery and supplies behind.

The final shot of the battle was fired by an elderly southern volunteer. Edmund Ruffin, a prominent 67-year-old writer and an ardent secessionist, had fought all day long on the Confederate side. It was to him that went the honor of pulling the lanyard that signaled the end of the battle. The shot flew into the center of the Cub Run bridge hitting a Federal wagon, wrecking it and completely blocking the bridge, causing even more confusion to the fleeing Federals on the Warrenton turnpike. Ruffin survived the four years of the war only to commit suicide in 1865 rather than live out the rest of his life under the US government.

The Confederate victory at 1st Manassas was greeted with great jubilation all throughout the South. However, it was now very clear to both sides that they were in for a long and difficult struggle. Casualties on both sides, considering that the battle lasted only a single day, were heavy. The Federals lost 2,896 men killed, wounded, or missing; the Confederates, 1,982.

After the battle, Manassas settled down and once again became the sleepy little backwater it had been before the war, but not for long. A little more than a year later, in August of 1862, two great armies would once again do battle in the fields around Manassas Junction.

Where to Stay, What to Do in Manassas

Attractions:

The Manassas Museum: 9101 Prince William Street. Museum features collections dealing with the Northern Virginia Piedmont history from prehistoric to modern times with special emphasis on the Civil War. Open daily except Monday, closed Jan. 1st, Thanksgiving, Dec. 24th & 25th. Phone 368-1873.

Annual Events:

Prince William County Fair: Carnival, entertainment, tractor pull, exhibits. Phone 368-0173. Mid-August.

Re-enactment of Battle of Manassas: Long Park. Phone 361-7181. Last weekend in August.

Hotels:

Best Western: 8640 Mathis Ave. 703-368-7070. 60 rooms, under 12 free, crib free, cable TV, free continental breakfast, cafe adjacent, room service, check out 11 a.m., meeting rooms, free airport transportation, accepts credit cards.

Courtyard By Marriott: 10701 Battlefield Pkwy. 703-335-1300. 149 rooms, under 19 free, crib free, cable TV, pool, cafe, room service, check out 1 p.m., meeting rooms, accepts credit cards.

Days Inn: 10653 Balls Ford Road. 703-368-2800. 113 rooms, under 18 free, crib free, cable TV, pool, free coffee in lobby, check out 11 a.m., meeting rooms, accepts credit cards.

HoJo Inn: 7249 New Market Ct. 703-369-1700. 159 rooms, under 18 free, crib free, cable TV, free continental breakfast, cafe adjacent, check out 11 a.m., meeting rooms, accepts credit cards.

Ramada Inn: 10820 Balls Ford Rd. 703-361-8000. 121 rooms, under 18 free, crib free, cable TV, pool, cafe, room service, check out 11 a.m., meeting rooms, accepts credit cards.

Shoney's Inn: 8691 Phoenix Dr. 703-369-6323. 78 rooms, under 18 free, crib free, cable TV, pool, cafe adjacent, check out noon, meeting rooms, accepts credit cards.

Holiday Inn: 10800 Vandor Lane. 703-335-0000. 160 rooms, under 18 free, TV, pool, free continental breakfast, cafe, room service, check out noon, meeting rooms, accepts credit cards.

Quality Inn: 7295 Williamson Blvd. 703-369-1100. 125 rooms, under 18 free, crib free, cable TV, pool, free continental breakfast, check out 11 a.m., meeting rooms, accepts credit cards.

Restaurants:

Carmello's: 9108 Center St. 703-368-5522. Children's meals, specializes in fresh seafood, veal, chicken, own pasta; accepts credit cards.

Red, Hot & Blue: 8637 Sudley Road, 703-330-4847. Children's meals, specializes in smoked prime rib, pulled pork sandwich, Memphis pit barbecue. Accepts credit cards.

Chapter 3

Fort Donelson

February, 1862

Fort Donelson is on US 79 one mile west of Dover and 30 miles west of Clarksville, Tennessee. The Visitor Center is open daily from 8 a.m. to 4:30 p.m. During the summer months park service employees portray Confederate life around the reconstructed log hut encampment and give hourly demonstrations of musketry. There is a picnic area in the park, rest rooms, and several country walks for the energetic visitor. Admission is only $1. Phone 931-232-5348.

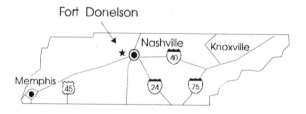

Fort Donelson National Military Park stands on the banks of the Cumberland River and is second only to Lookout Mountain for its natural beauty. The park is well worth a visit. The naval forces under the command of Union Flag Officer Andrew H. Foote thought otherwise. On February 14, 1862, after one and a half hours of withering Confederate cannon fire, the damage to Foote's ironclad gunboats was so extensive that he was forced to retreat up-river, and General Ulysses S. Grant was left to fend for himself. It would seem that he did very well, for only two days later he accepted the "unconditional surrender" of the Confederate garrison.

Gen. U.S. Grant.

The campaign for Forts Henry and Donelson began early in February 1862. The war so far had not been going well for President Lincoln and his armies; he desperately needed a victory. Ulysses S. Grant was, at that time, a nondescript brigadier general with what many perceived to be a real drinking problem. Be that as it may, he was, even then, one of the North's most aggressive commanders. He wrote of the situation on the two rivers in the West: *"The enemy at this time occupied points on the Tennessee and Cumberland rivers. The work on the Tennessee was called Fort Henry and that on the Cumberland Fort Donelson, at which points the two rivers approached within eleven miles of each other. These positions were of immense importance to the enemy and, of course, correspondingly important for us to possess ourselves of. With Fort Henry in our hands, we had a navigable stream open to us up to Muscle Shoals in Alabama. Fort Donelson was the gate to Nashville – a place of great military and political importance. These two points in our possession, the enemy would necessarily be thrown back to the boundary of the cotton states."* (From the *Personal Memoirs of U.S. Grant*, L. Webster & Co, New York, 1894). And so, when he heard that Confederate General P.G.T. Beauregard with a full division of infantry was marching at full speed to reinforce the two forts, he decided the best course of action was to capture them before Beauregard could get there.

The Confederate side of the story at the two forts was one of lost opportunities, poor judgment, and downright incompetence. General Albert Sidney Johnston was the darling of the Confederacy. President Jefferson Davis described him as the finest soldier in North America, but during the campaign for the river forts he made fundamental mistakes, the consequences of which would have a monumental effect upon the Confederate theater in the West.

Johnston's task, with an army of 75,000, was to defend the Confederacy in the West over an area stretching from the Appalachian Mountains to the Mississippi River. He was well aware of the fact that the

Gen. Albert Sidney Johnston.

Cumberland and Tennessee rivers offered the Union armies of Don Carlos Buell and Henry Halleck two major lines of communication straight into the heart of the Western Confederacy. To seal off the two rivers he had Fort Henry constructed on the Tennessee and Fort Donelson, less than eleven miles away, on the Cumberland. Neither position was a strong one, and neither fort was strongly garrisoned. By January of 1862 General Johnston had deployed his forces in a line that ran southeast from Columbus, Kentucky, to Forts Henry and Donelson, and then northeast again to Bowling Green.

In a joint effort with the United States Navy, General Grant moved against Fort Henry on February 6th. The fort's commander, Lloyd Tilghman, realizing he would be unable to hold the position, transferred the bulk of his Confederate garrison across the ten miles or so of swampy hinterland to Fort Donelson, thus swelling the defenders there from 5,000 to more than 16,000. Fort Henry fell to the ironclad gunboats of Union Flag Officer Foote before Grant had time to reach the field. Thus the stage was set for the battle over Fort Donelson.

You will find you have several options available to you when you arrive at the Visitor Center: First you might like to take either, or both, of the two hiking trails that wind their way around the battlefield. If you elect the hiking option your tour can be as short as three miles or as long as seven miles, depending upon the route you decide to take. If you take the walking tour you can leave your vehicle in the Park Service lot at the Visitor Center and obtain a Trail Guide at the information desk. If you are lucky with the weather, the walking tour is without doubt the best way to see all the points of interest in the park, and to enjoy an area of great natural beauty.

The second option, the one described here, is to take the driving tour: a seven-mile route around the park, out onto the highway to Dover, then back again to the Visitor Center. Whichever option you decide upon please be sure to observe all the rules of the countryside. Remain on the trails and walk facing the oncoming traffic when on the roads. Be alert for poison ivy, poisonous snakes, ticks, and spiders. Use extreme caution when walking down by the river. Do not walk or stand on rock walls, cannon or the earthworks. And be prepared for a strenuous walk in some of the wilder areas.
Your driving tour of the battlefield begins when you leave the Visitor Center and proceed along the tour route to Stop Number 1, Fort Donelson Proper, where you can leave your vehicle in the Park Service lot and visit stops one, two, and three on foot.

Fort Donelson Proper:
By now you are probably surprised to find only earthen ramparts instead of the tall stone or wooded walls we normally associate with the word "fort." However, you may be sure, that in every sense of the word, this was a fort to be reckoned with. The earthen ramparts were built by cutting and placing trees along the lines of defense and then covering them with earth. The earth would be taken from the outside of the intended rampart leaving a great trench, a moat if you will, that further enhanced the fortification. The walls on the inside of the fort originally were about six feet

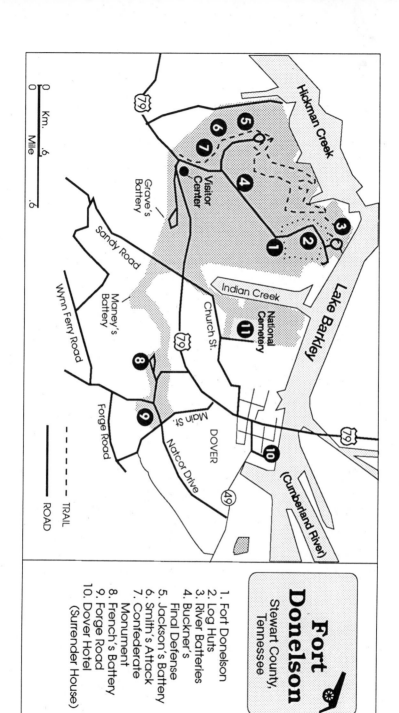

Fort Donelson
Stewart County, Tennessee

1. Fort Donelson
2. Log Huts
3. River Batteries
4. Buckner's
   Final Defense
5. Jackson's Battery
6. Smith's Attack
7. Confederate
   Monument
8. French's Battery
9. Forge Road
10. Dover Hotel
    (Surrender House)

TRAIL
ROAD

Km.
Mile

Hickman Creek
Lake Barkley
(Cumberland River)
DOVER
Indian Creek
National Cemetery
Visitor Center
Grave's Battery
Maney's Battery
Sandy Road
Wynn Ferry Road
Forge Road
Natcor Drive
Main St.
Church St.

in height; on the outside, to the bottom of the trench, about 12 feet.

The fort itself covers some 15 acres. It was built over a seven-month period by soldiers and slaves of the Confederacy. It was abandoned after the war and left to the ravages of time and the elements, until 1929 when it was refurbished and dedicated as a National Battlefield Park.

Inside the fort proper you will find several log huts, and possibly some Park Service employees acting out for you the everyday life of a soldier stationed at the fort in the early 1860s. The huts you see, by today's standards, are primitive, but in the long dark winters of the 19th century they were a veritable luxury. These few reproductions are a fair repre-

Water Battery, Fort Donelson.

sentation of the several hundred that housed first the Confederate garrison in early 1862, and then the Union force of occupation after the fall of the fort on February 16th 1862.

When you are ready to continue your tour take the footpath that leads to the River Batteries where you will find the fortified positions of the Upper and Lower Water Batteries. It was here that the battle for Fort Donelson commenced on the afternoon of February 14th.

Rear Adm. Andrew H. Foote.

The River Batteries:

The two batteries here were both armed with heavy coastal artillery. The Lower Battery consisted of eight 32-pounder cannon and one 10-inch colombiad. The Upper Battery was armed with two 32-pound caronades and a 6 1/2-inch rifled colombiad. The 32-pounders were capable of firing a 32-pound shot a distance of up to a mile; the colombiad was capable of hurling a 128-pound projectile more than three miles. As you can see, the great guns were mounted on fixed, wooden carriages and the two water batteries completely commanded the river approaches to the fort.

Flag Officer Andrew Foote, flushed with confidence after his easy victory at Fort Henry, was certain that the same tactics that had been so effective there some two weeks earlier would work here, too. He approached the fort with his fleet of gunboats comprising the four ironclads (*Louisville, Pittsburg, St. Louis,* and *Carondelet*) and two wooden gunboats (the *Conestoga* and the *Tyler*).

Once again, as he had at Fort Henry, Foote and his fleet approached the fort at close range hoping to batter the defenders into submission. It was not to be. As the ironclads rounded the river bend the Confederate cannoneers opened fire first with the 10-inch colombiad and 6 1/2-inch rifled gun. Foote was not to be deterred. On and on up the river he came until the fleet came within range of the 32-pounders; and still he pressed on, ignoring the devastating hail of heavy shot from the coastal batteries in the fort. Finally at a range of only 400 yards he opened fire with broadside after broadside from the mighty ironclad gunboats. But he had misjudged; the range was too close. His gunners, confined by the tiny gun ports on their boats, were unable to elevate their guns sufficiently to hit the defenses of the fort on the high ground. The gunners in the fort, however, were at no such disadvantage. They were able to batter the Union fleet at will. Eventually, after an hour and a half of sustained bombardment by both sides, three of Foote's ironclads, badly disabled, were drifting helplessly with current. Foote himself had been wounded and was left with no alternative but to withdraw his fleet. General Grant was left to finish the job alone.

Here's what one anonymous young Union sailor had to say about the engagement: *"The gunboats carefully steamed around the bend and maneuvered into position. Before they were ready to commence operations I noticed a puff of smoke appear at a certain point in one of the embankments. In a moment afterward I heard a boom and a terrible screech which filled the air. The leading gunboat returned the fire, that boat being the St. Louis under Flag Officer Foote. In a moment the Louisville also was in the action, and then the other ironclads of the fleet, the Carondelet and the Pittsburg, followed at some distance downstream by the wooden gunboats, the Tyler and the Conestoga.*

"When each boat arrived at the proper post, it delivered its fire and then circled around to reload and give the other boats opportunity to deliver their broadsides. Once in a while a solid shot from the fort would strike an iron-plated ship, make a deep dent in its armor and then glance off with a terrific splashing into the water. Then a shell would burst just over the deck,

Gun explosion on the Carondelet.

sending a perfect storm of iron hailstones down on the metal plates.

"At the very height of the engagement I saw a well-aimed bomb-shell enter the porthole of the Carondelet, exploding just within the opening, dismantling the cannon and wounding a dozen or more men. Through the din and confusion there could be distinguished officers' voices giving commands to the gunners, the cries of the wounded and the battering and hammering of the detail of men who at once were set to work to clear away the wreckage which had been made by the shell, so as to get the decks ready for action again. Thick and fast came the shells and bombs from the batteries, crashing on the iron plates, skipping across the waves, going clean through the smokestacks, tearing down the rigging; but still the lucky Commodore Foote kept his flagship, the St. Louis, in the forefront of the fight, and kept signaling to the others what to do. He had been wounded in the ankle, but he would not leave the field.

"After an hour and a half of this sort of work a couple of the boats, the flagship St. Louis, and the Louisville, were noticed to be in trouble. they moved wildly and falteringly hither and thither, and it was seen that the officers could not manage them. The

signals soon told the fleet what was wrong; the steering appara-
tus on both boats was out of gear, the pilothouse of the St. Louis
had been almost destroyed by round shot, and the machinery
injured so that the ships could not be maneuvered and soon
began to drift helplessly down the stream. The loss of the two
disabled ships so weakened the fleet that it was found necessary
to suspend the gunboat attack." (For more, see James Murfin's
Battlefields of the Civil War, Colour Library Books Ltd., (UK)
Surrey, England, 1988).

When you are ready to continue your tour you should make
your way back along the road the way you came until you
reach **Stop Number 4.**

Buckner's Final Defense:
Even though the fort's defenders had won the naval battle on
the river, the land engagement with Grant to the south of the
fort was not going quite so well. During the day Grant had
moved his army south and, by nightfall on the 14th, he had
completely surrounded the fort. It looked as though the defenders might be in for a long siege, a situation that could lead only
to one conclusion: the surrender of the fort. Obviously this was
not a viable option as far as the Confederate commanders were
concerned. Rather than wait for Grant to dig in and make ready
for a long engagement, they decided upon a bold plan to break
out of the fort, save the army, and march it to Nashville and to
safety. It was a bold plan.

On the morning of the 15th the Confederates launched a full-
scale attack on the Union right flank close to the position of
stops eight and nine on your tour. Grant was taken by surprise
but, knowing the numbers of the Confederate defenders in the
fort, he decided that for the Confederates to commit the bulk of
the army to an all-out assault on his right flank, they must have
weakened their lines elsewhere. He was, of course, right. Grant
picked his spot and ordered General Charles F. Smith to attack
the Confederate right flank at a point close to **Stop Number 6**
– we will visit that position a little later on the tour. Smith hit
the weakly defended Confederate line with everything he had
driving it back to the ridge in front of you. General Simon

Bolivar Buckner and his small force of infantry managed to hold this position until reinforcements arrived.

To continue your tour drive on back toward the Visitor Center until you reach the Confederate Monument – the monument is **Stop Number 7**; we will return to it a little later – and turn right. Continue on along the road until you reach **Stop Number 5**, Jackson's Battery. You can leave you vehicle in the Park Service lot.

Jackson's Battery:

This four gun light battery was positioned here during the fighting of the 14th. It is typical of the mobile light artillery units that fought all through the Civil War and, as you can see, much different from the heavy coastal guns of the River Batteries. Each gun would be hitched to a limber – a two-wheeled ammunition chest – and could be transported very quickly from one position on the battlefield to another by a team of six horses. Each piece would be supported by a caisson – a four-wheeled unit with three more ammunition chests – also pulled by a team of six horses.

The standard cannon used by both sides during the Civil War was the 12-pound Napoleon howitzer. This gun was a smoothbore piece, effective only to distance of about 1,700 yards, and it could not be depressed – tilted to fire downhill – because the load would fall out of the barrel.

Also used extensively by both sides were the James and the Parrott Rifles, both named for their inventors. These guns weigh about 1,750 pounds each and feature rifled barrels that gave them great accuracy and extended their range to about two miles. Most types of cannon could fire a variety of loads: the standard solid shot used for battering, exploding shells that broke-up into shrapnel, and the canister – a sort of giant shotgun shell filled with one-inch diameter metal balls – which was used at close range with devastating effect to decimate massed, charging infantry.

The roll of the light artillery in the Civil War was quite varied but mostly it was a supporting one. The highly mobile light units could rapidly be brought to bear on an enemy, defensive or offensive, and often made the difference between defeat or victory. The cannon was the Civil War equivalent of the modern machine gun.

After being held here in reserve all day, the 14th, Jackson's battery was moved to a position on the Wynn's Ferry Road as a part of the preparations for the Confederate breakout attempt on the 15th.

From here at Jackson's Battery you can proceed back the way you came until you reach **Stop Number 6**, the site of General Smith's attack.

Smith's Attack:

This is the position of the Confederate extreme right flank on the morning of February 15th. The earthworks in front of you were defended that morning, as we already know by General Simon Buckner's brigade. Smith himself led the charge against these rifle pits. Slowly, but surely, the Confederate line began to crumble. Buckner had no other option but to withdraw to a new defensive position – the one you saw at Stop Number 4.

From here it's only a short distance to **Stop Number 7**, the Confederate Monument, close to the Visitor Center.

The Confederate Monument:

The Confederate Monument is constructed of Georgia gray marble and is a little more than 33 feet tall. It was erected in 1933 by the Tennessee Division of the United Daughters of the Confederacy. The monument is dedicated to the memory of the southern soldiers who died here during the battle for Fort Donelson. Here, as was the case on most Civil War battlefields, the Confederate dead were not buried in the National Cemetery. The cemeteries were, for the most part, all constructed and dedicated after the war was over. As the United States forces were the victors, and therefore the Confederacy no longer existed, when the time came for the bodies of the fallen soldiers to be disinterred from the makeshift mass graves on the battle-fields, it was only natural that it was the Union dead that were removed and buried with honor in the National Cemeteries; the Confederate dead were left to rest as they were buried, in haste, and in mass graves, most of which are now lost forever.

The monument here, so local folklore has it, is located close to one of those mass graves. And it's very likely that it is, because most often the easiest way to bury a large number of dead was to place them in an abandoned rifle pit, trench, or earthworks and then simply cover it over. This area on the outer defenses of the fortification was literally crisscrossed with such works. But even if the story is no more than a romantic legend, or perhaps just wishful thinking, it doesn't really matter. Because the sentiment that built the monument is just as valid as if the grave was really here beneath the monument itself. The Confederate dead were really no different from those of the Union. They fought for causes just as dear to them as those of their Northern brothers. They all were Americans. The only difference between them is that one was the victor; the other the defeated.

To go to Stop Number 8 on your tour, French's Battery, you will need to return to the park entrance near the Visitor Center and turn right onto Highway 79. Proceed along the highway until you see a sign at Cedar Street pointing the way to the next stop on the tour. Turn right onto Cedar Street and continue along it until you see the two rock columns that indicate the entrance to this section of the park. You will find **Stop Number 8** just beyond the two columns.

French's Battery:
This four-gun battery, along with that of Maney just across the fields to the west, was a part of Fort Donelson's perimeter defenses. From here the two batteries could sweep all the approaches from the south and southeast. It was close to this position that the Confederate forces under Generals Buckner and Pillow attempted to break out of the fort on the morning of February 15th.

As we already know, on the evening of February 14th the three Generals commanding the garrison at the fort, Floyd, Pillow and Buckner, met together to consider their options, and they decided to break out of the fort and move the army to Nashville. It was decided that the attempted breakout should be made against the Union right flank, and accordingly, under cover of darkness the bulk of the Confederate army was moved to its own left wing. General Pillow's division was stationed at the Confederate center just to the west of here along what is now Natcor Drive and would lead the attack against the Union Line. General Buckner's division was stationed here, close to Stop Number 8 and would be held in reserve to fight a rearguard action should the breakout be successful. He was also orde red to be prepared to take advantage of any situation that might indicate a complete Union route.

All night long the Confederate commanders moved thousands of men, horses, and artillery from one end of the field to the other, leaving only a minimum of defenders in the earthworks; the massive movement of troops went unnoticed by the Federal pickets. By dawn everything was ready for the Confederate attack on the Union right flank.

The attack came as a complete surprise. General Grant, not expecting any serious or immediate action by the fort's garrison, had left the field for a conference with Flag Officer Foote on board the ironclad gunboat, *St. Louis*. General McClernand's division was not long up and about when Pillow's brigades smashed into them from the direction of what is now highway 49. For a while McClernand was able to hold his position but soon, inevitably, he was forced to fall back under the ferocious Confederate onslaught.

Union General Richard Oglesby's brigade on McClernand's right flank was the first to give way. General W.H.L. Wallace, next in line on Oglesby's left looked across the field to his right and watched the line crumble under the determined Confederate attack. More important, as far as he was concerned, he saw Nathan Bedford Forrest and the Confederate cavalry bearing down on his own position, also from the right. His men, by now

out of ammunition and ready
to panic, had no alternative
but to retreat. By noon, all
along the line, the Union
army was in confusion and retreat. It was at this point the
Confederate General, Pillow,
made a fatal mistake. Had he
continued his attack and followed through with the plan
as agreed the night before,
there is no doubt the Confederate army would have made
good its escape to Nashville.
As it was, Pillow, excited by
the complete success of the
early morning attack, de-
ceived himself into thinking

Brig. Gen. John B. Floyd.

that he had defeated the entire Union army and that they were
fleeing headlong from the field. With his head now full of
thoughts of personal glory he abandoned the plan to take the
army to Nashville. But General Buckner insisted they stick to
the original plan and take the army out of danger. Pillow,
euphoric in his perceived success, accused Buckner of coward-
ice, maintaining that Napoleon always followed up on his success and the Confederates would do no less; General Floyd
agreed with Pillow who immediately sent a messenger to General Albert S. Johnston in Nashville telling him that he had won
a great victory.

By mid-afternoon Grant, alerted to the Union army's desperate
plight, had arrived back on the field and had taken control of the
situation. During an inspection of the Confederate dead he
discovered that each soldier had been issued three days rations;
it was then he realized the Confederate army was attempting to
break out of the fort rather than defeat his army. Within an
hour he had regrouped and reformed his crumbling brigades
and had ordered a counter attack. This time it was the Southerners who were taken by surprise. Generals Lew Wallace and
McClernand hit the Confederate line hard and soon had driven

the brigades of Generals Buckner and Pillow back to their
original line of defense. The Confederate breakout had been
stopped.

When you are ready to continue your tour you will need to
leave here and go to the traffic island ahead. The small
monument indicates **Stop Number 9**, Forge Road. The
intersection is with modern-day Main Street; at the time of
the battle Main Street was called Forge Road.

Forge Road:
This was to have been the Confederates' main route out of
the fort had the breakout been successful, and so it would
have been had it not been for General Pillow's disastrous
bout of self indulgence and indecision. The monument you
see here was erected in 1964 and is dedicated to the Texas
infantrymen that fought here during the battle for Fort
Donelson in 1862 and the battle of Dover in 1863.

As you proceed to **Stop Number 10**, the Dover Hotel, you
will need to turn left on Main Street and continue along it
until you reach the intersection with Highway 79. Turn right
onto 79 and proceed along it until you reach the intersection
with Highway 49 in the center of Dover. Turn right onto 49
and go two blocks to Petty Street, turn left and make your
way to the end of the street where you will find the old hotel,
tour stop ten.

The Dover Hotel:
This fine old hotel was the site of General Simon Buckner's
headquarters, and of his surrender. The Dover Hotel was built
in the 1850s to service the steamboat traffic on the Cumberland
river. It continued to operate as a hotel long after the war ended
until it was finally closed for good in 1925.

On the evening of February 15th, after the abortive Confederate
breakout, the three Generals, Floyd, Pillow and Buckner, met
at Floyd's field headquarters to discuss the situation. After a
lengthy conference it was decided the only course open to them
was to surrender the fort. At some point during the discussion

the Confederate cavalry commander, Nathan Bedford Forrest entered the room and at once sized up the gloomy expressions on the faces of the Generals. He demanded to know if they intended to surrender. He was told that they did, whereupon he turned and stormed out of the room. Forrest gathered together his officers and men saying: *"Boys, these people are talking about surrendering, and I'm going out of this place before they do or bust hell wide open."* And with that he led them through the streams and swamps to

Col. Nathan Bedford Forrest.

safety. Meanwhile, back at headquarters, Floyd said to General Buckner, *"General, I place you in command; will you permit me to draw out my brigade?"* *"Yes, Provided you do so before the enemy can act upon my communications."* Turning to Pillow, Floyd said, *"General Pillow, I turn over my command."* *"I pass it,"* replied Pillow. *"I assume it,"* Buckner said grimly. *"Bring on a bugler, pen ink, and paper."* With those final words ringing in their ears, Floyd and Pillow dashed off to a waiting steamboat and made good their escape leaving Buckner to this hotel and to negotiate terms with the enemy. The following two letters between General Buckner and General Grant made history of their own:

"Sir: Yours of this date, proposing armistice and appointment of commissioners to settle terms of capitulation, is just received. No terms except an unconditional and immediate surrender can be accepted. I propose to move immediately against your work.
Your obedient servant,
U.S. Grant"

Buckner was astounded. More than that he was bewildered and somewhat worried. He did not know what Grant meant by the words, "Unconditional Surrender." The term had not been used before and the implications of it were, to say the least, not clear. Even so, in response to his historic letter, Grant received the following reply:

"Sir: The distribution of forces under my command, incident to an unexpected change of commanders, and the overwhelming force under your command, compel me, notwithstanding the brilliant success of the Confederate arms yesterday, to accept the ungenerous and unchivalrous terms which you propose.
I am sir,
Your very obedient servant,
S.B. Buckner, Brig. Gen. C.S.A.

And, with that, it was over. On the morning of the 17th of February, 1862, General Simon Bolivar Buckner surrendered the fort and more than 13,000 Confederate soldiers. The Tennessee and Cumberland rivers were open to Union traffic. General Grant had won for President Lincoln his much needed victory and, for himself, the reputation of a hard-nosed, no-nonsense military commander who could and would win victories for the northern cause. The terms "Unconditional Surrender" were not used again until it became Allied policy in World War II.

When you have finished your tour of the hotel – two rooms are open to the public and have been furnished and maintained just as they were in 1862 – you can proceed back to highway 79, turn left onto the highway and then right onto Church Street. You will find the National Cemetery about a half-mile down the street to your right.

The National Cemetery:
This is the last stop on your tour, **Number 11**, the National Cemetery. Established in 1867 it contains some 655 Union dead, of which 504 are unknown. As is typical of the times, there are no Confederate dead buried here. They still lie in unknown graves somewhere on the battlefield. When the Fort Donelson National Cemetery was established here by act of Congress in 1867 the Union dead were disinterred and reburied in this place with all the honors usually awarded to

those who gave their lives for cause and country. Since 1867 the cemetery had been expanded to take in the spouses and children of American Veterans. Today the cemetery contains more than 1,500 graves.

Where to Stay, What to Do

The closest city of any size to Fort Donelson is Clarksville, TN about 24 miles away to the east on US 79. Clarksville offers something for just about everyone.

Attractions

Clarksville-Montgomery County Museum: 200 S. 2nd Street. Built in 1898 as a US Post Office and Customs House. It houses changing history, science, and art exhibits. Open daily except Mon., closed major holidays. Phone 931-648-5780.

Dunbar Cave State Natural Area: 5 miles SE via US 79, Dunbar Cave Rd. 110-acre park with small scenic lake. Was once a fashionable resort; the cave itself once housed big dance bands, The old bath house has been refurbished to serve as a museum. The park is open daily. The cave is open June-August, weekends, by res. only. Phone 931-648-5526.

Beachhaven Vineyard & Winery: I-24 exit 4. Tours of the vineyard and winery; tasting room & picnic area. Open daily, closed Jan. 1, Thanksgiving, Dec. 25th. Phone 931-645-8867.

Annual Events

Old-time Fiddlers Championship. Late March.
Historical Tour Of Homes. Mid-May. 931-648-0001.
Walking Horse Show. Fairgrounds. Early June.

Hotels

Days Inn: 100 TN 76-Connector Rd. at I-14 exit 11. 931-358-

3194. 86 rooms, under 16 free, cable TV, pool, free continental breakfast, cafe adjacent, check out noon, accepts credit cards.

Econo Lodge: 201 Holiday Rd. 931-645-6300. 61 rooms, under 12 free, cable TV, pool, free coffee in lobby, free continental breakfast, cafe nearby, check out 11 a.m., accepts credit cards.

Holiday Inn Downtown: 803 N. 2nd Street. 931-645-9084. 135 rooms, under 18 free, crib free, cable TV, pool, cafe, check out noon, accepts credit cards.

Best Western Covington Inn: 3075 Guthrie Hwy. 931-645-1400. 125 rooms, under 12 free, crib free, cable TV, pool, cafe, meeting rooms, check out noon, accepts credit cards.

Ramada Inn Riverview: 50 College Street. 931-647-5005. 155 rooms, under 18 free, crib free, cable TV, pool, free continental breakfast, cafe, meeting rooms, check out noon, accepts credit cards.

Restaurant

Sadie's: 2801 Guthrie Hwy. 931-645-5997. Specializes in fried chicken, corn bread. Accepts credit cards.

Camping

Clarksville Campground: Open level sites. From junction of I-24 exit 1, to Highway 48, go 700 feet north on Hwy. 48, then follow the signs for 1/4 of a mile. **Facilities:** 41 sites, 19 full hook-ups, 22 water & elect. (15, 20, & 30 amp receptacles), 41 pull-throughs, tenting available, flush toilets, hot showers, sewage disposal, laundry, public phone, LP gas, ice, tables, fire rings, wood. **Recreation:** Rec. room, pool, playground, planned group activities, badminton, horseshoes, volleyball. Open all year round. 931-648-8638.

Chapter 4

Shiloh

April, 1862

Shiloh Military Park is on US 22 at the Tennessee/Mississippi border to the north of Corinth MS. It can also be reached via US 64 going west from Memphis. There are picnic areas on the battlefield. The Visitor Center is open daily from 8 a.m. until 5 p.m. during the winter, and until 6 p.m. during the summer. Admission is $1. Phone 901-689-5275.

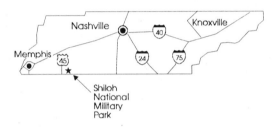

Shiloh, or Pittsburg Landing as it was called by many in the north, was never meant to be a battlefield. Instead it was intended to be a staging area from which the Federal Army of Tennessee under the command of Major General Ulysses S. Grant could mount an assault upon the Confederate positions and vital railroad junction at Corinth, Mississippi just 25 miles to the south. By April 1st, 1862, almost a year after the opening shots of the Civil War had been fired at Fort Sumter, the war had spread across almost the entire southern half of the divided nation. Major battles had been fought from Virginia to Florida in the east, and to Southern Missouri in the west. And although the battles of 1st Bull Run in Virginia, Wilson's Creek in Missouri, Gulf Islands in Florida, Forts Henry and Donelson in Tennessee, and Pea Ridge in Missouri had been bloody enough, they had given little indication of the carnage that was to come. The concept of war on both sides was still a romantic one.

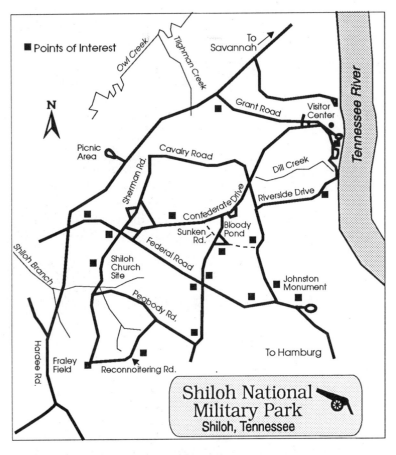

Thoughts of great deeds and personal heroism were bolstered by the swashbuckling attitudes of the officers and by the stirring new tunes of glory. Within a single week all the horrors of war would be brought home to both nations in an avalanche of death and destruction. The capture by Grant of the Confederate forts Henry and Donelson on the Cumberland and Tennessee rivers early in 1862 had been the beginning of the campaign. By the middle of March the Confederate army numbering some 44,000 men under the command General Albert Sidney Johnston had regrouped and were determined to hold at all costs the railheads and supply depots at Corinth.

Meanwhile, General Grant, surprised by the complete collapse of the Confederate defenses in Middle Tennessee, was on the move and planned to join up with the Army of the Ohio under Major General Don Carlos Buell at Savannah, Tennessee and from there continue the campaign on into Mississippi with the ultimate goal of destroying the Confederate army at Corinth.

Major Gen. Don Carlos Buell.

Brigadier General William Tecumseh Sherman, having led an abortive raid to sever the major east-west Memphis & Charleston Railroad, ultimately was responsible for bringing about of the tumultuous series of events that became the battle of Shiloh. Forced by bad weather to abandon his raid on the railroad, he returned by boat upriver along the Tennessee from Mississippi. The Tennessee river was in flood, swollen by the several days of torrential rain, and offered no accessible landing site but Pittsburg Landing.

Sherman arrived there with his division and that of Brigadier General Stephen A. Hurlbut on March 16th. Sherman, no doubt relieved to find a suitable landing site, declared that Pittsburg landing offered not only a strategic position from which to strike at the Confederate railroads, but an "admirable campground for a hundred thousand men," and "admits of easy defense by a small command."

The rest of Grant's army began arriving in dribs and drabs and continued to do so throughout the rest of the month until by the

31st of March Pittsburg Landing and the surrounding area had been transformed into a vast and seething military encampment some three miles square, bounded to the north-west by Owl Creek, and to the south by Lick Creek and the Tennessee river. As far as the eye could see the countryside was covered by the clutter of wagons, tents, pile-upon-pile of supplies, and everywhere men teeming, moving this way and that, drilling

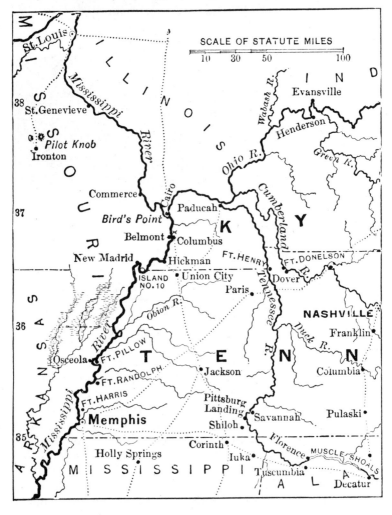

Gen. Johnston caught Grant's army in camp near Shiloh.

forward and back, carrying on the everyday chores of what had virtually become a major, though temporary, military township. Day after day steamships ferried Grant's army and its mountain of supplies down-river to the limited access at the landing site; and slowly but surely General Buell's Army of the Ohio, 50,000 strong, struggled southward from Nashville, overland along 122 miles of rutted and muddy backroads. By the evening of April 5th Grant's army at Pittsburg Landing had grown to more than 35,000 and Buell with his more than 50,000 men had arrived at Savannah, Tennessee, only nine miles away to the north-east. The stage was set.

Realizing he could not afford another defeat after the fiascoes at forts Henry and Donelson, Confederate General Johnston, at the urging of his generals, had decided to take the initiative. He knew that his position at Corinth was vulnerable, and that Grant's army was encamped at Pittsburg Landing, expecting the imminent arrival of Don Carlos Buell and his Army of the Ohio. So he decided to surprise the Federal force by attacking it

Confederate Generals Beauregard, Polk, Breckenridge, Johnston, Bragg, and Hardee in council before the Battle of Shiloh.

when and where they least expected it – in their own front yard. He determined to start his assault at dawn on April 4th, but bad weather caused one delay after another. By the evening of April 5th his army of 44,000 had moved into position just two miles south of Shiloh Church, the outer perimeter of Grant's army.

The original plan had been to attack the Federal positions "corps abreast." In other words the three Confederate corps of William Joseph Hardee, Leonidas Polk, and Braxton Bragg would advance in line, side-by-side, and attack simultaneously along the entire Federal front. General P.G.T. Beauregard, however, persuaded Johnston that an attack "corps-in-tandem" – one corps behind the other – would be the most effective formation. It was a battle formation modeled after Napoleon's order of battle at Waterloo; it didn't work there either. Unfortunately, though, Beauregard was allowed to have his way.

Johnston attacked the Federal positions early in the morning of the April 6. The attack by any estimation was a complete surprise. The action as it took place during those fateful two days in April of 1862 is best described as you tour the battlefield. Turn right out of the Visitor Center and proceed along Grant

Road to **Stop Number 1**. If you are to follow the battle in chronological order this position is out of sequence. It is, however, fitting that you are aware of it, as it plays a large part in the rest of what you are about to see. The road itself is the position of Grant's "Final Line" of battle on the afternoon of April 6th. It is, as you can see, a strong defensive position. The Federal troops that held this line were the hodge-podge remnants of assorted Union brigades that had been involved in the battle in one part of the field or another throughout the day; each driven inexorably backward from one defensive position to another. By the end of the day more than 18,000 Federal troops had converged upon, and had been organized into, this final line of defense.

Before the battle this ridge was the campsite of General W. L. Wallace's division. General Sherman's division was camped about two miles to your left, and Hurlbut's division was encamped about a half-mile away to your left and to the rear. You will be able to identify the actual positions of these campsites and other important positions by the yellow markers distributed throughout the battlefield.

At **Stop Number 2**, just a few yards along Federal Road, you will find a pyramid of cannon balls, the position of Colonel John A. McDowell's field headquarters on the morning of April 6th and the extreme right flank of Sherman's three brigades. About 200 yards away through the woods and to your right Union General Buckland was encamped on a ridge that stretched almost to Shiloh Church with Sherman's second brigade. General Hilderbrand with the third brigade held a position on the high ground behind the church. These three brigades formed a line almost a mile long that stretched from the banks of the Owl Creek to Shiloh Church.

At **Stop Number 3**, along the old Corinth Road, now Confederate Drive, you will find Shiloh Church. The church itself is close to the ridge upon which Sherman's three brigades were positioned on the morning of the 6th; his headquarters were just across the road behind you. As you can imagine this ridge formed a formidable defensive position. All morning long the

Gen. William Joseph Hardee.

Confederate commanders threw one assault after another up the ridge against the brigades of Buckland and McDowell only to be thrown back in confusion. Confederate General Patrick Cleburne lost a third of his brigade on these slopes. Sherman himself had four horses shot out from under him.

Against this ridge it became apparent that Beauregard's Napoleonic strategy would not work. The three Confederate corps advancing one behind the other and stretching across a three-mile front were led by General Hardee's corps, followed by that of Braxton Bragg and then Leonidas Polk. Johnston's plan had been to hit the Union army not here, but some two miles to the east, and to roll up the Federal left flank and then push the entire Union army back and away from Pittsburg Landing, finally destroying them on the banks of the Owl Creek. Unfortunately this was not to be, for the main weight of the Confederate force became engaged here instead. And with the Confederate corps stretched over such a wide line of battle there was no way the corps commanders could effectively supervise the action. Add all this to the rugged nature of the terrain and you can begin to understand the weakness of Beauregard's strategy. As Hardee's brigades were slowed down by the heavy woodland and the murderous fire of Sherman's defenders, the second and third Confederate corps soon came piling in one on top of the other, creating confusion and disorder, and allowing Sherman to hold this position until late morning.

At that time, with his left flank to the east of Shiloh Church in danger of collapsing, he was able to pull most of his division back to a second defensive position.

Further on along Confederate Drive at **Stop Number 5** is Fraley Field. It was in this 40-acre field to your right that the battle of Shiloh began. Sherman, for some reason, refused to believe that there was any real concentration of Confederate troops any closer than Corinth, some 22 or more miles away from here to the south. Somehow, though, General Johnston had

Then Brigadier Gen. William Tecumseh Sherman.

been able to move more than 40,000 men into position just a few hundred yards to the south of Fraley Field. For several nights Sherman had been receiving intelligence that the Confederates were close by and in force, but he refused to believe it. And anyway, he was under orders not to engage the enemy and so bring about a major battle before the second Union army under Don Carlos Buell arrived. All through the nights of the 4th and 5th Confederate campfires burned in long lines to the south of this field, and all through the same two nights the Confederate drums and bugles could be heard echoing across these fields and woods; they must have been hard to miss. However, during the early morningh hours of the 6th an extremely nervous Federal Colonel, Everrett Peabody, acting without orders and with a strong premonition of his own impending death, decided to send out a patrol in force. It was this patrol that, shortly before five o'clock in the morning, ran into the advance Confederate pickets posted in and around this field. The fighting here lasted for more than an hour until Peabody's Federal force of five companies was forced to withdraw to the cotton field at your left where they were joined by five more companies that had been sent forward in response to the sounds of the battle in Fraley Field. The new position of the reconnoitering party, now reinforced by the five new companies, was just along Reconnoitering Road to your left. The fighting there did not last long, however. Heavily outnumbered, outgunned, and outflanked by Shaver's Confederate brigade the small Federal force was compelled to pull back into the field on your right; there they were joined by four more companies from a Wisconsin regiment of rookies barely experienced enough to load and fire their weapons. Almost immediately the Union party was outflanked and force to pull back once again; the battle was about to move into the next stage.

The Confederate line now comprised elements of Brigadier General S.A.M. Wood's brigade, which had started the battle in Fraley Field, and Shaver's Arkansas brigade which had pushed the Federal party back through the cotton field, But already, due to the speed of the action and the heavily wooded terrain, it was having trouble maintaining its lines of communication.

One member of Shaver's Confederate force fighting Peabody's Federal reconnoitering party that morning was a young Welshman. John Rowlands had sailed from England as a cabin boy and had been adopted by a New Orleans merchant. He later took the merchant's name (Stanley) and enlisted in the Dixie Grays – "gentlemen volunteers" – where he soon found himself at Shiloh fighting in the fields in front of you. Private Henry Morton Stanley, soon to become a prisoner of war, later achieved fame as a journalist and explorer; he was the man who went to Africa and uttered the immortal words, "Dr. Livingstone I presume." Here, from his original memoirs, is a small part of his account of the fighting, on that morning in April, 1862.

"Forward, gentlemen, make ready!' urged Captain Smith. In response, we surged forward, for the first time marring our alignment. We trampled recklessly over the grass and young sprouts. Beams of sunlight stole athwart our course. Nothing now stood between us and the enemy.

"'There they are!' was no sooner uttered than we cracked into them with our muskets. 'Aim low, men!' commanded Captain Smith. I tried hard to see some living thing to aim at, for it appeared absurd to be blazing away at shadows. But, still advancing, firing away as we moved, I, at last, saw a row of little globes of pearly smoke streaked with crimson, breaking-out with spurtive quickness, from a long line of blue figures in front; and simultaneously, there broke upon our ears an appalling crash of sound, the series of fusillades following one another with startling suddenness, which suggested to my somewhat moidered sense a mountain upheaved, with huge rocks tumbling and thundering down a slope, and the echoes rumbling and receding through space. Again and again, these loud and quick explosions were repeated, seemingly with increased violence, until they rose to the highest pitch of fury, and in unbroken continuity. All the world seemed involved in one tremendous ruin.

"Though one's senses were preternaturally acute, and engaged with their impressions, we plied our arms, loaded and fired, with such nervous haste as though it depended on each of us how soon this fiendish uproar would be hushed. My nerves tingles, my pulses beat double-quick, my heart throbbed loudly, and almost painfully; but amid all the excitement, my thoughts, swift as the flash of lightning, took all, sound, and sight, and self, into their purview. I listened to the battle raging away on our flanks, to the thunder in front, to the various sounds made by the leaden storm. I was angry with my rear rank, because he made my eyes smart with the powder of his musket; and I felt like cuffing him for deafening my ears! I knew how Captain Smith and Lieutenant Mason looked, how bravely the Dixie Grays' banner ruffled over Newton Story's head, and that all hands were behaving as though they knew how long all this would last. Back to myself my thoughts came, and, with the whirring bullet, they fled to the blue-bloused ranks afront. They dwelt upon their movements, and read their temper, as I should read time by a clock. Through the lurid haze the contours of their pink faces could not be seen, but their gappy, hesitating, incoherent, and sensitive line revealed their mood clearly.

"We continued advancing, step by step, loading and firing as we

went. To every forward step, they took a backward move, loading and firing, as they slowly withdrew.

"After a steady exchange of musketry, which lasted some time, we heard the order: 'Fix Bayonets! On the double-quick!' in tones that thrilled us. There was a simultaneous bound forward, each soul doing his best for the emergency. The Federals seemed inclined to await us; but, at this juncture, our men raised a yell. Thousands responded to it, and burst out into the wildest yelling it has ever been my lot to hear. It drove all sanity and order from among us It served the double purpose of relieving pent-up feelings, and transmitting encouragement along the attacking line. I rejoiced in the shouting like the rest. It reminded me that there were about four hundred companies like the Dixie Grays, who shared our feelings. Most of us, engrossed with the musket-work, had forgotten the fact; but the wave after wave of human voices, louder than all other battle-sounds together, penetrated to every sense, and stimulated our energies to the utmost.

"'They fly!' was echoed from lip to lip. It accelerated our pace, and filled us with a noble rage. Then I knew what Berserker passion was! It deluged us with rapture, and transfigured each South-erner into an exulting victor. At such a moment nothing could have halted us. Those savage yells, and the sight of thousands of racing figures coming towards them, discomfited the blue-coats; and when we arrived upon the place where they had stood, they had vanished."

Stop Number 6 on Reconnoitering Road marks the campsite from which Colonel Peabody sent out the Federal scouting party that started the action that morning. Although he was blamed for bringing about the action in direct contravention of general orders, there's no doubt that his action did in fact save the entire Federal army from destruction. He was killed, somewhere close to here, trying to restore order to his fleeing troops.

Continue along Reconnoitering Road to the junction with Peabody Road and turn to the right, then proceed until you reach **Stop Number 7** at the junction of Peabody and Gladden Road.

At the start of the battle, just beyond the junction of Peabody and Gladden roads, in a field on the other side of the woods in front of you, Brigadier General Benjamin M. Prentiss' 2nd brigade, untrained, undisciplined, and certainly unprepared for the battle that lay ahead, was encamped and eating breakfast. This brigade was swept away to the northern edge of the field by General Adley H. Gladden's Confederate brigade. There the Federal troops were able to establish a new line of defense and repulse the enthusiastic but unruly Confederate attack. The Federal force, with Prentiss in command, comprised more than 2,000 men and two batteries of artillery. The fighting on Prentiss' line of battle continued unabated until at last the raw recruits were once again able to repulse, for a while at least, the screaming horde of Confederate infantry. In the heat of the action General Gladden was mortally wounded, but his Confederate brigade, now commanded by Colonel Daniel W. Adams, regrouped, reformed, and attacked again. This time they were successful and General Prentiss and his rookie brigade was driven back through the woods in total disorder.

The destruction of Prentiss' division was at this point in the battle almost complete. His artillery batteries had been captured or disabled. Only two of his seven brigades, and whatever dribs and drabs of the others that could be rounded up, had any fight left in them. These two brigades withdrew to a new position, close to the junction of Federal Road, and just to the rear of two brigades of Union General Hurlbut's division on the edge of the Peach Orchard.

Turn left now onto Gladden Road and go to **Stop Number 8** at the junction of Federal Road.

So, by 8:30 in the morning of April 6th, Prentiss' division had been driven back in panic and confusion. The Confederate brigades of Shaver and Wood had moved on through this position and were actively engaging McClernand's division which had moved back to join up with Sherman. Confederate General Cleburne was engaging Sherman's division on its right flank. And about a mile away to your right a second Confederate force was about to attack the lone Union brigade of Colonel David

Stuart on the high ground at the extreme left flank of the Federal line of battle as it originally was in the early morning.

As you make the turn to your right and proceed along Federal Road to **Stop Number 9** you will be entering a section of the battlefield that saw some of the bloodiest and most desperate fighting of the entire Civil War.

The field to your left, at Stop Number 9, is where the Federal army tried to stem the advancing Confederate tide. General Hurlbut, with two brigades, took up a defensive position here on the edge of the field. The line of guns you see in the center of the field indicates the supporting Union artillery. The second line of guns in the forward position away to your far left indicates the position of a second Union battery. Unfortunately, this battery was placed too far forward, and was manned by raw and inexperienced troops. At the first sight of the advancing Confederate force, the men at that forward battery panicked, abandoned their guns, and fled in confusion and abject terror from the field, leaving the battery in front of you to cope, single-handed, with the Confederate advance.

Try to imagine the scene as it must have been during the early morning hours of that fateful day; put yourself at the head of the advancing Confederate line of battle. Hurlbut's two brigades are slowly but surely falling away in front of you. The field you see ahead is obscured by a dense pall of smoke. Your ears are ringing from the constant crash of musket fire all around you. To a man you and your companions are rushing forward at the double-quick, bayonets at the point, musket barrels almost too hot to handle. Nothing, it seems, can stand in the way of this insanely driven Confederate charge. Suddenly, the smoke ahead begins to clear, just a little. You now find yourself staring down the barrels of that line of cannon you see in the open field in front of you. Before you can even think, the battery opens fire at point-blank range. The first broadside of double-loaded canister fills the air with thunder and a whirring of a million angry hornets, delivering a horrendous firestorm around you. Your companions are literally blown away beside you. More than a hundred men are wiped from the face of the earth in that single devastating second on the southern approaches to the Peach Orchard. The unstoppable Confederate advance is thrown back in confusion as broadside after broadside screams across the open ground ahead. Henry M. Stanley had this to say about it:

"The world seemed bursting into fragments. Cannon and musket, shell and bullet, lent their several intensities to the distracting uproar. If I had not a fraction of an ear, and an eye inclined towards my Captain and Company, I had been spellbound by the energies now opposed to us. I likened the cannon, with their deep bass, to the roaring of a great herd of lions; the ripping, cracking musketry, to the incessant yapping of terriers; the windy whisk of shells, and zipping of minie bullets, to the swoop of eagles, and the buzz of angry wasps. All the opposing armies of Gray and Blue fiercely blazed at each other.

"After being exposed to this fearful downpour, we heard the order to 'Lie down, men, and continue your firing!' Before me was a prostrate tree, about fifteen inches in diameter, with a narrow strip of light between it and the ground. Behind this shelter a dozen of us flung ourselves. The security it appeared to offer restored me to my individuality. We could fight, and think, and observe, better than out in the open. But it was a terrible! How the cannon bellowed, and their shells plunged and bounded, and flew with screeching hisses over us! Their rending explosions and hurtling fragments made us shrink and cower, despite our utmost efforts to be cool and collected. I marveled, as I heard the unintermitting patter, snip, thud, and hum of bullets, how anyone could live under this raining death. I could hear the balls beating a merciless tattoo on the outer surface of the log, pinging it vivaciously as they flew off at a tangent from it, and thudding into something or other, at the rate of a hundred a second. One, here and there, found its way under the log and buried itself in a comrade's body. One man raised his chest, as if to yawn, and jostled me. I turned to him, and saw that a bullet had gored his whole face and penetrated into his chest. Another ball struck a man a deadly rap on the head, and he turned on his back and showed his ghastly white face to the sky.

"'It's getting too warm, boys!' cried a soldier, and uttered a

vehement curse upon keeping soldiers hugging the ground until every ounce of courage was chilled. He lifted his head a little too high, and a bullet skimmed across the top of the log and hit him fairly in the center of his forehead, and he fell heavily on his face. But his thought had been instantaneously general; and the officers, with one voice, ordered the charge; and cries of 'Forward, forward!' raised us, as with a spring, to our feet, and changed the complexion of our feelings. The pulse of action beat feverishly once more; and though overhead was crowded with peril, we were unable to give it so much attention as when we lay stretched on the ground. . . .

"My physical powers were quite exhausted, and to add to my discomfiture, something struck me on the belt clasp, and tumbled me headlong to the ground. I could not have been many minutes prostrated before I recovered from the shock of the blow and the fall, to find my clasp deeply dented and cracked. My company was not in sight. I was grateful for the rest and crawled feebly to a tree. . . . Within half an hour, feeling renovated, I struck north in the direction my regiment had taken, over a ground strewn with bodies and the debris of war.

"The desperate character of this day's battle was now brought home to my mind in all its awful reality. . . . Close by was a young Lieutenant, who judging by the new gloss of his uniform, must have been some father's darling. A clean bullet-hole through the center of his forehead had instantly ended his career. A little further on were some twenty bodies, lying in various postures, each in its own pool of viscous blood, which emitted a peculiar scent, which was new to me, but which I have since learned is inseparable from a battle field. Beyond these, a still larger group lay, body overlying body, knees crooked, arms erect, or wide-stretched and ridged according as the last spasm overtook them. . . . It was the first Field of Glory I had seen in my May of life, and for the first time that Glory sickened me with its repulsiveness, and made me suspect it was all a glittering lie. . ."

Continue along Federal Road for three-quarters of a mile until you reach Johnston Road; then bear right until you reach **Stop Number 10** and the hospital site turn-around.

This was, on the morning of the 6th, the field headquarters of a Union brigade commanded by Colonel David Stuart. It was just a little further on along Johnston Road from this point that Stuart's brigade was positioned on the extreme left flank of Sherman's division overlooking a small ravine into Lick Creek. When the Confederate artillery opened fire the first regiment of Stuart's brigade immediately drew back some 150 yards, but the second two regiments were able to hold their ground for almost two hours before falling back to a better defensive position on higher ground just to the north.

It was here on this site, too, on the evening of the second day of battle, the 7th of April, that General Nelson, a division commander of Buell's Army of the Ohio had his medical staff establish a field hospital. The arrangements here, so Nelson declared, "are as perfect as the circumstances would allow. The wounded were all promptly attended and cared for." If this were true, then, it was indeed a unique situation, for at this period of the Civil War there was no established ambulance corps, nor would there be until August, 1862. Until then it was not unusual for the wounded to lie unattended upon the battlefield for days; many of them dying unnecessarily of relatively minor wounds. So, as far as the Battle of Shiloh was concerned, this was a fairly important site. Significant also is the fact that the field surgeons on either side were treated no differently from any other battlefield officer, and rather than being left alone on the field to do whatever good they could for the wounded of either side, they were often taken as prisoners of war, or forced to retreat along with their regiments leaving the wounded on the field to fend for themselves as best they could. Not only that, medicines and dressings and general cleanliness were always in short supply, and those of the wounded who might have been "lucky" enough to find themselves in one of these field hospitals could expect only the most rudimentary of services. Amputation was, for the most part, the order of the day. The stomach wound was, almost without exception, a ticket to the cemetery. The large caliber, low velocity minie ball inflicted the most devastating of wounds, tearing great holes in flesh and muscle, and shattering entirely any bone it might strike.

The Hornet's Nest.

At this point in the proceedings you will need to leave here and proceed back along Johnston Road to the junction with Federal Road and bear left until you reach the intersection with Gladden Road and **Stop Number 11**.

By mid-morning the Federal divisions of Hurlbut and Prentiss, now reinforced by a brigade under the command of Brigadier General John A. McArther of W.H.L. Wallace's division, had, along with Stuart's brigade on the extreme left, been pushed steadily backward. They now formed a line that, when joined with McClernand's, and then with Sherman's, division on the extreme right, extended almost the entire width of the battlefield. The three Confederate corps of Hardee, Polk, and Bragg had by now been joined on their extreme right flank by that of John Breckinridge, and were pressing the beleaguered Federal line very hard. By noon the Union forces had been pushed back to the Sunken Road – soon to be called "The Hornet's Nest."

At the Union center, Hurlbut's division, with more than 5,400 men and three batteries of artillery, were deployed behind an old, split-rail fence with the Peach Orchard and a clear field of fire in front of them. What was left of Prentiss' division had been joined by the two remaining Peabody brigades, and, further strengthened by the addition of eight field guns, they were deployed along an old sunken road on Hurlbut's right flank. W.H.L. Wallace with 5,800 men was at Prentiss' right. These three positions formed a great semi-circle more than a half-mile wide at the center of the Union line of battle. And it was across this road and the field in front of you that more than 18,000 Confederate

Major Gen. Braxton Bragg.

infantrymen of Braxton Bragg's corps hurled themselves a dozen times at a Federal force less than half their size.

Turn right off Federal Road onto Gladden Road and go to the stop sign at the junction with Hornet's Nest Road. Turn right on Hornet's Nest and go to the turn-out and then turn right. The battery of cannon you see on your right is stop number 12. At this point in the tour you might like to take a walk along the Sunken Road to the right. It leads past Prentiss' position to Hurlbut's line of battle in the Peach Orchard. If you have any imagination at all you will find the atmosphere here heavy with the shadows of the past. Do the unseen spirits of a thousand Union and Confederate dead still drift through the trees and blossoms of the Peach Orchard and along this old, well worn, cart track? Stand, for a moment, by yourself, and on a quiet summer day, as you listen to the breeze whispering through the leaves of trees that shade the Sunken Road, it's not difficult to believe that they do.

Had Bragg been a better tactician than he was an organizer he might have seen the weakness on the Union left flank. And had he done so, an all-out attack there surely would have swept away David Stuart's brigade and initiated a total collapse of the entire Federal army. Bragg opted for the obvious, and flung his corps across the Peach Orchard at the Union center time and again in a series of desperate but futile attacks on the Sunken Road.

Confederate Brigadier General Benjamin F. Cheatham's brigade was the first to see action at the Sunken Road. At 11 o'clock, without support, he hurled his three regiments against the left of W.H.L. Wallace's line. His men were slaughtered by the hundred in the open field. So badly were they mangled that they had to be withdrawn from the fight entirely. Next, Bragg ordered a lone brigade of four regiments under the command of Colonel Randall Lee Gibson into the fray. They, too, were mowed down like so much hay on a summer's day. The ground, literally, was covered with the Confederate dead. Bragg, incensed by what he regarded as Gibson's premature withdrawal ordered them back again. Gibson protested, but did as he was ordered, and once again the brave soldiers of Louisiana and Arkansas charged across the killing field. This time they made it, weary and exhausted, to the very brink of the Sunken Road only to be repulsed in fierce hand-to-hand combat by the determined Federal defenders.

The survivors of that second charge by Gibson's gallant brigade gave the Federal stronghold its famous name, "The Hornet's Nest." Unfortunately, the day was not yet done for Gibson and his brigade. Bragg ordered them back against the Sunken Road a third time; and, incredibly, a fourth time.

To follow the action as it unfolded that day you should now turn right onto Hornet's Nest Road and continue along it until you reach the stop sign at Confederate Drive, then turn left and go to **Stop Number 13**: the site of Ruggles' Battery.

The normal order of battle in the early days of the Civil War dictated that, for the most-part, each brigade had, and independently operated, a battery of artillery. It was unusual for a division to "mass" it's artillery. The line of guns you see in front of you indicates the position of the largest concentration of field artillery ever seen on any American battlefield to this point in the war. Confederate Brigadier General Daniel Ruggles, a division commander in Bragg's corps, was appalled by the devastation being caused by the Federal units of Wallace and Prentiss in the Sunken Road. And so, acting without orders, he directed his staff officers to round up every field gun they could lay their hands and bring it to this position. Soon, Ruggles had amassed 62 assorted pieces of artillery and had deployed them in a line more than a thousand feet long. Ruggles ordered the battery to open fire at about four o'clock in the afternoon. General Wallace's men took the brunt of this devastating firestorm. It has been estimated that the combined firepower of the 62 guns was some 180 rounds per minute. The effect of this inordinate concentration of fire was immediate. General Wallace, realizing that his position had now become untenable, ordered his men to retreat. In an attempt to escape capture, he tried to gallop past the Confederate artillery position and in so doing took a mortal wound to the head. General Prentiss, with eight regiments numbering almost 2,000 men, realizing he was now caught in a deadly trap, fought on. Then, at about five o'clock in the afternoon, assailed on three sides, he finally gave the order for his men to retreat, but it was too late. In the space of half an hour some 2,000 Union soldiers had surrendered and the remnants of Hurlbut's and Wallace's brigades had been turned and pushed back. An eye-witness to the events in The Hornet's Nest that day was Leander Stillwell. He later published his diaries, letters, and recollections as: The Story of a Common Soldier of Army Life in the Civil War, 1861-1865. He had this to say about it: *"From one end of the regiment to the other leaped a sheet of red flame, and the roar that went up from the edge of that old field doubtless advised general Prentiss that the Rebels had at last struck the extreme left of his line. . . . We retreated from this position as our officers afterward said, because the troops on our right had given way, and we were flanked. Possibly those boys on our right would give the same excuse for their leaving, and*

*probably truly, too. Still, I think we did not fall back a minute
too soon. As I rose from the comfortable log from behind which a
bunch of us had been firing, I saw men in gray and brown
clothes, with trailed muskets running through the camp on our
right, and I saw something else, too, that sent a chill all through
me. It was a kind of flag I had never seen before. It was a gaudy
sort of thing with red bars. It flashed over me in a second that
thing was a Rebel flag. It was not more than sixty yards to the
right. The smoke around it was dense and kept me from seeing
the man who was carrying it, but I plainly saw the banner. It was
going fast, with a jerky motion, which told me that the bearer was
on the double-quick. About that time we left. We observed no kind
of order in leaving; the main thing was to get out of there as quick
as we could."*

So, General Prentiss and more than 2,000 men were overrun
and forced to surrender. Prentiss himself was taken prisoner.
But the efforts of the few brave defenders on the Sunken Road
and in The Hornet's Nest had not been in vain. They had
delayed the Confederate advance by more than five and a half
hours of sustained fighting. And they had won for General
Grant the time he needed to organize his Final Line of defense
on the ridge in front of Pittsburg Landing.

At this point it would a good idea if you drove on to the
intersection of Federal Road. Turn left on Federal and continue on past the junction of Gladden Road to the junction of
Johnston Road. This time you will need to turn left and go
to stop fourteen and the Johnston Monument. The monument, as you can see, is simply the stump of an old oak tree.

General Albert Sidney Johnston, the commander of the entire
Confederate army, unable to find any high ground from which
to observe and direct the course of the battle was compelled,
throughout the day, to ride from one position to another directing the course of the action as best he could. It was sometime
after noon that he arrived with Brigadier General John S.
Bowen's brigade of Breckinridge's corps at the far western
section of his line of battle. Colonel David Stuart, the anchor of
the Union left flank, already was considering pulling back.

Breckinridge told Johnston that Statham's brigade had refused to press the attack on the Federal left flank. Johnston, recklessly, decided to lead the attack himself. He passed along the line of infantry and assured them man-to-man that he would lead them into the attack. Word was passed along the Confederate line that there was to be a concerted effort to break and roll up the entire Federal left flank. Union General McArther was the first to break under the pressure of the combined Confederate attack. General Johnston led the bayonet charge aimed at the Peach Orchard and General Hurlbut, but he encountered heavy resistance, as did Stephen's brigade, and took cover. It was some half an hour later, as Johnston was issuing orders for a renewed attack, that it was noticed he was severely wounded. He had in fact been hit four times, but it was a minie ball wound to his right leg behind the knee that severed an artery

Gen. U.S. Grant.

and brought about his demise. The wound must have been bleeding into his boot for more than half an hour before it became apparent that Johnston was in serious trouble. There were no doctors on hand to treat the wound, but even if there had been, by the time the wound was noticed it probably would have been too late. Ironically, Johnston was in possession of the means by which he could have saved his own life. There was a tourniquet in the pocket of his uniform coat. Beneath the tree in front of you, its stump now preserved as a monument to one of the South's greatest generals, that Albert Sidney Johnston expired, a little after two o'clock in the afternoon of April 6th, 1862. General Pierre Gustave Toutant Beauregard, Johnston's

second in command, was immediately notified of Johnston's death and he assumed overall command of the Confederate army. Many would say that it was Johnston's death that saved the Union army that day; maybe it was, but that is something we shall never know.

> The next stop on your tour is **Number 15**, The Bloody Pond. Continue along Johnston Road and you will find it just past the Peach Orchard on your left.

The pond you see today is much the same as it was in 1862. However, after General Hurlbut was forced to pull back from the Peach Orchard it lay between the two armies and, so it is said, the wounded soldiers from both sides crawled in their hundreds to drink from the pond and wash their wounds. It is also said that men and horses from both sides fell from the effects of their wounds into the pond staining it dark red, hence the name: The Bloody Pond.

> Continue along Johnston Road until you come to the junction with Riverside Drive and then turn right and continue on to stop number 16. The Indian mounds you see here are interesting, but they played no part in the battle. When you have finished here you can continue on to **Stop Number 17**, the River Overlook at Pittsburg Landing, but before you take time out to visit the National Cemetery there you might like to visit **Stop Number 1** once again, Grant's Final Line. Grant's position will mean more to you then than it did when you began your tour.

By late afternoon on April 6th the Federal line with Hurlbut on the left had been smashed and had pulled back again and again, from one new defensive position to another. Sherman and McClernand, too, had been forced back all along the line of battle.

General Grant, now anticipating that the Confederates would press home their advantage in an all-out attack on Pittsburg Landing, had taken good advantage of the time so hard won by his corps commanders. Quickly he had made plans to defend the landing. Colonel Joseph D. Webster spent most of the afternoon moving a battery of five 24-pounder siege guns into position on what was to become Grant's Final Line. The monster guns were to be the mainstay of Grant's defensive line. By six o'clock in the afternoon, the line had been strengthened by at least ten more batteries of field guns. All afternoon the remnants of the decimated brigades of Hurlbut, Wallace, Stuart, and others fell back and reformed along Grant's Final line.

Across the river from Pittsburg Landing the first elements of Don Carlos Buell's Army of the Ohio were beginning to arrive. But the Confederate corps of Bragg, Polk, and Breckinridge already were in sight and preparing for one final, massive push to carry the Federal army into the Tennessee River. Chalmers and Jackson began the attack on Grant's defensive position at six o'clock. But Webster's monster guns spoke and Chalmers was beaten back at once by the deadly firestorm. Soon, Jackson, too, had pulled back behind the crest of the ridge to avoid the deadly barrage. Then, as darkness began to fall over the battlefield, Beauregard called an end to the day's fighting.

By dawn on April 7 Grant's army, reinforced overnight by General Don Carlos Buell and advance elements of his Army of the Ohio, numbered more than 55,000 men. The fighting was resumed at 6 a.m. but Beauregard, now facing vastly superior numbers and mounting casualties, knew he could go no further, and withdrew his forces from the field. The battle of Shiloh was over. The cost of the two days in lives alone had been terrible. Union casualties numbered more than 13,000, Confederate casualties were in excess of 10,500; a total of more than 23,000 were killed, wounded, or missing.

"Shiloh!" There's something magical about the name. It can conjure up a thousand tales of heroism or tragedy. And who has not heard of Johnny Clem, the "Drummer Boy of Shiloh?" He was only ten years old when he served there with the 22nd Michigan. He retired from the army in 1916 with the rank of Major General. Johnny Clem died in 1937 and is buried at Arlington National Cemetery. Today, the wild beauty of this isolated field of war is overwhelming. The air on a summer's day is often still and heavy and the silence is broken only by the dull buzz of insects. Pittsburg Landing is now a National Cemetery, the Hornets' Nest a pleasant country walk, and the Peach Orchard blooms again each spring. The Bloody Pond teams with tiny fish and the old oak tree under which General Johnston died is only a rotted stump.

Where to Stay, Things to Do

Although the Shiloh National Battlefield Park is easily located, it is quite a distance from the nearest major city. To the south is Corinth, Mississippi, to the west, Memphis, and to the northeast is Nashville. All of these major metropolitan areas can provide dining, entertainment and accommodation to suit most budgets.

Chapter 5

2nd Manassas

August, 1862

After the Federal defeat at 1st Manassas on July 21st, 1861, President Lincoln removed General Irvin McDowell from command of the Union army and replaced him with General George B. McClellan. During the year that followed the first battle of Manassas the war in the west had gone badly for the Confederacy. With the fall of Forts Henry and Donelson, and the major Union victory at Shiloh, Missouri, all of Tennessee west of Nashville belonged to General Grant. He would spend the rest of 1862 preparing for his campaign into Mississippi.

In the east the Confederate fortunes had fared better. Even though Generals Joseph Johnston and James Longstreet had bungled, the battle of Seven Pines, Virginia, 1862, had ended indecisively with both sides claiming victory. The battles around Richmond, known as the "Seven Days," lasting from June 25th to July 21st 1862 (Mechanicsville, Gaines Mill, Savage Station, Glendale, and Malvern Hill) resulted in a somewhat tenuous victory for the Confederate forces and put an end to Union General George B. McClellan's Peninsula Campaign.

McClellan re-equipped and re-trained the army for combat so that by the spring of 1862 the raw Union recruits, including the survivors of 1st Manassas, had become veterans ready and able to deal with any wartime situation. These troops were then moved to Fort Monroe, Virginia from which position McClellan made ready to drive up the peninsula and attack Richmond.

Meanwhile a second Union army, The Army of Virginia, had been placed under the command of General John Pope and charged with the protection of Washington. Pope's army was

Gen. John Pope.

made up of three army corps under the commands of Generals Banks, Sigel and Irvin McDowell.

On August the 26th Confederate General Stonewall Jackson attacked the Union supply depot at Manassas. His troops made free with everything they could lay their hands on, from boots and saddles, to food and medicine. Everything they couldn't carry away with them was destroyed so that it couldn't be used by the enemy. The attack on the depot told Pope where Jackson was, so he immediately turned his army toward Manassas and set forth to find him. In the meantime McClellan and his Army of the Potomac was already on its way from the east to join him.

Confederate Generals Lee and Longstreet, too, were on the move. They were making all speed to join Jackson. Jackson, knowing that if McClellan were allowed to join Pope the Union force would be able to overwhelm them by sheer weight of numbers, decided it would be best to bring Pope to battle before the two Federal armies could combine.

At five o'clock on the afternoon of August 28th, 1862, a lone rider on a ridge overlooking the Warrenton Turnpike observed a long column of Union soldiers making their way slowly eastward. For a while the rider could be seen observing the column, then he turned and trotted away toward the woods in the distance and was gone. The column of Union soldiers was Rufus King's division of Irvin McDowell's corps, and the lone rider was Stonewall Jackson. The second battle of Bull Run was about to begin.

Your tour of the battlefield will take you over a 12-mile route designed to show you all the of most important sites on the field. Please be careful when driving on the two highways that divide the park – US 29, the old Warrenton Turnpike; and VA 234, the old Manassas-Sudley Road – and observe the speed limit of 45 miles per hour when you are on them; the speed limit in the park itself is 25 miles per hour. The first stop on your tour is Battery Heights. Leave the Visitor Center and go down the driveway and then turn right onto route 234, go about a half-mile until you reach the intersection at the Stone House and then turn left at the red light onto route 29, the Warrenton Turnpike. Follow the road for about a mile and watch for the Park Service sign on the right. When you reach it, pull off the road and park your vehicle.

Battery Heights:
The second battle of Manassas began here in the late afternoon of August 28th, 1862. General Rufus King's division was marching east along this road when it was seen by Jackson, whose wing of General Lee's Army of Northern Virginia, more than 24,000 troops, was waiting behind an old, unfinished railroad embankment a little less than a half-mile away to the north. All day long Jackson's army rested, recovering from the several days of marching that had brought them to this position. Late that afternoon one of Jackson's staff officers brought him the news he had been waiting for: a long column of Union soldiers was marching along the Warrenton Turnpike. Jackson went to see for himself and quickly realized that the opportunity he had been awaiting was at hand. When he returned from the ridge he told his officers, *"Bring up your men, gentlemen."* Within minutes two Confederate batteries were in position on the ridge in front of you and the first cannon shells were falling on the Federal column.

King's division was taken completely by surprise, but not particularly bothered. Union Brigadier General John Gibbon was leading the second brigade in the column. He believed that the cannon fire was coming from an isolated section of J.E.B. Stuart's Confederate cavalry, and that they needed either to be chased off or captured before the column could continue. Gibbon, himself an ex-artillery officer, called for his old battery "B" of the 4th U.S. Artillery commanded by Captain J.B. Campbell. Campbell placed his guns in this field close to the position marked by the 12-pounder Napoleons to your right. Campbell's battery "B" opened up with all six of his Napoleons and soon was engaged in a lively duel with the two Confederate batteries on the ridge; the battle had begun.

Gibbon ordered his infantry forward toward the ridge. In what seemed like only seconds his full brigade had become involved, and this entire section, from the farmhouse of John Brawner beyond the woods to your left, to the hollow in front of you, had turned into a raging, flaming hell-hole. For more than an hour and a half the two battle lines stood, less than 100 yards apart, locked in a deadly shooting battle.

The casualties mounted at an alarming rate. Confederate General Taliaferro went down, wounded three times and Colonel John Neff of the 33rd Virginia was killed. During that hour and a half 200 Confederates were killed, and more than 1,200 Federals lay dead or wounded. Every field officer of the 7th Wisconsin had gone down either killed or wounded. By this time the daylight was almost gone but still the battle continued. As the sky darkened the men fought on by the light of the muzzle flashes from cannon and musket until at last, at about 9 p.m., the gunfire began to subside. The first day of the battle of 2nd Manassas was over; the cost in human lives had been enormous. The next morning it could be seen that the fields from here to Brawner's farm lay thick with the bodies of the dead of both sides.

The next stop on your tour is the Stone House. Leave the parking lot and turn left onto Route 29. Continue along the road until you reach the intersection with Route 234 where you will find a picnic area at **Stop Number 2** on your left.

The Stone House:

To make the best of this historic site park your vehicle and make the short walk to the top of Buck Hill just to the rear of the house. Buck Hill was the site of General Pope's battlefield headquarters at second Manassas.

It's difficult to imagine today the scene as it must have been on top of this hill during the two days of August 29th and 30th, 1862. The crest here had been turned into a tented military village. The entire area was a hive of activity with general officers, staff officers, colonels, captains, and an assortment of couriers hurrying back and forth to all points on the battlefield as General Pope tried to maintain control of the battle.

From the top of the hill you have an excellent view of the southern half of the battlefield and several of its most important features and landmarks. Just below you is, of course, the Stone House – a 19th-century structure and one of only two original Civil War period buildings on the battlefield. During both battles of Bull Run it served as a field hospital. To the south you can see a two-story house on the top of Henry Hill. It, too, saw action during both battles. To the right of Henry Hill, about a fourth of a mile away, you can see Chinn Ridge, and about a half-mile away to the west on this side of the Warrenton Turnpike you can see the house that replaced the original Dogan House, and Dogan Ridge itself. It was on that ridge, on August 30th, that General Pope assembled a massive concentration of Union artillery. Just to the north you can see Matthew's Hill, the scene of the early action at the battle of 1st Manassas more than a year earlier.

After you have taken time out to view the Stone House itself you can leave the Park Service lot and turn right onto Route 234, the old Sudley Road. Go about a half-mile until you reach the picnic area at the top of the hill on your left and Dogan Ridge.

Dogan Ridge:
All through the long night of August 28th Confederate General Stonewall Jackson prepared to meet the Union attack he knew must come the next morning. He ranged his more than 24,000 men and artillery in a line of battle across a one-and-a-half-mile front that ran from his right flank at Brawner's Farm to your left, almost to Sudley Church about a mile away from here to

the north. By the morning of the 29th Jackson's line was extended along an almost impregnable line of ready-made, heavily fortified breastworks which incorporated the cuttings and embankments of an abandoned, unfinished railroad spur which runs north and south through the woods about a half-mile from here to the north-west in front of you.

At about 5:30 on the morning of August 29th Union General Franz Sigel moved to attack the Confederate positions on the abandoned railroad. He advanced with his entire 1st Army Corps of more than 9,000 men in two divisions across the fields in front of you. General Robert C. Schenk and the 1st division moved westward along the Warrenton Turnpike to threaten Jackson's right flank while General Carl Schurz and his division headed out across the fields to attack the Confederate breastworks head on. He would be supported by artillery fire from the low ridge ahead of you.

Suddenly, the line of woods in the distance erupted in a hailstorm of Confederate musket and cannon fire. The effect on the Federal line was devastating. All throughout the morning, in one desperate frontal attack after another, the Federal brigades assaulted the Confederate fortifications along the abandoned railroad, all to no avail. Desperate as the Union attack on Jackson's front was, it was not meant to be Pope's main thrust to destroy Jackson's beleaguered force. That dubious honor was to have gone to Union General Fitz John Porter.

Pope, knowing that he had Jackson outnumbered by more than two to one, felt that if he could hold Jackson's attention by sending General Sigel and the 1st Corps against him in an all-out frontal attack it would give Porter the time and the cover needed to march his army corps of 11,000 men from Manassas Junction toward Gainsville, make a sharp turn toward the north, and then fall on Jackson's right and rear flanks. It would then be simply a matter of rolling up the entire Confederate line from one end to the other and the battle would be over.

So, as the morning wore on, Generals Sigel, Schenk, and Schurz fought a series of disjointed, uncoordinated, and for the most part, half-hearted and futile actions against Jackson's almost impregnable line of breastworks, and all through the morning General Pope waited for the sound of gunfire from the southwest that would herald the commencement of General Porter's flanking attack; it never came.

Shortly before noon, unknown to General Pope, Confederate General James Longstreet arrived on the field with the entire second wing of Robert E. Lee's Army of Northern Virginia – more than 28,000 men. When the rest of the army arrived later that afternoon Lee's strength had increased to more than 55,000; General Jackson was no longer alone.

When you are ready to continue your tour leave the parking lot and turn left onto Route 234. Go for about a mile until you see the sign for **Stop Number 4** and then turn into the parking lot on your left.

Sudley Church:
This is the position occupied by Jackson's extreme left wing. The abandoned railroad and the earthworks are still in good condition and, as you can see, they are located just to the south of this parking lot. It was the left wing of Jackson's line that saw most of the fighting all day long on August 29th. Confederate General Ambrose Powel Hill and his division held the position here, the scene of some of the heaviest fighting. During the morning he weathered the attacks from Sigel's 1st Army Corps as they tried to separate him from the Sudley Road and Jackson's potential escape route to the north. During the afternoon it was Union General Samuel P. Heintzelman's 3rd Army Corps that took up the attack on Hill's positions. Then at around 5:30 in the afternoon Union General Phil Kearny's "thieves" supported by Steven's division of Reno's corps and "Fighting" Joe Hooker with his division, smashed into these positions on Jackson's left wing in an all-out frontal attack that was designed to turn the Confederate flank. As the action raged around this position the battle-weary Confederates began to run out of ammunition. Still they fought on, at times reduced to throwing rocks at the enemy, and, during the rare lulls in the fighting, they ransacked the pouches of their fallen comrades for ammunition.

As the hour grew late the fighting became desperate and often hand-to-hand; for almost an hour the bayonet ruled the embankments on the abandoned railroad. It was only the timely intervention of Jubal Early with reinforcements from Virginia and Georgia, and the typical lack of cohesion among the attacking Federals, that finally saved the day. General A.P. Hill and his men had been engaged, almost continuously, for more than ten hours. Stonewall Jackson, on hearing the good news and with a rare smile on his face, was heard to say, *"I knew he could do it."*

Union General Kearny, his men by now in retreat, went to Pope on Buck Hill in search of reinforcements; there were none to be had.

> To continue your tour leave the Park Service lot and once again turn left onto the old Sudley Road, Route 234. Go for about two-tenths of a mile and then turn left onto Route 622. Route 234 is an extremely busy road and the turn onto 622, just beyond the church, is almost concealed so keep a sharp lookout for it and be watchful of the traffic. Go for about a mile on 622 until you reach the parking lot on your left and **Stop Number 5.** Leave your vehicle and make the short walk across the road and into the woods where you will find the unfinished earthworks of the railroad.

The Abandoned Railroad:
This position was held by Confederate General A.R. Lawton and marks a point roughly at the center of Jackson's line. At four o'clock on the afternoon of August 29th Union Colonel James Negley's brigade of Reno's 9th Army Corps smashed through the trees and attacked this position. The Confederate defenders in front of them and on both sides unleashed such a hailstorm of fire the Federals became convinced they were under fire from their own 48th Pennsylvania regiment. Negley's standard bearer angrily waved the Stars and Stripes from the top of the embankment only to receive a further firestorm of minie balls and canister. Negley's men turned and ran. The Confederates, whooping and yelling, stormed out of the woods in pursuit and ran slap bang into the surprised Excelsior brigade of Union

General Nelson Taylor, turning it into a fleeing, panic-stricken mob. The Confederates were elated. Colonel Negley had lost almost 50% of his brigade; more than 500 of 1,300 men.

During the afternoon Confederate Generals Longstreet and Robert E. Lee began consolidating their position in preparation for the battle they were sure would come the following morning. It's interesting to note that by late afternoon on the 29th of August Longstreet had been able to move more than 28,000 men and equipment into position on the Confederate right and General Pope was completely unaware of it. In fact, by the morning of August 30th, Pope had managed to convince himself that the battle was over and that Jackson had left the field and was retreating back toward the Bull Run Mountains. Never had a battlefield commander been so wrong.

That morning, August 30th, Stonewall Jackson held the same positions as he had the day before. Longstreet, however, had joined his own left flank to Jackson's right flank; a small gap between the two Confederate wings was plugged by the 36 massed cannon of two Confederate artillery battalions under the command of Colonel Stephen D. Lee, a formidable array of death and destruction. Longstreet's line of battle extended southward from Brawner's farm and overlapped the Union lines by almost a mile. So, by mid-morning Lee's army of more than 55,000 was positioned in a great "vee" shaped formation, the mouth of which resembled a gigantic trap ready to engulf any Union force that Pope might send against it. When noon came Pope still believed that Jackson was on the run. He was not aware that Lee had taken the field with the entire Army of Northern Virginia.

To continue your tour leave the parking lot and turn left onto Route 622, The Groveton-Sudley Road. Go for about a half-mile until you reach the parking area at **Stop Number 6**, the Deep Cut. From here you can take a short walking tour of about 30 minutes that will lead you across the field in front of you, into the woods, and on to the Deep Cut in the railroad embankment where most of the action here, on the afternoon of August 30th, took place. The walk is a fairly easy one and is well worth the effort, for rarely will you have such an opportunity to relive, via the ship of the imagination, the action almost exactly as it took place.

The Deep Cut:

General Porter with his 5th Army Corps was by now in position at the center of the Union line close to the John Dogan house. Pope, still clinging to his belief that Jackson was in retreat, ordered Porter to move forward and smash Jackson's rearguard, and then he ordered his entire army to make ready to pursue the fleeing Confederates. Within minutes Pope's illusions were shattered. Porter's brigades ran slap into the still firmly entrenched Confederate brigades holding Jackson's right flank in the railroad fortifications.

Pope, however, was undaunted and ordered Porter to press on with his attack. A little after mid-day Porter, with more than 10,000 men including his own 5th Army Corps, moved into the woods to the east of this road, and then the Groveton-Sudley Lane. They were met by a veritable firestorm of Confederate artillery fire, and for more than two hours the entire Union division commanded by Brigadier General Daniel Butterfield lay face-down among the trees waiting for the holocaust to subside. General George Sykes and his brigade assumed a similar position on Butterfield's left.

> The first stop on your walking tour here at Deep Cut is the Cedar Pole Monument at the white sign in the middle of the field in front of you. As you walk across the field you should be aware that the woods to the left didn't exist at the time of the battle; the entire area in front and to the left was one vast open field.

At three o'clock in the afternoon as Butterfield's division, now supported by General Hatch's division, moved out of the woods and started across this field toward the Confederate positions they were met by a storm of canister and shells. For a moment or two the blue-clad line faltered, and then they pressed forward at the double-quick. Volley after volley of cannon fire smashed into and tore great gaps in the advancing Federal line; on they went. Then, at a distance of about 200 yards, the entire Confederate line of breastworks erupted in a cauldron of flame and minie balls as several thousand muskets opened fire, almost as one.

The next point on your walking tour is the stone obelisk you see at the top of the hill. It was here that the fighting reached a crescendo as the men of Butterfield's and Hatch's divisions came under the combined Confederate musket and cannon fire of Stafford's, and Johnston's brigades. The air around them was filled with lead and iron. Great gaps were blown into the Federal lines as they advanced into what, for most, must have seemed like certain death. But not for a single second did the Yankees hesitate. The massed Federal infantry charged on up the hill and, eventually, the steady and continuous fire they poured upon the enemy began to take its effect. The two opposing lines closed to a distance that could be measured only in feet. The carnage they wrought upon each other was incredible.

Jackson, realizing that his front line was in trouble, and in real danger of collapsing, ordered his second rank forward in support. They, too, were decimated by the deadly Federal firepower. Confederate brigade commander Colonel Baylor, seeing his men beginning to falter, grabbed his unit's battle flag and, waving it high in the air, charged the Federal line screaming and yelling for his men to follow him. And they did, only to see the brave colonel fall dead under a hail of bullets.

As you walk along the railroad cutting to your right you should be able to imagine what it must have been like at the height of the battle as the men of Starke's Confederate division struggled to hold their position here, and waited for reinforcements to arrive from General Longstreet's corps.

All along the embankment in front of you Colonel Leroy Stafford's Louisiana brigade poured forth volley after volley into the ranks of the New Yorkers as they scrambled up the embankment. So intense was the firestorm from the embankment the Federals were unable to raise their heads to aim their weapons; instead they poked their rifles over the top and fired blindly down on the southerners below. At one point a single, mounted Union officer with sword waving over his head managed to reach the top. Many of the Confederates screamed to their comrades not to kill him, but it was no use. Down he went, horse and rider, riddled with Confederate minie balls.

For more than 30 minutes Stafford and his men held their position. All this time Union reinforcements tried in vain to reach the beleaguered New Yorkers trapped here in front of the breastworks. As they charged across the fields to your right they, too, came under fire from the massed guns of Stephen D. Lee's artillery battalions and were driven back again in confusion. Ammunition on the Confederate side of the embankment began to run low. Soon the rebel army was reduced to throwing cannon ball sized rocks down on the Federal ranks; the situation became grim.

Then, at last, Confederate reinforcements from General A.P. Hill's division began arriving with ammunition enough for all. Confederate fire all along the embankment and from both sides now combined with Stephen D. Lee's artillery and began to rake and devastate General Porter's divisions in the fields to your right. It was the beginning of the end. The Union forces had no alternative but to fall back the way they came. As they did so the Confederate batteries redoubled their efforts, firing barrage after barrage of double-loaded canister into the decimated ranks of retreating Federals.

Panic set in and the Union retreat turned into a wild race across the fields to the cover of the trees beyond. More than a third of Porter's Federal force were left dead and wounded upon the field. For the survivors of both sides it had been an afternoon they would remember above all others for the rest of their lives.

When you have finished your walk and are ready to continue your tour return to your car, leave the parking lot and continue along Route 622 for about a half-mile until you reach the intersection with Route 29. Turn left there and you will see a sign indicating the parking lot for the Dogan House Confederate Cemetery on your left.

Groveton:

In 1862 this was Groveton, a tiny community of perhaps eight or so small houses. During the battle of second Manassas the small white house you see just to the west was the home of Mrs. Lucinda Dogan and her family. Today it has been lovingly restored to its Civil War era condition and is the second of the two remaining original structures on the battlefield; the other is, of course, the Stone House.

The nearby Confederate Cemetery was established in the 1870s. Of the thousands of Confederate soldiers that died on these fields during the two battles for Manassas, the 260 buried here are but a tiny representation of the total. Many of the Confederate dead still lie in unknown mass graves somewhere on the battlefield. Only 40 of the 260 buried here have been identified. After the war, the Union dead were, for the most part, disinterred from their hurriedly dug mass graves and taken home to be reburied, some in National Cemeteries and some close to the families they left behind.

The next stop on the tour is New York Avenue; to reach it you must leave the parking lot here and turn left onto Route 29. Go for about a tenth of a mile and then turn right onto New York Avenue. Follow the road for just a short distance until you reach the parking area between the two New York monuments.

The New York Monuments:

At about four o'clock in the afternoon Confederate General James Longstreet seized the initiative. You will remember that his wing of Lee's army was in a line of battle that stretched from Brawner's farm on Jackson's right, almost a mile and a half to the south, and formed one entire arm of a great, inverted Confederate "vee" shaped formation. What was left of General Porter's 5th Army Corps now held the high ground at the John Dogan House.

It was at this point, so it seems, that General McDowell had a temporary loss of sanity, for, without thinking, he ordered General Sigel's troops out of position and sent them in support of General Porter, leaving only a single battery under the command of Lieutenant Charles Hazlett here, on the ridge overlooking Groveton, to face the entire might of Longstreet's 28,000 strong army; not even the pickets were left behind to defend Hazlett and his lone battery. Hazlett was horrified, and quickly sent for help. All that was available was a single volunteer brigade commanded by Colonel G.K. Warren, about 1,000 men in all, of General Sykes' division comprising the 5th New York Zouaves and the 10th New York infantry. These few, hurriedly took up a position to Hazlett's left and prepared to meet whatever General Longstreet might send toward them; they did not have long to wait. At about 4:30 in the afternoon the great Confederate counterattack began.

Longstreet's entire wing of 28,000 men began to move forward. Five full Confederate divisions led by General John B. Hood's Texans advanced upon this position held by the two lonely New York regiments.

Imagine, if you can, what it must have been like that afternoon for those few brave men as they faced the combined might of the entire Confederate army. In less than a minute the fields as you look toward Groveton had turned gray, and had seemed to have taken on a life of their own as thousands upon thousands of Longstreet's men moved into view in front of them. The 10th New York had been sent to a forward position to act as skirmishers some 500 yards to the front. They were immediately overrun and barely had time to fall back to join the 5th New York Zouaves here, resplendent in their red pantaloons, blue jackets and tasseled fezzes. The air around them was filled with thousands upon thousands of Confederate minie balls. The New Yorkers began to drop like so many flies. In less than five minutes the 5th New York Zouaves suffered the highest percentage of men killed outright in a single Civil War battle: 124 were killed and 180 were wounded. Lieutenant Hazlett, unable to help them, desperately limbered his guns and dragged them away at the full gallop toward the rear. A cry went up among the New Yorkers "every man for himself," and they, too, turned and ran for cover.

Twenty minutes later, when the New Yorkers rallied round their flag once more, only 40 of the original 490 soldiers that took to the field as 5th New York Zouaves remained.

Stop Number 9 on your tour is Hazel Plain, the site of the old Chinn House. When you are ready to continue, you should drive back down New York Avenue and turn right onto Route 29. Go to the intersection with Route 234 and turn right. Continue on to the top of the hill and turn right opposite the Visitor Center onto the park road and follow it until you come to a tee junction and then turn right and go to the top of the hill, where you will find the Hazel Plain parking area to your left.

Hazel Plain:

The stone foundations you see in front of you are all that remain of Benjamin Chinn's plantation. During the first battle of Manassas it was a Confederate artillery position; during both battles the house saw service as a field hospital.

Take a few moments to look around and then, when you are ready, continue on along the park road for about a quarter of a mile until you reach the pull-off on your right, **Stop Number 10**. Park your vehicle there and make the short walk out to the lone oak tree to the right of Webster's Grove. There, as you look back toward the site of the Chinn House, you will have the best view of the scene of the fierce fighting on Chinn Ridge as the Union generals struggled to buy enough time for General Pope to save his battered army.

Chinn Ridge:

As Longstreet's wing of the great Confederate "vee" shaped formation began to wheel left toward the northeast it seemed inevitable that it would destroy every Federal position in its path. Longstreet's objective was Henry Hill just to the east of here. If he could take it he would command the Warrenton Turnpike and the destruction of Pope's entire army would seem to be inevitable. It was imperative, then, that Pope should get enough men onto Henry Hill to defend it, but to do that he had to buy some time. He ordered General Reynolds and his two remaining brigades, along with those of Generals Sykes and Reno to Henry Hill. The four brigades of Generals Tower, Hartsuff, Milroy, and Krzyzanowski were sent to Chinn Ridge with all speed and orders to hold it all costs.

On and on rolled the Confederate juggernaught. Like some great land-locked storm it swept across the fields until it reached the slopes of Chinn Ridge. As the first Confederate units approached the ridge, the only Union troops in position here were the men of Colonel Nathaniel McLean's Ohio brigade and a single battery of artillery. As they prepared to receive the advancing Confederate units from the right flank, Brigadier General Nathan Evans' brigade of South Carolinians came charging out of the woods some 75 yards to the front. The Ohio regiments turned and fired by file: two men at a time fired their muskets from one end of the line to the other. The cannoneers double-loaded their pieces with canister and, for a moment at least, Evans' brigade staggered, and then stopped altogether under the withering, Union firestorm.

Evans was soon reinforced by Micah Jenkins' South Carolina brigade, and then by two more Virginia brigades under the command of Colonels Eppa Hunton and Montgomery Corse, all moving north up the slopes of the ridge. Union Colonel McLean ordered a section of the battery to turn and drive them back when someone yelled that the advancing Virginians were Union reinforcements. Through the dense clouds of smoke all McLean could see of the advancing soldiers were their dark uniforms, so he held his fire. The Virginians charged and sent a hailstorm of minie balls into the Ohio regiments on the ridge.

Then, as McLean's men began to withdraw, the Union reinforcements began to arrive. The fighting here on Chinn Ridge grew to monumental proportions as thousands of men from both sides shot, thrust, cut and slashed beneath the dense clouds of choking gunsmoke. For more than an hour the four Union brigades of Generals Tower, Hartsuff, Milroy, and Krzyzanowski fought resolutely on as they struggled to hold the ridge and buy time for General Pope but, inevitably, the overwhelming odds they faced began to tell. The hillside around and below the Chinn

House was seething, for as far as the eye could see, with Confederate soldiers.

Slowly, but surely, with Confederate fire now pouring in upon them from every direction, the thin blue lines were driven backward until, at last, they were forced from the field in retreat. Confederate Lieutenant Colonel F.G. Skinner, riding ahead of his 1st Virginia regiment, charged the union battery here and, with a single slash of his sword, almost decapitated one of the cannoneers. He killed another with a single thrust almost at the same time as a Union infantryman plunged a bayonet into him and unhorsed him. Declining aid he said, *"Bah! Witness gentlemen, I took this battery."*

A Federal artilleryman jumped astride the lead horse of his limber and careened off at full gallop pulling the gun to safety. As he did so he came under fire from a half-hundred Virginia marksmen. He escaped unscathed and, once out of range, stopped his wild gallop and turned and waved his cap at the enthusiastically cheering Confederate sharpshooters.

Alexander Hunter of the 17th Virginia was among the Confederates who fought here on the ridge that afternoon in 1862. Here's how he described the action: *"The Seventeenth was on the right of the line, and the other regiments dressed by our colors as we bore right oblique toward the battery, which was now hidden by a volleying fume that settled upon the crest.*

"Still the advance was stayed or the ranks broken. We neared the Chinn House, when suddenly a long line of the enemy rose from behind an old stone wall and poured straight into our breasts a withering volley at pointblank distance. It was so unexpected, this attack. Many were falling killed or wounded, and but for the intrepid coolness of its colonel, the Seventeenth would have retired from the field in disorder. His clear, ringing voice was heard and the wavering line reformed. A rattling volley answered the foe, and for a moment or two the contest was fiercely waged. Then the colonel fell with his knee frightfully shattered by a minie-ball. Once down, the calm, reassuring tones heard no longer, the line broke. Now individual bravery made up for the

disaster. The officers surged ahead with their swords waving in the air, cheering on the men, who kept close to their heels, loading and firing as they ran. The line of blue was not fifty yards distant and every man took a sure, close aim before his finger pressed the trigger. It was a decisive fight of about ten minutes, and both sides stood off gamely to their work. Our foes were a Western regiment from Ohio, who gave and received and asked no odds. The left of our brigade having struck the enemy's right and doubled it up, now sent one volley into their flank.

"In a moment the blue line quivered and then went to pieces. Officers and men broke for the rear, one regimental colors were captured by Jim Coleman, of the Seventeenth. In a few moments there were none left except the dead and wounded." (James Murfin, *Battlefields of the Civil War*, Colour Library Books Ltd., (UK) Surrey, England, 1988).

As General Robert E. Lee rode out to inspect one of his Confederate batteries he was told that one of the gunners would like to have a word with him. *"Well, my man,"* he said, *"what can I do for you?"* The young man looked up at him, smiled, and then said, *"Why General, don't you know me?"* The General looked closely at him and then, beneath the dirt and grime that covered the young man's face, Lee recognized his youngest son, Private Robert E. Lee Jr.

> When you are ready to continue the tour return to your car, drive back to the Visitor Center and leave your vehicle in the parking area there. The last stop on the tour is Henry Hill and it's just a short walk from the Visitor Center.

Henry Hill:

As the afternoon wore on it became obvious to Pope and his generals that the Army of Virginia was beaten. By 7:00 p.m. Pope had realized that all he could hope for now was to make an effective withdrawal and save what was left of his beleaguered force. To do that he had to keep open the line of retreat over the Stone Bridge. If the Confederates were allowed to gain control of the bridge all would be lost. Pope looked upward at the darkening sky and shuddered; as if the Federal army hadn't suffered enough already, storm clouds were gathering in the heavens overhead; it already was beginning to rain.

The battle on Chinn Ridge raged on for more than an hour and the Federals there, locked in some of the most desperate fighting of the war, struggled to hold their ground and buy time enough for Pope to secure his lines of retreat. But for his beleaguered force on Chinn Ridge, all that now stood between Pope and total destruction at the hands of General Longstreet was a single, thin, rag-tag Union line: two brigades of the Pennsylvania Reserve Division under the command of General John Reynolds. These few were drawn up in two ranks on Henry Hill behind the rubble of the one-time home of Mrs. Judith Carter Henry; a lady who had met her end at the hands of the Union artillery almost a year earlier during the first battle of Bull Run.

The grim-faced Pennsylvanians watched from here as Longstreet's Confederate brigades on Chinn Ridge smashed the last remnants of the retreating Union forces and moved resolutely toward this position. Then, the ecstatic Confederates, screaming the Rebel yell, charged toward the slopes of Henry Hill.

Gathering himself together, General Reynolds took a deep breath and shouted at the top of his lungs, *"Forward, reserves!"* And, forward they went at the double-quick. The two armies came together in a cataclysmic collision at the Sudley Road. In minutes the entire area had turned into a holocaust. General Reynolds himself grabbed the battle flag of the 2nd Pennsylvania and, taking his life in his hands, galloped the entire length of the Federal front, screaming and yelling encouragement to his men. The Confederate advance was stopped dead in its tracks.

General Richard Anderson joined in the fray on the Confederate side. Reynolds was joined by General Sykes and his regulars. The battle raged on but, this time, the Union brigades would not give way. The sky turned dark and Longstreet had no choice but to break off the engagement and withdraw his forces back to the heights of Chinn Ridge.

At 8:00 p.m. General Pope ordered his army to retreat across the Bull Run toward Centerville. By this time it was raining hard and the dejected Union army began its long march through the mud and the downpour away from the Bull Run river toward the relative safety of the one-time Confederate defenses along the heights at Centerville. The battle of Second Manassas was over. The cost to both armies had been heavy. Pope had lost more than 20% of his army: almost 15,000 casualties. General Lee had fared only slightly better with some 9,000 casualties, about 17% of his total force of 55,000 effectives.

There's an interesting sidelight to the fighting at Manassas on the 29th of August. Due to Porter's failure to carry out Pope's planned flanking attack against Stonewall Jackson, and Pope's unwillingness to accept responsibility for his own defeat, Pope had Porter court marshaled for disobedience of orders and misbehavior in the face of the enemy. Porter was found guilty and dismissed from the army. He spent the next 15 years trying to clear his name. It was not until 1878 when his case was reheard at West Point, and new evidence was introduced and new witnesses, including Confederate Generals Longstreet and Jubal Early, gave evidence on his behalf, that he finally won his case. He was restored to the army rolls with full honor and retirement benefits almost 20 years after the battle.

The Manassas National Military Park is 26 miles south of Washington DC near the intersection of I-66 and VA 234 at 12521 Lee Highway, Manassas, VA 22110. The phone number is 703-754-1861. The Visitor Center is open daily except Christmas.

Where to Stay, What to Do

Attractions

The Manassas Museum: 9101 Prince William Street. Museum features collections dealing with the Northern Virginia Piedmont history from prehistoric to modern times with special emphasis on the Civil War. Open daily except Monday, closed Jan. 1st, Thanksgiving, Dec. 24th & 25th. Phone 368-1873.

Annual Events

Prince William County Fair: Carnival, entertainment, tractor pull, exhibits. Phone 368-0173. Mid-August.

Re-enactment Of The Civil War Battle Of Manassas: Long Park. Phone 361-7181. Last weekend in August.

Hotels

Best Western: 8640 Mathis Ave. 703-368-7070. 60 rooms, under 12 free, crib free, cable TV, free continental breakfast, cafe adjacent, room service, check-out 11 a.m., meeting rooms, free airport transportation, accepts credit cards.

Courtyard By Marriott: 10701 Battlefield Pkwy. 703-335-1300. 149 rooms, under 19 free, crib free, cable TV, pool, cafe, room service, check-out 1 p.m., meeting rooms, accepts credit cards.

Days Inn: 10653 Balls Ford Road. 703-368-2800. 113 rooms, under 18 free, crib free, cable TV, pool, free coffee in lobby, check-out 11 a.m., meeting rooms, accepts credit cards.

HoJo Inn: 7249 New Market Ct. 703-369-1700. 159 rooms, under 18 free, crib free, cable TV, free continental breakfast, cafe adjacent, check-out 11 a.m., meeting rooms, accepts credit cards.

Ramada Inn: 10820 Balls Ford Rd. 703-361-8000. 121 rooms, under 18 free, crib free, cable TV, pool, cafe, room service, check-out 11 a.m., meeting rooms, accepts credit cards.

Shoney's Inn: 8691 Phoenix Dr. 703-369-6323. 78 rooms, under 18 free, crib free, cable TV, pool, cafe adjacent, check-out noon, meeting rooms, accepts credit cards.

Holiday Inn: 10800 Vandor Lane. 703-335-0000. 160 rooms, under 18 free, TV, pool, free continental breakfast, cafe, room service, check-out noon, meeting rooms, accepts credit cards.

Quality Inn: 7295 Williamson Blvd. 703-369-1100. 125 rooms, under 18 free, crib free, cable TV, pool, free continental breakfast, check-out 11 a.m., meeting rooms, accepts credit cards.

Restaurants

Carmello's: 9108 Center St. 703-368-5522. Children's meals, specializes in fresh seafood, veal, chicken, own pasta; accepts credit cards.

Red, Hot & Blue: 8637 Sudley Road, 703-330-4847. Children's meals, specializes in smoked prime rib, pulled pork sandwich, Memphis pit barbecue. Accepts credit cards.

Chapter 6

Antietam

September, 1862

Antietam National Battlefield Park is located to the north and east of Sharpsburg, Maryland along MD 34 and 65. Both routes intersect either US 40 or 40A and I-70. The address is PO Box 158, Sharpsburg MD 21782. The Visitor Center is north of Sharpsburg on MD 65 and is open daily except Thanksgiving, Christmas and New Years Day. The Visitor Center houses a museum and offers information, with a 26-minute orientation movie shown on the hour. All Visitor Center facilities and most tour route exhibits are wheelchair accessible. The phone number is 301-432-7648.

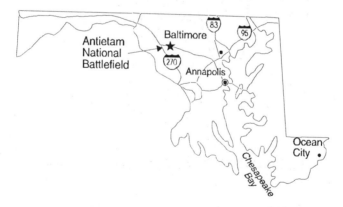

The battle of Antietam was the culmination of General Robert E. Lee's first attempt to take the war onto Union territory. Lee crossed the Potomac river into Maryland on September 5th, 1862 following his stunning victory at the second battle of Manassas on August 29th and 30th, with every intention of capitalizing on the initiative he and his Army of Northern

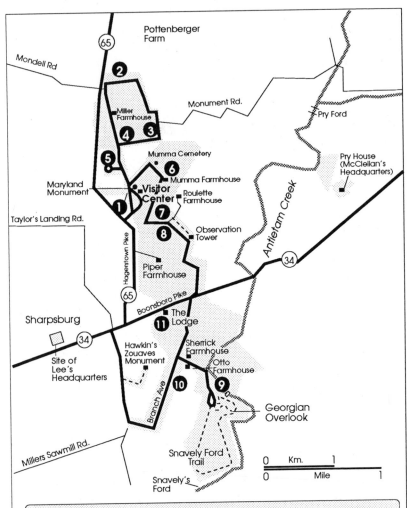

Antietam National Battlefield

1. Dunker Church
2. North Woods
3. East Woods
4. The Cornfield
5. West Woods
6. Mumma Farm
7. Roulette Farm
8. Sunden Road (Bloody Land)
9. Lower Bridge
10. The Final Attack
11. Antietam National Cemetery

Virginia had fought so hard to win. It was not his intention, however, to attack the Federal fortifications around Washington itself. His main objectives were first political: if he could wage a successful war against the North on its own territory he would be able to gain not only a great tactical victory but a moral one as well, and might even gain foreign support for the Confederacy into the bargain. Second, he needed to resupply his exhausted army. Most of his men were hungry and had lived off the land for more than two weeks. They were short of even the most basic necessities, including shoes. Third, he was determined to tempt Union General George B. McClellan away from the fortifications around the Federal capitol and then bring him to battle at a place of his own, Lee's, choosing.

With these three objectives in mind, Lee decided to risk it all. He did something that was against all the rules of warfare, something so bold that it was thought by many of his contemporaries to be at best reckless, and at worst bordering on the insane: he divided his army. Lee had crossed the Potomac with a force of some 40,000 men. McClellan would oppose him with more than twice that number, about 88,000. Lee, however, knew his adversary very well, and while he regarded him as a competent general he knew also that the man was timid, and his own worst enemy into the bargain. And though Lee's judgment of McClellan was basically correct, and he would decisively outgeneral him, the consequences of a series of mistakes and misjudgments on both sides would leave his army badly mauled and his first invasion of Northern territory in tatters.

The first of those mistakes involved Lee's General Order Number 191. Somehow two copies of this general order from Lee, instead of the usual one, were sent to one of his field commanders by mistake. One of those copies was handled properly; the other went missing. It became famous as "The Lost Order" and by the afternoon of September 13th it had wound up in the hands of none other than General McClellan himself. It outlined General Lee's entire plan of campaign including that fact that he had divided his army and sent General Stonewall Jackson with six divisions to take the Federal supply depot and garrison at Harpers Ferry.

Major Gen. George McClellan, fourth from right, with his staff in March, 1862.

General McClellan now was in possession of information that told him a swift advance would place him solidly between the divided elements of Lee's army. To President Lincoln he promised he would lose no time, and would catch Lee in his own trap. *"My general idea is to cut the enemy in two and beat him in detail,"* he said. What exactly he meant by "lose no time" is anybody's guess for it wasn't until the next day, some 18 hours after receiving Lee's Order 191, that he finally moved toward the Confederate positions in the passes through South Mountain where, after a short but bloody battle on the afternoon of September 14th, Lee withdrew his tiny army of less than 15,000 men and reformed them on the high ground to the west of Antietam Creek, and to the northeast of Sharpsburg.

Had McClellan pursued his enemy and brought him swiftly to battle at first light the next morning he might well have avoided the terrible bloodshed that was shortly to follow. As it was he allowed Lee to escape and time to reform and reorganize his tiny force. The first of McClellan's troops did not begin arriving on the eastern banks of the Antietam until mid-afternoon on the 15th. McClellan himself arrived sometime after 3 p.m. when he made a cursory inspection of the situation and then decided *"it was too late in the day to attack."*

At eight o'clock that morning of September 15th, 17 miles away at Harpers Ferry, General Jackson had received the surrender of the Federal garrison. Included in the spoils were 13,000 small arms, 73 cannon and an enormous stock of supplies including food and a great many badly needed pairs of boots.

"Stonewall" Jackson.

McClellan heard the news of the fall of Harpers Ferry almost at the same time as General Lee. This and the fact that he knew Lee was preparing to make a stand at Sharpsburg did nothing to bolster his confidence. He was convinced that Lee had crossed the river into Maryland at the head of an army of more than 120,000 and, by those numbers, he was greatly outnumbered. In addition to that, he knew that Jackson must soon march north to rejoin Lee at Sharpsburg. Even so, Lee, by McClellan's own reckoning, after having split his force, could not have more than 30,000 men arrayed against him; he, McClellan, had more than 60,000. In actuality he outnumbered Lee by more than four-to-one.

Lee, too, was well aware of his predicament. So why did he decide to stay and face McClellan down? First, he believed the

Union soldiers to be disorganized and demoralized after their recent defeats; he was wrong. Second, he had supreme confidence in his abilities as a general. General McClellan had brought not only a superior force to Sharpsburg, he had brought himself – a fact, as far as General Lee was concerned that more than evened the odds. Lee was convinced beyond doubt that he could beat George McClellan on any field of battle. So, Lee stood on the heights overlooking Sharpsburg and Antietam Creek, daring McClellan to attack him. It was one colossal bluff, and for two days it worked; McClellan simply did not believe that Lee intended to bring him to battle. To General Franklin in Pleasant Valley he wrote, *"I think the enemy has abandoned the position in front of us, but the fog is so dense that I have not yet been able to determine. If the enemy is in force here, I shall attack him in the morning."*

But he didn't attack him in the morning. By the time the fog had burned off at around 10:30 a.m., and the Confederate army was seen to be in line of battle, *"It became evident from the force of the enemy and the strength of their position that desperate fighting alone could drive them from the field, and all felt that a great and terrible battle was at hand."* With that McClellan devoted the rest of the day, the 16th, to preparation, reconnoitering the field, positioning his troops, and *"perfecting arrangements for the attack."*

At mid-day the vanguard of Jackson's force began arriving at Sharpsburg. By the evening three divisions had reached the field and two more under the command of Confederate Generals Lafayette McLaws and Richard H. Anderson would arrive early on the morning of the 17th. A courier was sent at all speed to Harpers Ferry with orders for General Ambrose Powel Hill, whom Jackson had left to manage the details of the Federal surrender, to move out at first light and join Lee as soon as possible.

By the end of the day, the 16th, Lee had posted his meager forces in line of battle north and south along a ridge over a four-mile front that was parallel to, and just in front of, the Hagerstown Pike. The line ran from the Poffenberger Farm at the north end, down past Sharpsburg itself, and on to the lower bridge across the Antietam. General Jackson was placed in command of the left flank, General James Longstreet the right flank. A brigade of Major General J.E.B. Stuart's cavalry was posted at the northern flank of Lee's line and another was posted at the southern end. To the north Stuart had positioned 14 guns on the high ground known as Nicodemus Hill.

General McClellan decided, after a full day of planning, that he would attack the enemy to the north on Lee's left flank. The bridge there across the Antietam was undefended and out of range of the Confederate artillery. General Joseph Hooker and his 1st Army Corps, supported by General Joseph K.F. Mansfield's 12th Corps, would lead the attack on the Confederate left. General Porter and his 5th Corps would be held in reserve ready to take advantage, in case of victory, or as a defensive position should it become necessary. They would cross the Antietam that afternoon and make ready to do battle early the following morning, the 17th. General Sumner, the oldest general officer on the battlefield, was to hold his 2nd Corps in readiness behind the Antietam.

The Union cavalry, some 4,300 strong under the command of Brigadier General Alfred Pierson, was put in position at the Federal center with Porter's 5th Corps ready to deliver the coup-de-grace should the enemy be seen to be on the verge of defeat.

Major General Ambrose E. Burnside, McClellan's long-time friend, now out of favor, would be sent to the south to join Brigadier General Jacob Cox and the 9th Corps with the intention of moving across the lower bridge against Lee's right flank. It was a disgruntled Burnside that joined the 9th. General Cox offered to turn over command of the corps to Burnside; Burnside did not accept, and it was never really clear who did in fact command the 9th Corps at Antietam. To complicate matters even further neither general seemed to know what the 9th Corps' roll was to be in the upcoming battle. It seems that McClellan discussed his battle plan only with General Hooker; every one else was kept in the dark. Either that or McClellan had no plan after Hooker was to make his move against the Confederate left and was preparing to fight the battle as circumstances dictated. As it was, Burnside and Cox decided that they were meant to mount a diversion at the lower bridge while the main battle was to be fought by Hooker to the north. If that were so, then obviously if the diversion was to succeed it would have to made at precisely the same moment as Hooker opened his attack; that never happened.

Burnside, sulking over his perceived mistreatment at the hands of General McClellan, determined to do no more than carry out to the letter whatever orders he might receive from his commanding general.

That afternoon Hooker moved across the upper bridge and took position opposite Lee's left flank. At sunset there was a brief but fierce clash between Hooker's advance units and the Confederate outposts on Lee's extreme left, but by that time it was too dark for any real fighting. And so the long night of waiting began. The stage was set for what was to become the bloodiest single day of the entire Civil War.

To enable you to easily find your way around the battlefield the Park Service has clearly marked the route with a series of white arrows that lead the way to each major stop on the tour. All you have to do is follow them and you can't go wrong. Please observe the rules of the countryside: don't litter the park, don't climb on the cannon or the monuments, and please keep to the speed limit of 25 miles per hour.

To begin your tour of the battlefield leave the parking lot at the Visitor Center, turn right and drive to the first stop, The Dunker Church. Leave your vehicle in the parking lot and visit the church. Though it was rebuilt after collapsing during a storm in 1921 it is much the same today as it was in 1862. Much of the original material was reused in its reconstruction.

The Dunker Church:
At first light on the morning of September 17th General Hooker

The Dunker Church.

rode out to his picket line on the Poffenberger Farm to inspect the site of his intended assault on the Confederate left. As he looked southward across the fields he could see a small white building on the fringe of the woods next to the Hagerstown turnpike. It was a church, this church. It was built in 1853 by a pacifist sect of the German Baptist Brethren. Because of their belief in the practice of baptism by total immersion they became known as the Dunkers; hence the Dunker Church.

Hooker observed that morning that the Confederates had positioned several artillery batteries just across the turnpike from the church. He decided that the Rebel artillery position would his first objective. It seems strange that he gave no consideration to J.E.B. Stuart's massed guns just to the west on Nicodemus Hill. Those guns would play a major roll in the fighting of the early hours of the morning.

When you are ready to continue, leave the parking lot and proceed straight on for about a mile along the old Hagerstown turnpike, through the intersection with Cornfield

Avenue and then turn right onto Mansfield Avenue. You will find the parking lot on the left-hand side of the Avenue.

The North Woods:

Jackson, fully aware that Hooker had moved across the Antietam with his 1st Army Corps and was preparing to attack him, swung his line anti-clockwise to face him; forcing Hooker into such a position that any move he might make against the Confederate left must come in the form of a frontal attack.

Hooker, so it would seem, had no real instructions from McClellan other than to attack the Confederate left flank. How he was to do it, and in what force, seems to have been left entirely up to him. He decided to go forth with his own 1st Corps of some 8,500 men in three divisions and leave General Mansfield's 12th Corps in reserve to the rear.

Hooker's left flank was held by Brigadier General James Rickett's division, his right by Brigadier General Abner Doubleday's division. Jackson would face Hooker also with three divisions: Brigadier General John R. Jones held a position some 500 yards to the north of the Dunker Church, Brigadier General Alexander R. Lawton with his division was placed just to the south facing Hooker toward the East Woods, while Brigadier General John Bell Hood was held in reserve with his division in the West Woods. Jackson faced his enemy's 8,500 men with about 7,700 of his own.

September 17th dawned overcast with patchy ground fog hanging in the hollows and woodlands along the ridge. At 5:00 a.m. the battle opened on both sides with the artillery commanders opening fire as soon as it was light enough to see. Colonel Stephen D. Lee, the Confederate artillery brigade commander, joined in with his batteries posted close to the Dunker Church. These were answered by the Federal, long-range, rifled guns on the far side of Antietam Creek.

At 6:00 a.m. Hooker's three divisions began to move out from the fields of the Poffenberger Farm here in front of you, southward and on through Miller's farm to the Cornfield and the East

Woods. Three regiments of Pennsylvanians under Brigadier General Abram Duryee led the attack for Rickett's division on the Union left, three regiments from Wisconsin and one from Indiana, all under the command of Brigadier General John Gibbon, led the advance for Doubleday's division on the right. Gibbon's men marched forward toward the West Woods and immediately came under devastating artillery fire from J.E.B. Stuart's divisional batteries on Nicodemus Hill; Gibbon's force began to take horrible losses. Meanwhile General Duryee's men had already entered the northern end of The Cornfield.

Next on your tour is Stop Number 4, The Cornfield. Stop Number 3, the East Woods, and Stop Number 4 are, for the purposes of this tour, just about the same. Leave the parking area, proceed along Mansfield Avenue, and follow the white arrows on the road to **Stop Number 3**, then **Stop Number 4** on Cornfield Avenue and the parking area on your right.

The Cornfield:
Here in front of you is Miller's Cornfield, the scene of some of the bloodiest fighting, not only in this battle, but in the entire Civil War. By the end of the day this cornfield would change hands six times and many thousands of young men from both sides would lie dead or wounded among the cornstalks.

In the pasture at the southern end of the Cornfield Confederate Colonel Marcellus Douglass was waiting with his brigade of Georgians behind odd piles of fence rails and in the small hollows. As Duryee's Pennsylvanians entered the Cornfield Douglass told his men each to take aim at his own row of corn. Suddenly, the first of Duryee's men appeared out of the corn. The Georgians stood up and delivered an horrendous volley of fire that completely devastated the first rank of the advancing Union line. The two battle lines now stood almost toe-to-toe less than 200 yards apart, each man firing as fast as he could load.

General Ricketts had intended to quickly reinforce Duryee's Pennsylvanians with two more brigades. Unfortunately that was not to be. One brigade was delayed when its commander was wounded by artillery fire, the other was left leaderless when its colonel lost his nerve and fled from the field. Duryee, left to fend for himself against superior numbers and the withering Confederate firestorm, had no alternative but to withdraw back through the cornfield, leaving more than 350 (over a third of his brigade) on the battlefield.

Eventually Rickett's remaining brigades began to move forward and the killing began again. Confederate General Lawton had reinforced Douglass' Georgians with a brigade of Louisianians under the command of Brigadier General Harry T. Hayes. Together they mounted a Confederate counter attack that drove right through the Cornfield almost to the edge of the East Woods. This time it was the Confederates' turn to face the firestorm. The Confederate attack faltered and then crumbled. Colonel Douglass was killed and the two Confederate brigades fell back to the pasture at the southern end of the Cornfield.

And so it went, back and forth, first one side, and then the other. The early morning fog lifted sometime around 8:00 a.m., only to be replaced by a dense pall of gunsmoke that lay across the Cornfield like a great choking blanket. The confusion was complete. The acres of the Cornfield here were soaked red with the blood of both sides. One man said he could have walked the length and breadth of the field across the bodies of the fallen and never would have had to lay a foot upon the bare earth.

Hooker's 1st Army Corps alone suffered more than 2,600 casualties in the Cornfield – 30% of its numbers. Jackson's divisions fighting against Hooker's 1st Corps suffered more than 3,000 casualties. General Lawton lost almost half of his division and Lawton himself was wounded, and one of his brigade commanders was killed and another wounded. By the close of day the Cornfield had cost both sides more than 12,000 men.

During the changing tides of battle in the Cornfield General Hooker himself was severely wounded in the foot and had to be taken from the field. At almost the same time that Hooker received his wound, General Mansfield, who had arrived on the field with his 12th Corps of 7,000 men, was positioning his men in and around the East woods. While doing so he noticed that the 10th Maine regiment had opened fire on targets hidden among the trees. Mansfield had only just come from a briefing by General Hooker and he knew that some of Ricketts' troops were still thought to be in the woods. He quickly rode forward shouting that they were firing upon their own men. But these men from Maine knew what they were about and told Mansfield so. It was at that moment that the general took a Confederate minie-ball in the chest. The handsome general with the flowing white beard was taken from the battlefield to a field hospital where he died the next day. Mansfield was the first of six general officers to die in the battle of Antietam: three Union and three Confederate. Twelve more suffered serious wounds and had to be removed from the field. Again the numbers were evenly distributed: six for either side.

In the meantime, just to the west, Union General John Gibbon's Iron Brigade was spearheading the attack for Abner Doubleday's division. These men, as you will remember, were advancing toward Jackson's left. As they entered the battle zone they came under the deadly fire of J.E.B. Stuart's artillery on Nicodemus Hill and Stephen D. Lee's batteries at the Dunker Church. The effect of the combined Confederate artillery was devastating, but Gibbon's men pressed on southward on both sides of the Hagerstown turnpike; half of the force passing through a pasture on the western side of the pike, the other half through Miller's peach orchard and into the Cornfield. These men were advancing upon the best of the Confederate army, Stonewall Jackson's own Stonewall Brigade now under the command of Colonel Andrew Grigsby. Once again the deadly pattern was repeated. As the Federals came within range Grigsby's men rose and fired volley after volley of withering musket fire into the ranks of the Iron Brigade. Gibbon immediately rushed reinforcements to his embattled regiments. Billy Yank and Johnny Reb slugged it out toe-to-toe. Inevitably the weight of the superior numbers on the Federal side began to tell. With almost half of his men lying dead and wounded upon the field Grigsby's brigade began to fall back.

Confederate General Starke moved to stem the Federal tide with his two remaining brigades, about 1,200 men from Virginia, Alabama, and Louisiana. Starke's brigades moved out of the West Woods toward the Cornfield at the double-quick and soon were engaging the enemy at point-blank range.

Major Dawes: "*Men and officers are fused into a common mass, in the frantic struggle to shoot fast. Everybody tears cartridges, loads, passes guns, or shoots. Men are falling in their places or running back into the corn. . . . The men are loading and firing with demoniacal fury and shouting and laughing hysterically.*"

Starke's counter attack stopped the Federal advance. Unfortunately Starke himself was killed during the fighting. By now it was clear to Jackson that he would have to commit all of his reserves in order to prevent a major Union breakthrough by Hooker's 1st Corps. At 7:30 a.m., on his order, General John Bell Hood's division of 2,300 soldiers moved out of the West Woods and took the place of General Lawton's embattled division fighting in the Cornfield where they soon overran the remnants of Rickett's brigades in the East Woods. It was at about this time, as you will remember, that Union General Mansfield's 12th Corps entered the battle.

All this time General McClellan had been calmly observing the course of the battle from the high ground east of the Antietam and at the center of the Federal line. At the sight of Hood's division sweeping across the Cornfield he decided it was time to move more troops into the action. At about 7:30 he gave the order for General Sumner to move across the Antietam with two of the three divisions that made up the 2nd Corps and reinforce Hooker. At the same time, Confederate Major General D.H. Hill, commanding Lee's center, moved one of his own brigades forward in support of Hood's counter attack. An hour later his entire force of some 3,500 soldiers was engaged against the combined might of Hooker's and Mansfield's 1st and 12th Corps. By 9:00 a.m. the tide had turned against the Confederates and they had been driven from the Cornfield leaving it littered with more than 8,000 casualties, Union and Confederate; but there was more yet to come. Only Jackson had managed to keep the Confederate left intact and was desperately trying to hold a tenuous line of battle in the area of the West Woods.

The next stop on your tour, **Number 5**, is the West Woods. Continue on along Cornfield Avenue and follow the white arrows until you reach the parking area.

The West Woods:
As it became clear to General D.H. Hill that he was not going to be able to stop the Union advance he sent Colonel Stephen D. Lee to General Lee with word that the entire Confederate left flank would collapse unless he received reinforcements. The artillery commander found Lee already in control of the situation; establishing a new line of batteries on the high ground behind the West Woods. Lee had ordered General Lafayette McLaws, newly arrived from Harpers Ferry to march his men to the aid of the embattled left flank. "Don't get excited about it, Colonel. Go tell General Hood to hold his ground, reinforcements are now rapidly approaching. . . . Tell him I am now coming to his support."

At 9:00 a.m. Union General Williams reported to McClellan as follows: "*General Mansfield is dangerously wounded. General Hooker severely wounded in the foot. General Sumner I hear is advancing. We hold the field at present. Please give us all the aid you can. It is reported that the enemy occupy the woods in our advance, in strong force. . . .*"

As Union Major General John Sedgewick's division of 5,400 men, Sumner's advance vanguard, arrived in the East Woods the battlefield fell strangely silent. The fog had lifted and only the thinning wisps of gunsmoke rising slowly into the sky blocked the morning sunlight. The silence seemed ominous; the harbinger of the horrors yet to come. The silence must have had much to do with Sumner's feelings that the Confederates had fled the field and that the battle was all but over. In any case throwing caution to the winds, full of thoughts of personal glory and too impatient to wait for his second division under the command of General William H. French to catch up, he ordered Sedgewick's division forward with himself at its head.

It's not clear what happened when French arrived in the East Woods. What is clear is that Sumner and Sedgewick's division

Major Gen. Edwin Sumner, oldest Union corps commander.

had already gone, and that for one reason or another French did not follow him; Sumner, without the support of French's division was heading for disaster. He was about to enter a deadly ambush alone and without hope of reinforcement.

Jackson's forces by now were ranged in giant crescent shaped formation in the West Woods: Stuart was on your right, Jackson himself was in front of you at the center with McLaws and Walker to your left. The mouth of the crescent faced northeast toward Sedgewick's advancing division. General J.E.B. Stuart had withdrawn his artillery from Nicodemus Hill and had placed them on the heights of Hauser's Ridge behind the West Woods. The trap was complete.

Sedgewick's men pushed forward through the Cornfield with Stuart's cannon inflicting heavy losses on the advancing columns. Closer and closer to the jaws of Jackson's crescent they came. Then, it must have seemed that hell had opened up on earth. A hailstorm of musket fire from left, right and center shattered the Federal ranks. The Union troops tried to hold their ground but the withering Confederate fire was overwhelming and they broke and ran. In less than 20 minutes Sedgewick's division suffered more than 2,350 casualties, almost 44% of his entire force. The Confederates pursued the fleeing Sedgewick brigades once more into the Cornfield, and once more they came under the devastating Federal artillery fire, and then they, too, fell back. McClellan's efforts of the morning all had been in vain; Jackson and his valiant few still held their position and McClellan would leave him to lick his wounds in relative peace for the rest of the day. The remaining two divisions of General Sumner's 2nd Union Army Corps were by this time approaching the Confederate center to the south and an old, well worn cart path soon to become known forever as "The Bloody Lane."

As you tour the battlefield you will notice several cannon mounted upside-down. There are six of them. Each is a memorial to a general of either side who lost his life during the battle. You may already have seen the one at Stop Number 3 where Union General Joseph Mansfield fell mortally wounded in the East Woods. The one here on your right as you leave to continue on to the next stop marks the spot where Confederate Brigadier General William Starke fell during the charge from the West Woods. When you are ready to continue your tour follow the white arrows to **Stop Number 6**, the Mumma Farm.

The Mumma Farm:
From the parking area you should have the Mumma farm buildings in front of you and the family cemetery to your left. When it became clear to Samuel Mumma that his farm was about to became a central feature on a major battlefield he decided to evacuate his family until the conflict was over. When he returned his home was gone, burned to the ground by the Confederates so that it couldn't be used by Federal sharpshooters. It would not have been unusual for buildings to have been destroyed during the heat of battle; in fact that was often the case. The destruction of the Mumma farm, however, was unique in that it was the only civilian property on this battlefield to have been purposely destroyed in an act of wartime strategy.

Follow the arrows along the tour route to reach **Stop Number 7**. When you have parked your car you will see the Roulette farm to your left and the Bloody Lane in front of you.

The Roulette Farm:
As you will remember, when Union General William French

with the second division of General Sumner's 2nd Corps reached the East Woods he found that Sumner and Sedgewick had already left. French, not knowing which way Sumner had gone, had to make a decision. He could hear the sounds of battle raging away to the west as Sedgewick engaged the Confederates in the West Woods, and he could see Greene's Federal unit off to his left in front of the Dunker Church. He decided to take up a position on Greene's left flank. So, at about 9:30 a.m., General French moved his division of almost 6,000 men southward and away from the embattled Confederate left flank.

Generals Lee, Longstreet, and D.H. Hill watched from a hill on the Piper farm, just behind you, as French's Federals moved resolutely toward the Confederate center and D.H. Hill's brigades waiting east of the Hagerstown pike in an old, well-worn, sunken road. As the three Confederate generals discussed the situation a shot fired from a Union cannon more than a mile away to the east cut the front legs from under General Hill's horse; it was the third horse shot from under him that day.

As French's brigades crossed the fields of the Roulette Farm they encountered some resistance from an unexpected enemy. A lucky shot from a Confederate cannon bowled over farmer Roulette's beehives. Swarms of angry bees caused chaos in the ranks of the rookie soldi ers of the 132nd Pennsylvania. They quickly reformed, however, and moved on through these fields to the sunken road – **Stop Number 8** on your tour.

The Bloody Lane:
This small, sunken cart path is 600 yards to the south of the Dunker church. It ran eastward from the Hagerstown turnpike for about a fourth of a mile, turned to the southeast for about a fourth of a mile more, and then turned southward to join the Boonboro Turnpike about a half-mile further on. To defend the position Confederate General Hill had some 2,500 men made up of a mish-mash of odd brigades from Alabama and North Carolina under the commands of Brigadier Generals Robert Rodes and George Anderson, along with a brigade from Lafayette McLaws division under the command of General Roswell Ripley. Hill was outnumbered by French more than two-to-one.

Confederate General John B. Gordon in his memoirs describes some of the action here at "Bloody Lane:" *"My troops held the most advanced position on this part of the field, and there was no supporting line behind us. To comfort General Lee as he rode away I called aloud to him, "These men are going to stay here, General." Alas! Many of the brave fellows are there now.*

"The predicted assault came. The men in blue formed in my front, four lines deep. The brave Union commander, superbly mounted, placed himself in the front, while his band in the rear cheered them with martial music. It was a thrilling spectacle. To oppose man against man was impossible, for there were four lines of blue to my one line of gray. The only plan was to hold my fire until the advancing Federals were almost upon my lines. No troops with empty guns could withstand the shock. My men were at once directed to lie down upon the grass. No shot would be fired until my voice should be heard commanding, "Fire!"

"There was no artillery at this point on either side and not a rifle was discharged. The stillness was literally oppressive, as this column of Union infantry moved majestically toward us. Now the front rank was within a few rods of where I stood. With all my lung power I shouted "Fire!"

"Our rifles flamed and roared in the Federals' faces like a blinding blaze of lightning. The effect was appalling. The entire front line, with few exceptions, went down. Before the rear lines could recover my exultant men were on their feet, devouring them with successive volleys. Even then these stubborn blue lines retreated in good order.

"The fire now became furious and deadly. The list of the slain lengthened with each passing moment. . . ."

It was inevitable, then, that under such a firestorm, the Federals would be repulsed; and they were. As the three regiments under the command of Brigadier General Nathan Kimball fell back he was heard to whisper, "God save my poor boys." French's division was finished. More than 1,750 of its number were left on the field at the Bloody Lane – losses second only to those of General Sedgewick. It was now General Richardson's turn to try his hand at the Bloody Lane. The first unit of his division to arrive on the scene was the famous Irish Brigade, the 63rd, 69th, and 88th New York regiments, along with the 29th Massachusetts, under the command of Brigadier General Thomas H. Meagher. They marched proudly toward the Sunken Road and slightly to the left of the position just left by French's devastated division. The men of General Hill's division in the Bloody Lane waited with rifles at the ready, and watched as the Irish Brigade fixed bayonets and, with the emerald banners waving gaily over their heads, prepared to charge. General Meagher, heavily fortified with strong Irish whiskey, gave the order and the famous brigade moved forward at the double-quick.

Once again the deadly firestorm from the Confederate ranks decimated the front line of the advancing Federals. In less than five minutes the Irish Brigade lost more than half its number as the Confederate riflemen in the Bloody lane doubled their rate of fire, with the rear rank loading and passing their rifles to those in the front rank. Meagher himself was saved only because the effects of an over-abundance of whiskey finally became too much for him and he fell from his horse and had to be carried from the battlefield.

And then, something went wrong in the Confederate ranks. A misheard order was taken as an order to withdraw and retreat. In moments the Confederates were abandoning their easily defended positions all along the Sunken Road and were running for the rear. With that one mistake the entire center of Lee's line was shattered. The Federals stormed cheering and whooping into the Sunken Road and on through the cornfields of Piper's farm beyond.

General Hill, unable to believe that he was about to be defeated, took up a rifle and began rounding up his men. With only 200 soldiers he charged the onrushing lines of Richardson's division. Incredibly the tactic worked. The Confederate troops rallied and the Federals, surprised by Hill's counter-attack, were, for the moment at least, stopped in their tracks.

General Longstreet, seeing what was happening to Hill and the Confederate center, ordered his own personal staff to man some abandoned cannon and commence firing on Richardson's division. With double loads of canister the involuntary artillery battery began to inflict devastating losses on the Federal line. Longstreet's battery was joined by another and then another and soon more than 20 guns were pouring canister into Richardson's brigades at the rate of almost two rounds per minute per gun. The effect on the Federal positions was devastating. Richardson's advance faltered and finally stopped. His men had fought themselves to a standstill. They were exhausted and almost out of ammunition. Richardson's brigades had no alternative but to withdraw back across the sunken road to the shelter of the ridge beyond. By 1:00 p.m. the battle at The Bloody Lane was over and the center of Lee's line, though tenuous, still held. General Richardson himself had been killed by cannon fire on the hill to your right; the spot is marked, as you can see, by an inverted cannon.

T.F. DeBurgh Galway saw action at the Bloody Lane on the Union side. He was with the Eighth Ohio and describes what he saw after it was all over as follows:

"What a sight was that lane! I shall not dwell on the horror of it; I saw many a ghastly array of dead afterward, but none, I think, that so affected me as did the sight of the poor brave fellows in butternut homespun that had there died for what they believed to be the honor and a righteous cause."

Before you leave the Sunken Road you might like to take time out to visit the observation tower to your right. It offers a panoramic view of the entire battlefield. Perhaps you will be able to take a trip, via the ship of the imagination, back to that fateful day in September, 1862. If so, you cannot fail to moved as war correspondent George Smalley was: *"Four miles of battle, its glory all visible, its horrors all hidden, the fate of the Republic hanging on the hour – could anyone be insensible of its grandeur?"*

The next stop on your tour is the Lower Bridge. When you're ready to leave you will need to pay close attention to your battlefield map as you follow the arrows to **Stop Number 9**. Leave your vehicle in the parking area and proceed down the stairway to the Wayside exhibit where you will have a much better view.

Burnside Bridge (The Lower Bridge):

This, on August 17th, 1862, was the scene of much confusion, and since then, much conjecture. Here it was that Union Generals Ambrose E. Burnside and Jacob Cox sat for most of the morning with the 12,500 men of the 9th Army Corps and did practically nothing. McClellan always maintained that he ordered Burnside to attack the Confederate right across this bridge simultaneously with Hooker's attack on the Confederate left. Burnside maintained that McClellan gave no such order, but that he was to wait until he heard from McClellan before moving against the single Georgia brigade defending the bridge on the west side of the Antietam. Had Burnside moved across the bridge at the same time Hooker and Mansfield were assailing Jackson and the Confederate left, there's little doubt that by sheer weight of numbers alone the Union Army of the Potomac must have carried the day and swept Lee and his army from the field and into the Potomac river itself. But Burnside and Cox waited, and they waited, and then they waited some more. During the course of the morning McClellan sent several couriers to find out why Burnside had not begun his attack; but still he waited. It was not until 10:00 a.m., some five hours after the battle had begun, that McClellan's courier reached the dynamic duo with specific orders that they were to storm the bridge at once and open the attack against the enemy's right flank.

General Jacob Cox responded and ordered Colonel George Crook's brigade to storm the bridge; the 11th Connecticut would form a skirmish line along the east bank of the creek and prepare the way for Colonel Crook. At the same time Brigadier General Isaac P. Rodman was to go south along the banks of the Antietam and find a suitable place to ford the river. The Lower Bridge looked to Burnside and Cox like an exceedingly difficult prize to seize. It was a stone bridge with three supporting arches, 125 feet long and only 12 feet wide. If ever there was a bottle-neck, this was it.

Defending the bridge were 500 southerners: the 2nd and 20th Georgia under the command of Brigadier General Robert Tombs. His men were well dug in at an old quarry on the west side of the bridge in a position from which they were able to command the bridge's every approach. Tombs was supported in strength only by five batteries of artillery on the high ground to the rear.

The 11th Connecticut hit the banks of the creek just as had been expected. Almost immediately they came under the withering fire of the Georgian's guns across the river. The regimental commander was hit four times by Confederate minie-balls and went down mortally wounded. The Yankees from Connecticut retired from the field leaving almost a third of their number behind, either dead or wounded. But things got worse, for even though Burnside and the 9th Corps had been camped close by on the east side of the creek, neither he nor McClellan had bothered to reconnoiter the terrain around the bridge, and

The taking of "Burnside" Bridge over Antietam Creek, in a contemporary drawing by Edwin Forbes.

Burnside Bridge as it looks today.

Crook's brigade became lost in the woods on the east side of the creek. Eventually, instead of storming the bridge, they appeared on the river bank some 400 yards upstream where they, too, came under deadly Confederate fire from across the creek.

It was not until late morning that this comedy of errors finally sorted itself out, and not until 1:00 p.m. that Burnside's third assault finally carried the bridge. In the meantime General Rodman was making his appearance with his 3,200-strong division on the Confederate left. Under an indescribable barrage of Federal fire, after holding out for more than three hours, their ammunition running dangerously short, the Georgians began to withdraw from their positions. At the sight of this a great cheer went up from the Federal ranks here, and on the high ground behind you. Nothing now stood between the 9th Corps and Sharpsburg itself.

Before you return to your vehicle you might like to take time out for a pleasant stroll along the banks of the Antietam. Or perhaps you might like to sit for a while on the grassy slopes and look down upon the bridge. Either way, today's Burnside Bridge, although it has been restored to its Civil War appearance, offers a more pleasurable experience for us than it did for so many Union soldiers that dark day in 1862.

When you are ready to continue your tour return to your vehicle and follow the white arrows to **Stop Number 10** on the hill above the Otto farmhouse, the scene of the final attack.

The Final Attack:
The hill overlooking the Otto farmhouse is the one mentioned earlier – the position of the five batteries of Confederate guns that protected General Tombs and the Georgian defenders of the Burnside Bridge. The monuments you see here were erected by survivors of the Union regiments that took the hill.

When the Lower Bridge fell to Burnside and his 9th Corps, Lee knew he was in deadly danger of losing the battle. His forces were all committed and fighting to hold tenuous positions across the battlefield. But aid was indeed at hand from two directions. Ironically the first came in the form of Burnside himself. Instead of pressing home his advantage and smashing the Confederate right flank with everything he had as might have been expected, he delayed his advance for more than two hours, thus giving Lee breathing space and the time gather up the remnants of rag-tag brigades from around the battlefield and to the rear.

It was close to 3:00 p.m. when the 9th moved forward in three divisions: some 8,500 men in all. Slowly, but surely, the Union advance swept first one Confederate division and then another. Things began to look grim for Lee and his Army of Northern Virginia. It was just then, when it seemed as if all must be lost, that Lee rode to the top of a nearby ridge for a better view of the battle and saw something moving in the distance to the south. He called for a passing artillery officer to bring his telescope and asked him to view the advancing columns – his hands had been injured in a fall and were heavily bandaged. *"Who's troops are those?"* he asked. *"They are flying the Virginia and Confederate flags, Sir."* It was as if Lee had been expecting them, for he said calmly, *"It is A.P. Hill from Harpers Ferry."* And it was. Lee's army finally, with the exception of the enormous casualties of the day, was all in one piece. Hill, with more than 3,000 men, was arriving on the battlefield at exactly the right time and in exactly the right place.

A.P. Hill.

Lee's courier had arrived in Harpers Ferry early that morning and told him that it was requested that he march for Sharpsburg with all speed. Hill had covered the 17 miles in just seven hours and without breaking stride his lead brigade of South Carolinians under the command of Brigadier General Maxcy Gregg tore into the ranks of the 4th Rhode Island and the 16th Connecticut at the double-quick firing volley after volley as they went. The effect on the raw Federal troops was immediate and devastating. Panic set in as the untrained soldiers, many so inexperienced they were unable to complete the complicated task of loading and firing their muskets, turned and ran from the field with the South Carolinians pouring a devastating hailstorm of fire upon them. Burnside, unable to grasp what was happening around him, ordered his 9th Corps into retreat. A.P. Hill's counter-attack had saved the day. Lee's embattled Army of Northern Virginia had been pulled back from the edge of destruction. The bloodiest single day of the entire Civil War was at an end. Just how bloody the day had been was not discovered for several days and, in fact, even today it's not certain just how many casualties the Confederate army suffered. So many men were missing on both sides it was assumed that many were

Common Soldier Monument,
Antietam National Cemetery.

stragglers and would turn up sooner or later. The fact is that on September 17th the count for the Confederate side was 1,546 dead, 7,752 wounded, and 1,018 missing, a total of 10,318; for the Union army it was 2,108 dead, 9,540 wounded, and 753 missing for a total of 12,401 – in all some 22,700 casualties on both sides, a horrendous statistic by any measure. General Lee claimed shortly after the battle that his entire effective force numbered no more than 35,000. Of McClellan's 75,000 effective only 55,000 were actually involved in the fighting. Even though the battle ended without either side defeated, Lee's army, by reason that it still held its line much as it had at the onset of battle early that morning, might well be justified in claiming a technical victory against vastly superior odds. Whatever the opinion, it's certain that the Battle of Antietam changed the course of the war forever because, seven days later on September 22nd, Lincoln issued his Emancipation Proclamation that changed the struggle for state's rights into a war against slavery. Politically, it was a deathblow to the Confederacy.

The last stop on your tour is the National Cemetery. Leave the parking lot and go into the town of Sharpsburg. Turn left onto Main Street and continue on until you reach the cemetery. The parking area is on your right.

The National Cemetery:
The ground here was purchased by Maryland and the Northern

*President Lincoln meeting with McClellan near Sharpsburg,
October 3, 1862.*

States whose troops fought at Antietam. There are some 4,800
soldiers buried here. Almost 2,000 of them are unknown. The
Confederate dead were, for the most part, removed after the war
and taken home. The monument which stands in the center of
the cemetery was erected in memory of "The Private Soldier."
Many of the dead still lie where they fell, buried in unknown
graves upon the battlefield.

The evening of the battle, September 17th, Lee and his commanders met in Council of War to discuss the situation. His
generals reported to Lee on the extent of the army's appalling
losses, and were unanimous in their recommendations that the
army should be put into retreat and withdraw across the Potomac and to safety. Lee considered this advice and then told his
generals that if McClellan wished to continue the battle the
following morning he would find him, Lee, ready and waiting.

For some reason, known only to himself, McClellan gave orders
that the conflict was not to be resumed the next day, the 18th.
Even though he still outnumbered Lee almost two-to-one, he

maintained that it was his Army of the Potomac that was outnumbered and that he must await reinforcements even then on their way from Washington.

All day of the 18th the survivors on both sides buried their dead. During the night of the 18th Lee's army broke camp and stole away from the battlefield under cover of darkness and across the Potomac. They would live to fight another day. McClellan gave orders on the morning of the 19th to resume the battle; there was no one left upon the field for him to fight.

Where to Stay, Things to Do in Hagerstown, Maryland

Hagerstown is located 10 miles to the north of the Antietam National Military Park. It is the closest city of any size to the battlefield and offers the following amenities:

Museums

The Washington Museum of Fine Arts: City Park. South on US 11 (Virginia Ave.). Paintings, sculpture, changing exhibits, concerts, lectures. Open daily except Monday; closed on major holidays. Free. Phone 739-8393.

Jonathan Hager House and Museum: 19 Key St., in City Park. Stone house in a park setting; authentic 18th century furnishings. Open April to December except Monday. Phone 739-4665.

Hagerstown Roundhouse Museum: 300 S. Burhans Blvd., across the tracks from the City Park. Museum houses photographic exhibits of the seven railroads of Hagerstown; historic railroad memorabilia, tools and equipment; archives of maps, books, papers and related items. Gift shop. Open May to September in the afternoon; the rest of the year Friday to Sunday afternoons. Phone 739-8782.

Miller House: 135 W. Washington St. Washington County Historical Society Headquarters. Federal town house circa 1820; three-story spiral staircase; period furnishings; garden; clock, doll and Bell pottery collections; Chesapeake & Ohio Canal and Civil War exhibits; 19th century country store display. Open April through December, Wednesday to Sunday; closed major holidays and the first two weeks in December. Sr. citizen rate. Phone 797-8782.

Parks

Greenbriar State Park: 10 miles east via US 40. The Appalachian Trail passes near this 1,275-acre park and its 42-acre man-made lake. Swimming (Memorial Day to Labor Day, daily); fishing; boating (rentals; no gas motors). Nature, hiking trails. Picnicking. Standard fees. Phone 791-4767.

Fort Frederick State Park: 19 miles S&W via I-81 & I-70 to Big Pool, then one mile SE via MD 56, unmarked road. Erected in 1756 during the French and Indian War. The fort is a fine example of a pre-Revolutionary stone fort and overlooks the Chesapeake and Ohio Canal National Historical Park. Barracks, military re-enactments throughout the year. Fishing, boating (rentals), nature and hiking trails. Picnicking (shelter), playground. Unimproved camping. Museum, orientation film, historical programs. Standard fees. Winter hours may vary. Phone 842-2155.

Annual Events

Halfway Park Days: Helicopter rides, antique cars, dance bands, flea market, food. Late May.

Hagerstown Railroad Heritage Days: Special events centered on the Roundhouse Museum. Last week in May and early June. For more information and schedule phone 739-4665.

Frontier Craft Day: Colonial crafts demonstrated and exhibited; blue-grass music; food. First week in August.

Lietersburg Peach Festival: Peach-related edibles, farmer's market, blue-grass music, military reenactments. Second weekend in August.

Williamsport C & O Canal Days: Arts & Crafts, Indian village, National Park Service activities, food. Late August.

Alsatia Mummers Halloween Parade Festival: Saturday, the weekend closest to Halloween.

Hotels

Sheraton Inn Conference Center: 1910 Dual Hwy. (US 40). 301-790-3010.

Best Western Venice Inn: 431 Dual Hwy. (US 40). 301-733-0830.

Days Inn Williamsport: 310 E. Potomac St. Williamsport, MA 21795. 301-582-3500.

Howard Johnson Plaza: Halfway Blvd. at I-81, exit 5. 301-797-2500.

Holiday Inn: 900 Dual Hwy. (US 40), 301-739-9050.

Ramada Inn Convention Center: 901 Dual Hwy. (US 40) 301-733-5100.

Dagmar: 50 Summit Ave. at Antietam St., 301-733-4363.

Bed & Breakfasts

Lewrene Farm: 9738 Downsville Pike, MA 21740. A quiet farm, cozy colonial home with fireplace, antiques, candlelight breakfasts. Open all year. Spanish & some German spoken. 301-582-1735. Lewis & Irene Lehman.

Beaver Creek House: 20432 Beaver Creek Rd., four miles east on I-70, exit 32A, in the village of Beaver Creek. Antique-filled Victorian country home near I-70 & I-81. Clean, hospitable, relaxed; close to historic sites, golf, antique and shopping outlets. Open all year. Don & Shirley Day. 301-797-4764.

Restaurants

Railroad Junction: 808 Noland Dr., at the junction of US 11. Open 6:30 a.m. to 3:30 p.m.; closed Sunday, also weeks of 4th of July and Christmas. Children's meals. Specialties: stuffed chicken breast; veal parmigiana; Cajun steak; own pies. Located near the railroad tracks. Fun atmosphere with railroad-theme decor and tapes of actual trains; model trains circle the room at the ceiling. Credit cards. 301-791-3639.

Red Horse Steak House: 1800 Dual Hwy. (US 40). Open 4 p.m. to 10 p.m., Sunday to 9 p.m. Closed on major holidays. Reservations required on Fridays and Saturdays. Bar. Children's meals. Specialties: prime rib; broiled seafood; steak. Open-hearth grill. Colonial-style atmosphere. Family owned. Parking. Credit cards. Phone 301-733-3788.

Richardson's: 710 Dual Hwy. (US 40). Open 7 a.m. to 10 p.m. Children's meals. Specialties: fried chicken, seafood, crab cakes. Salad bar. Own pies. Cakes. Three dining areas. Railroad theme, memorabilia. Credit cards. Parking. 301-733-3660.

Camping

Fort Frederick State Park: From town: go 18 miles west on I-70, then one mile south on Hwy. 56. **Facilities:** 28 sites with 29 ft. max. RV length. No hookups. Pit toilets. Public phone, limited grocery store, ice, tables, fire rings, grills, wood. **Recreation:** pavilion, boating, canoeing, boat rentals, lake fishing, hiking trails. Open April through October. Phone 301-842-2155.

Greenbriar State Park: From town go eight miles east on US 40. **Facilities:** 165 sites (29 ft max. RV length), nine electrical, 156 no hook-ups, flush toilets, hot showers, sewage disposal, laundry, public phone, limited grocery store, ice, tables, grills, wood. **Recreation:** lake swimming, boating, canoeing, ramp, dock, boat rentals, lake fishing, playground, planned group activities, hiking trails. Open to public. No pets. Open April through October. Phone 301-791-4767.

KOA Snug Harbor: A riverside campground with shaded and open sites. From the junction of I-70 & I-81 go 1 1/2 miles west on I-70 (exit 24) then 1/4 mile south on Hwy. 63, then 2 1/2 miles west on Kemps Mill Road. **Facilities:** 90 sites, 43 full hook-ups, (20, 30 & 50 amp receptacles), 20 pull throughs, a/c allowed ($), cable TV, tenting available, flush toilets, hot showers, handicap restroom facilities, sewage disposal, laundry, public phone, grocery store, RV supplies, LP gas, ice, tables, wood, church services. **Entertainment:** rec. room, pavilion, coin games, swimming pool (heated), sauna, whirlpool, boating, dock, boat rentals, river fishing, basketball hoop, playground, planned group activities (weekends only), horseshoes, hiking trails, volleyball, local tours. KOA 10% value card discount. Open all year round. Member ARVC. Phone 301-223-7571.

Chapter 7

Fredericksburg

December, 1862

The Visitor Center at the National Battlefield of Fredericksburg is located on US 1, Lafayette Blvd., in Fredericksburg, VA. Picnic tables are provided and picnicking is allowed only in designated areas. All pets must be kept on a leash. Hiking, jogging, and bicycling are encouraged in the park and motorists are asked to be alert to these activities. The tour described here requires that you turn onto and off of several heavily traveled highways so please be careful at all times. Most of the facilities at Fredericksburg are accessible to wheelchairs. Phone 540-373-4510.

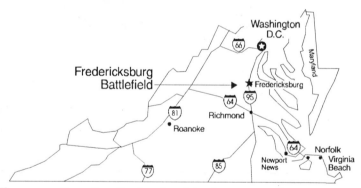

Three months after the battle of Antietam was fought on September 17th, 1862, the Army of Northern Virginia and the Army of the Potomac were once again facing each other across a river; this time the Rappahannock. The location was the little Virginia town of Fredericksburg, some seventy five miles to the south of Sharpsburg. The date was December 11th, 1862.

It had taken Union General George B. McClellan almost two

Fredericksburg and Vicinity, 1861 - 1865

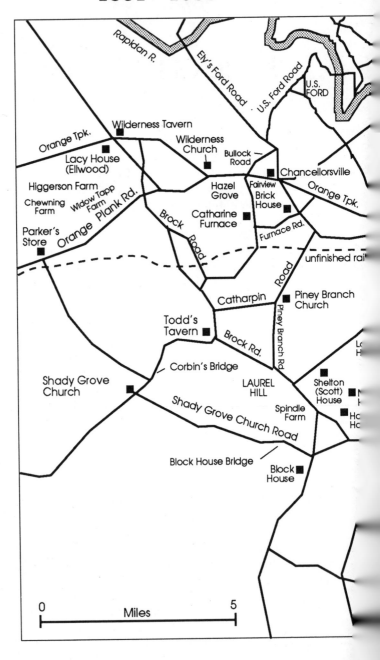

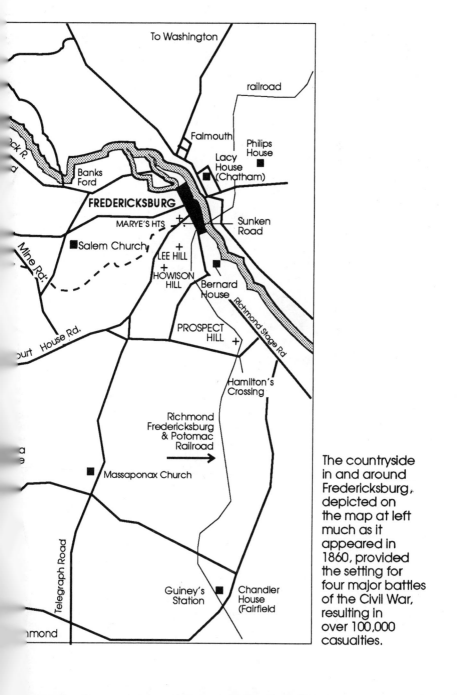

The countryside in and around Fredericksburg, depicted on the map at left much as it appeared in 1860, provided the setting for four major battles of the Civil War, resulting in over 100,000 casualties.

months after the battle of Antietam to gather himself and his 120,000-strong army together before he finally moved his army southward in pursuit of General Lee, whose army was by this time divided – the two wings separated by more than 100 miles of rolling Virginia countryside. Had McClellan moved quickly he might have defeated Lee and his much smaller army decisively, but he didn't. And Lee, knowing his adversary probably better than anyone else did, wasn't particularly worried.

President Lincoln, too, knew that as long as McClellan was in command of the Army of the Potomac things were unlikely to improve and so he finally removed him from its command and turned the army over to General Ambrose E. Burnside.

Burnside quickly swung into action. First he reduced the number of general officers reporting directly to him by forming

Maj. Gen. Ambrose E. Burnside.

the army into what he called three "Grand Divisions" under the commands of Generals Sumner, Hooker, and Franklin, and then he moved the army southward, feinting first toward Culpeper Court House, then moving rapidly to Falmouth, and then to Fredericksburg where he would cross the Rappahannock by pontoon bridges and advance on Richmond. At first Burnside showed all the fire and enthusiasm that Lincoln so badly needed, and the advance elements of the Union army already were at Falmouth before Lee could be certain that Fredericksburg was the major Union objective.

Lee knew he must bring the two widely separated wings of his army together, and quickly. So, on November 26th, he ordered General Thomas (Stonewall) Jackson to move his divisions from

Winchester to Fredericksburg. Jackson arrived there on December 1st. Lee, at first, was not certain exactly where Burnside would attempt the river crossing. It seemed possible, in light of the presence of Federal gunboats at Port Royal, that he might make his move there, and then make a flanking movement against Lee in an effort to turn his right flank just to the south of Fredericksburg. So, in an effort to provide for all possibilities, Lee positioned Longstreet and his divisions on the high ground to the west of the city; Jackson and his divisions were spread over a wide area to the south. Confederate cavalry commander General J.E.B. Stuart's brigades were posted on both right and left flanks of the army. General William Barksdale's Mississippi brigade was posted inside the city itself.

On December 9th Burnside issued orders that the army would cross the Rappahannock on the morning of Thursday December 11th and, in a two-pronged attack, General Sumner's Grand Division would take Fredericksburg and then move against the Confederate positions on the high ground to the west of the city; General Franklin's Grand Division would advance into the plain to the south of the city and move against Jackson on the high ground at Hamilton's Crossing; Fighting Joe Hooker and his Grand Division would be held in reserve, ready to take advantage of the situation as it might develop.

The crossing of the river was scheduled to begin at first light on the morning of the 11th. The noise of the equipment being moved into position, however, alerted the waiting Confederates on the other side of the river. General Lafayette McLaws, convinced that the long awaited crossing was at last under way, ordered two cannon to fire the prearranged warning signal and the Mississippians in the streets of the city made ready to receive their guests.

Soon the first pontoons began to appear through the mist of the early morning fog that blanketed the river. The Federal engineers were greeted by a hailstorm of Confederate minie balls and were driven back into the protection of the fog. Again and again they attempted to push the bridges on across the river, only to be driven back each time under a hail of Confederate

The pontoon bridges at Franklin's Crossing.

musket fire. By mid-morning the Federals decided they'd had enough of General Barksdale and they decided to drive him and his defiant brigade from the city with cannon fire.

Union artillery commander General Henry J. Hunt's 150 massed guns on Stafford Heights laid down a barrage against the city that lasted for more than two and a half hours, at a rate of fire of more than 60 rounds per minute. In all, more than 9,000 rounds slammed into the tiny city of Fredericksburg, setting many of the fine old houses on fire and demolishing many more. And it was all to no avail, for as soon as the barrage was over the Confederates emerged from their cellars and rifle pits unscathed, ready once again to decimate the Federal engineers on the pontoon bridges.

Finally, it was decided that a small force of Union volunteers should be ferried across the river in boats to establish a foothold whereby they could protect the engineers. Four regiments from New York, Michigan, and Massachusetts jumped aboard pontoon boats and, under cover of heavy Federal fire, they made it to the far side of the river. All through the rest of the afternoon and on into the darkening hours of the evening, with Federal soldiers streaming across the now completed bridges, Barksdale

Results of bombardment of Fredericksburg.

and his 1,600 Mississippians fought gamely in the city streets until at last he was forced to withdraw. By nightfall four bridges had been constructed across the river, two to the north at the Lacy House opposite Fredericksburg, and two to the south at Deep Run where General Franklin and his Grand Division would cross.

On the morning of December 12th the two Grand Divisions began crossing the river. General Lee, high on the top of the hills to west, watched from afar. He now knew from where the main thrusts of the Union army would be made. Urgent orders were dispatched to Generals A.P. Hill and Jubal Early to move northward from Port Royal and Skinner's Neck at once; they arrived during the night and moved immediately into position.

By daylight on the 13th Lee's divisions were ready and waiting. General Longstreet with his 40,000 men occupied a line of battle some five miles long on Marye's Heights to the west and in front of the city. General Jackson with 39,000 men to the south was in a line of battle only two miles wide, but almost a mile in depth. The stage was set. The battle of Fredericksburg was about to begin.

Sumner's advance Union skirmishers in Fredericksburg.

Your tour of the battlefield park at Fredericksburg begins at the Visitor Center. Leave the parking area and turn left but, except for your visit to Chatham, DO NOT follow the directional signs you will see along the way. Ins tead, follow the map and the directions in this book. Please be very careful of the traffic in the city.

Chatham Manor, the old Lacy House, is the first stop on your tour. After making the left turn out of the parking area at the Visitor Center, drive three blocks to Littlepage Street and then turn left again and drive four blocks to Hanover Street. Turn right there and drive for three blocks until you reach the "Y" intersection with George Street (it's one block past the traffic light), and then bear right and continue along Hanover Street until you reach the stop sign at the junction with Sophia Street. Turn left there and go two blocks to the traffic light, then turn right across the bridge and stay in the left-hand lane. Proceed on up the slope for a couple of hundred yards and turn left at the first traffic light onto VA Highway 218. Stay in the left-hand lane for about a tenth of a mile until you see the large sign directing you to Chatham Manor. Turn left at the sign and go to the Chatham parking lot where you can leave your vehicle while you visit the house and grounds.

Chatham Manor: The Lacy House:
It was here on Stafford Heights that General Edwin B. Sumner
arrived with his Grand Division of the Army of the Potomac on
November the 17th. The rest of the Union army arrived on the
eastern shores of the Rappahannock three days later. It had
been Burnside's intention to cross the river before Lee knew
what he was about, and he would have done so but for the long
delay in the arrival of the pontoon boats. And so the great army
had no alternative but to lay in wait.

General Lee, on the other hand, now had the time to move into
position ready to thwart Burnside's grand design, and he made
good use of it. By November the 19th Confederate General

The Lacy House, Sumner's headquarters.

James Longstreet and his corps of 40,000 men were installed in
a defensive position upon the high ground, Marye's Heights,
just to the west of the town on the opposite side of the river.
General Jackson arrived with his corps of 39,000 men a week
later.

Chatham, known as The Lacy House during the Civil War, was
the field headquarters of General Edwin Sumner. You might
like to take a short walk through the gardens down to the river
bank where you should be able to get some idea of the task the
Federal engineers faced when they set about building their
bridges across the tidal waters of the Rappahannock. And, as

you look out across the river and the town to the west, you should be able to see an American flag flying in the distance on the crest of Marye's Heights close to the Visitor Center.

Inside the Lacy House itself you will find exhibits that explain the history of the old house and its role during the Civil War. The house was built some 90 years before the outbreak of the Civil War. It had at first been the home of wealthy landowner William Fitzhugh, but by 1862 it was owned by J. Horace Lacy. After the war the plantation's fortunes declined and it changed hands several times. During the early part of this century the house and grounds were extensively renovated to a point where the estate had become known as one of the most beautiful in the entire state. The house and grounds were donated to the National Park Service by industrialist John Lee Pratt in 1975, and so it became a part of the Fredericksburg National Battlefield Tour.

> When you are ready to continue your tour, leave the parking area at Chatham and turn left at the bottom of the hill. Go one tenth of a mile to the stop sign, turn right across the river, and then turn right again onto Sophia Street. Drive on for four blocks to the Park Service Historical sign by the river at the end of Hawke Street and park your vehicle.

The Upper Pontoon Crossing Site:
This is the point where the Federal pontoon bridges crossed the Rappahannock. You can see General Sumner's headquarters, The Lacy House – or Chatham Manor if you will – across the river in the clearing on Stafford Heights. Behind you, on Sophia Street, were the houses where Brigadier General William Barksdale's 1,600 men held back the Federal engineers for almost the entire day of December 11th. Some of the original houses are still standing today.

The next day, December 12th, was spent by the occupying Union forces in ransacking the town. Fine furniture and paintings were thrown into the streets, and all sorts of goods were carried away from the city in a frenzy of looting and destruction. It was one of the more shameful episodes of the Civil War; an episode the Union side did their best to forget as quickly as possible.

From the parking area, move carefully out into the traffic and continue on along Sophia Street for one block, then turn left onto Pitt Street. Continue along Pitt Street for six blocks to Washington Avenue and turn left. Park your vehicle there for a few moments in front of the Washington Monument.

The Mary Washington Monument:
In 1862 this part of Fredericksburg and its fine buildings did not exist. The monument to your right honors our first president's mother, Mary Washington. President Grover Cleveland dedicated the monument in 1894. An unfinished earlier monument stood here at the time of the Civil War and acted as a landmark for both sides during the battle.

In 1862 there was a dam several miles above Fredericksburg where water was diverted into a canal that ran through the town. That canal, still in evidence here today, played an important part in the battle. There were also three main roads and several minor ones that led from the city across the battlefield; two of those roads would play a major role in the coming battle.

William Street became The Orange Plank Road and crossed over a drainage ditch of the main canal by way of a wooden bridge, continuing on over Marye's Heights to Chancellorsville. Hanover Street became The Telegraph Road and it crossed the Hazel Run and then continued on around the bottom of Marye's Heights where it became a sunken road with a four-foot high stone wall on the side facing the city.

The Confederate positions on Marye's Heights were at the closest point where Lee's line of battle approached the city and, as such, were the obvious first target of any Union attack. Unfortunately the terrain between the city and along the two roads offered the attacking Federals very little cover from the Confederate fire and was in fact a potential killing field.

*The Washington Artillery firing on Union troops charging
Marye's Heights.*

As you make your way to the next stop on your tour, The
Canal Ditch Crossing, you will pass the Fredericksburg
Confederate Cemetery to your right. The cemetery is the
final resting place of more than 3,500 Confederate soldiers
and six generals. It was dedicated by the Lady's Memorial
Association of Fredericksburg in 1870. If you would like to
take a little time out to visit the cemetery you may park your
vehicle along Washington Avenue. If not you should proceed
along Washington Avenue for six blocks and then turn right
onto William Street, the old Plank Road, and go one block to
the traffic light on Kenmore Avenue where you turn left.
Drive on for three blocks until you reach the traffic light at
Hanover Street and then turn right and park your vehicle at
the curbside.

The Canal Ditch Crossing:
In 1862 the old Canal Ditch ran under what is now Kenmore
Avenue; you drove along it to get here. It was close to noon on
December 13th when General French's leading brigades moved
out of the streets of Fredericksburg. General French describes

what he encountered. *"On the outskirts of town the troops encountered a ditch, or canal, so deep as to be almost impassable except at the street bridges, and, one of the latter being partly torn up, the troops had to cross single file on the stringers. Once across the canal the attacking forces deployed under the bank bordering the plain over which they were to charge."*

The ditch was 15 feet wide and more than six feet deep. The bank General French mentioned is visible to your left. You are now standing close to the final staging area for the Union troops as they made ready to attack the Confederates on Marye's Heights. The Federals were already taking casualties, especially from artillery fire, even while they were still in the streets of the city. They came under both musket and artillery fire as they made their way in single-file across the stringers. By the time they were able to take advantage of what little cover the bank ahead of them offered, the number of Federal casualties was beginning to mount at an alarming rate.

To continue your tour, move out into the traffic and go two blocks to the traffic light on Littlepage Street, then turn left and drive four blocks to the stop sign at Lafayette Blvd. Turn right onto Lafayette and go three blocks to battlefield Visitor Center, turn into the parking area, and leave your vehicle while you visit the Sunken Road.

At the far end of the parking area you will find a trail that leads to a reconstructed portion of the stone wall. Follow the trail to the Sunken Road and then walk along it for a short way until you reach a large painting behind the stone wall, then turn and face the large monument.

The Sunken Road:
The Sunken Road is, as you already know, a part of what was in 1862 the old Telegraph Road. As you stand here you will be able to get an idea of just how strong a defensive position this was. On the morning of December 13th this position along the sunken road on the Confederate right was occupied by General Cobb's Georgia brigade. The 24th North Carolina Volunteers of Cooke's brigade was located close by to the left. These units

*Confederate troops defending the stone wall at the foot of
Marye's Heights.*

were formed in two ranks behind the stone wall so that the front
rank was in a firing position with the second rank loading and
passing their rifles back and forth to the front rank. In this
manner they were able to maintain a steady and continuous
rate of fire against the attacking Federals.

That morning in December of 1862 Confederate Generals Lee
and Longstreet watched from the top of the hill on Marye's
Heights as the blue-clad lines marched across the plain toward
the Sunken Road. French's leading brigade under the command
of Brigadier General Nathan Kimball was met by a withering
hailstorm of Confederate fire from General Cobb's infantry
behind the Stone Wall. At a distance of 100 yards the leading
elements of Kimball's brigade planted their guidons and continued the advance. Under a devastating hail of fire from the
Confederate defenders in the Sunken Road they moved forward.
The soldiers in the front ranks began falling like so many flies,
only to be replaced by those following on behind. It was carnage
on a grand scale. Finally, within 60 yards of the Confederate
muskets – point-blank range – they were forced to withdraw.

The remaining brigades of French's division, and then the brigades of Hancock's division, each in turn tried their hand against the Sunken Road, each with no better luck than Kimball. Within the space of an hour, two entire Union divisions had been decimated as they attacked the Confederate position here in front of you. French's and Hancock's dead and wounded during that first hour of the battle totaled more than 3,200, and there was more yet to come.

General Couch had been watching the action, and the devastation of the two divisions, from a cupola on top of the Fredericksburg Court House. He determined that the only way to take the Confederate positions in the Sunken Road was to send his third division – all that was left of his corps – off to the right, from which direction they could then flank the Confederate position beyond the protection of the Stone Wall.

Couch ordered General Howard's division to move out to the right and then turn on the Confederate left. Alas, no one had bothered to reconnoiter the terrain and, as the hapless soldiers crossed the canal and turned right, they soon found the ground ahead of them marshy and impassable. They had no alternative but to wheel to the left and soon found themselves headed in the direction of the Stone Wall and destruction. Howard's division, too, was decimated by the sustained and withering fire from the Sunken Road. He left more than 900 of his men dead and wounded to join their fallen comrades on the field in front of the Stone Wall.

By now one would have thought that General Burnside had gotten the message: that the Confederate position in the Sunken Road in front of Marye's Heights was impregnable. Not so. He kept sending orders across the river to continue the attack. By mid-afternoon all seven divisions of the two corps of Generals Wilcox and Stoneman, the 9th and the 3rd, had been hurled into the battle in front of Marye's Heights. All to no avail. Burnside's commanders were beginning to wonder if he might have gone out of his mind. It was getting late into the afternoon and Burnside, perhaps now becoming desperate, ordered General Hooker and his reserve Grand Division to renew the attack against the Stone Wall. Hooker ordered two of his divisions to cross the river and make ready to continue the attack. While his men made the crossing, Hooker rode out to assess the situation for himself. His opinion was that further action on the plain in front of the Sunken Road would be suicidal. He then rode back to Burnside and made an attempt to persuade him that such was the case, and that the planned attack should be called off. Burnside refused to listen to Hooker and ordered him to continue his attack. By the time Hooker had re-crossed the river for the second time, however, the shadows were lengthening into evening, and it already was becoming too dark to continue. Hooker was able safely to call off the attack.

But the day was not yet quite over. General Couch was informed that the Confederates seemed to be abandoning their position in the Sunken Road and so, with great enthusiasm, he ordered General Humphreys' brigade to attack the retreating Confederates. Humphreys ordered his men to fix bayonets and charge.

Alas, the Confederate's movement was nothing more than one battalion relieving another. Humphreys' men, in their enthusiasm, didn't even bother to stop and load their weapons and they, too, failed to reach the Stone Wall. In minutes they returned from the fray, battered and bleeding, leaving a thousand of their number dead and wounded upon the field.

The total number of Union casualties at the Sunken Road now numbered almost 9,500. It had been a costly day indeed for General Burnside. Not a single Union Soldier had reached the Stone Wall.

The night of December 15th was a bitterly cold one. All night long the wounded lay moaning and wailing in the darkness. The sounds of approaching death among the fallen on the far side of the Stone Wall were more than one Confederate soldier could stand. Sergeant Richard Kirkland of South Carolina crossed the wall to give aid to the wounded Federals lying in ghastly heaps upon the field. The monument you see here in front of you is dedicated to the memory of that Confederate soldier, Richard Kirkland.

When you are ready to continue your tour, return to the Visitor Center. Before you do, however, you might like to take a moment or two to visit the National Cemetery located near the Visitor Center. There are some 15,000 Union soldiers buried there; many of them were killed here, in front of the Sunken Road.

The next stop on your tour is Lee Hill. Leave the parking area and go to the front of the Visitor Center. Turn right there onto Lafayette Blvd. Go six-tenths of a mile until you reach a Park Service sign directing you to Fredericksburg battlefield and Lee Drive. Turn left onto Lee Drive and go two-tenths of a mile and leave your vehicle in the parking area on your right. Then follow the trail up the hill to the site of General Lee's headquarters. It's a fairly stiff climb and, if you take your time, it's a walk of about ten minutes.

Lee Hill:
You are now walking in the footsteps of General Robert E. Lee. At the time of the battle this ridge was known as Telegraph Hill, and it was here that Lee established his field headquarters, from which he directed the course of the battle. As you can see, the position here is an ideal one. The Confederate engineers felled the trees on the crest of the hill and on the slopes in every direction, giving him a panoramic view of the entire battlefield from north to south – a battle line that extended for more than seven miles.

Today the view from Lee's headquarters site is not quite as it was then. The trees and shrubs have re-established themselves once more and the beauty of the surrounding country is unspoiled, leaving little evidence of the carnage that took place on the plains below. Even so, you should be able to identify many of the landmarks that General Lee would have seen back in the dark days of December, 1862.

If you look out into the middle distance you can see the three steeples in the town of Fredericksburg and the Lacy House on Stafford Heights.

General Lee constructed his line of battle all along the crest of Marye's Heights. General Longstreet held a five-mile-long line from the Rappahannock River on the left flank, to the Deep Run valley some two miles south of here to the right. General Jackson's corps continued the line two more miles southward from the Deep Run to Hamilton's Crossing. The entire Confederate line literally bristled with artillery that bore down upon the Federals in the plains below. The cannon you see here in the earthworks is one of two monsters brought in from Richmond by rail. It's a 30-pounder Parrott Rifle with an effective range of more than two miles.

As Lee watched his troops repulse one Federal attack against the Sunken Road after another, he had a couple of near misses himself. A shot from one of the Union long-range cannon located on the far side of the river buried itself at Lee's feet in the parapet of the gun emplacement to your right. Later, as Lee, Longstreet, and artillery commander Pendleton stood nearby, the breach of the great Parrott rifle burst, sending great chunks of iron flying in all directions. Fortunately no one was hit by the missiles.

When you have finished your visit to Lee's headquarters you can return to your vehicle and make your way to the next stop on your tour, Prospect Hill. Continue on along Lee Drive for four and a half miles, past the earthworks on either side of the road, through the junction with Landsdown Road, and on to Prospect Hill. The parking area is opposite the artillery display. Pull in, park your vehicle, and walk to the painting close to the artillery display.

Prospect Hill:
It was from here on the morning of the 13th of December that Stonewall Jackson directed the battle at the southern end of the Confederate line. General A.P. Hill held the line here on Jackson's right flank with General Hood's division on his left. General Taliaferro's division was held in reserve to the rear in the fields behind you. The gun emplacements around you were those of Confederate artillery Colonel Ruben Walker. Mobile artillery units of General Jeb Stuart's cavalry brigade were

posted forward and off to your left. The Confederate defensive line here was an exceedingly strong one, with one exception. If you look to your left, across the railroad tracks, you will see a stone pyramid and a clump of trees beyond it. That area, in 1862, was marshland. Much of it was covered by surface water and thick woodland. Neither Hill nor Jackson felt there was any need to defend such a position. That area was the weak link in the Confederate line; a gap almost 600 yards wide, open to the advancing Union attack.

At 8:30 that morning General Franklin's Grand Division, almost 60,000 men, began to move. General Burnside's plan was for Franklin to take the high ground at Prospect Hill and then to roll up the entire Confederate right flank toward Marye's Heights. General George Meade's division moved out across the fields first under cover of the early morning mist. He was closely followed by General Gibbon's division to his right and rear. Meade paralleled the river for some 600 yards and then wheeled his division to the right and headed for the Richmond Road.

As the heads of Meade's columns reached the road they came under fire from two cannon under the command of a young cavalry officer: Major John Pelham. For an hour the gallant young man held up the entire Federal advance. Only after a heavy and concentrated barrage from the Union divisional artillery had disabled one of his guns, and under direct order from General Stuart himself, was Pelham persuaded to withdraw.

By this time the sun had burned off the early morning fog and the Federal lines were visible for all to see. For the Confederate defenders here on the heights of Prospect Hill it was a magnificent, though daunting, sight. The bright sunlight flashing across thousands upon thousands of bayonets. Column after column of blue-clad infantry covered the plain and it seemed as if the land itself seethed, moving, almost with a life of its own. It was a sight that never would be forgotten by the Confederate troops here on Prospect Hill.

Meade resumed his advance at about 1:00 p.m. As the advancing Federal division approached within 500 yards of this position, Walker's guns opened up with a devastating barrage on the advancing columns. Great gaps were smashed into the Federal line as the Confederate cannoneers shattered them with double-loaded canister at a rate of fire of more than two rounds per minute per gun. The Confederate cannonade was answered in strength by the Union divisional artillery and the duel continued unabated for almost an hour. So many artillery horses were killed during the battle that the Confederates called the area "Dead Horse Hill."

Under cover of the Federal barrage Meade's men, with fixed bayonets, charged headlong across the plain and into the woods beyond the stone pyramid; unknowingly they had discovered Jackson's weak spot. With General Gibbon's division advancing on their right rear, Meade's division smashed through the woods, rushed the hill, and tore into the Confederate line; it was the breakthrough that they had been looking for.

> To continue your tour, you will need to retrace your route along Lee Drive for six-tenths of a mile to a large painting on your right.

Meade's Breakthrough:
It was here at this position that Confederate General Maxcy Gregg's brigade of South Carolinians faced the advance units of General Meade's advancing Federal division. As the first elements of Union infantry rushed from the trees in front, General Gregg, not realizing what was happening, ordered his men to hold their fire. As a result he was severely wounded and his line was shattered by the onrushing Federal infantry.

Two of Meade's brigades suddenly found themselves in the middle of the Confederate line. Unfortunately the breakthrough had happened so quickly and so completely that the Federals were almost as surprised as were the Confederates, and by this time were widely scattered and almost completely disorganized. Even so, the Union objective had been reached. All that was needed now was for Meade's division to receive reinforcements and the attack could be carried through in force.

Unfortunately for Meade, General Gibbon's division advanced only as far the railroad where, when Gibbon discovered that there were no supporting troops to his right, it began to waver, and he refused to answer Meade's urgent pleas for help. This gave Stonewall Jackson the time to rush reinforcements to A.P. Hill's aid, and with General Jubal Early's division heading into the fray at the double-quick a Confederate counter-attack was soon under way.

Gen. Thomas J. Jackson.

Suddenly the unearthly sounds of the rebel yell were echoing across the battlefield as Early's division smashed into the two beleaguered Union brigades. The fighting was desperate and hand-to-hand. In moments the once victorious Federal infantrymen were running in confusion back from whence they came. Almost 40% of Meade's division lay dead and wounded on the Battlefield. Meade was first distraught, and then angry. *"My God, General,"* he is said to have shouted at his corps commander, General Reynolds, *"did they expect me to whip Jackson's entire army by myself?"* The battle of Fredericksburg at the southern end of the field was over. It had ended, for all intents and purposes, in a draw.

At the other end of the field at the Sunken Road in front of Marye's Heights it was a different story. The battle there ended in a complete victory for Confederate defenders. The following morning it became evident just how devastating the previous day had been for the nine Federal divisions that had hurled themselves in one futile attack after another against the impregnable Confederate positions behind the stone wall. As the

The stone wall, from the Confederate side, after the battle.

fog lifted on the morning of December 14th a macabre sight met the eyes of those on both sides. The plain was literally carpeted with thousands of blue-clad bodies. Thousands more lay wounded and freezing upon the field, their pitiful cries for help echoing across the frozen landscape.

General Burnside had no stomach for renewing his offensive that day and General Lee was content to await whatever his Federal counterpart might decide to do next. He did nothing.

On the afternoon of the 15th Burnside requested a truce so that he might be able to bury his dead. Lee consented and then the waiting continued. The next morning, December 16th, Confederate scouts discovered that the entire Union army had recrossed the river under cover of darkness and a heavy rainstorm, and that the pontoon bridges had been removed from the river; the Union army had retired safely into encampment on the eastern side of the Rappahannock river. The battle for Fredricksburg was over; a complete and undisputed victory for General Lee and his Army of Northern Virginia.

Both armies spent the winter watching each other from opposite sides of the river. Before the next major engagement Burnside would be replaced in command of the Army of the Potomac by Major General Joseph (Fighting Joe) Hooker. In May the following year the two generals would test each other's metal in battle just a few miles away to the west at a lonely crossroads tavern: Chancellorsville.

Where to Stay, Things to Do in Fredericksburg

Attractions

Visitor Center: 706 Caroline St. Orientation film; information, obtain walking tour brochure and combination tickets.

Belmont (The Gari Melchers Estate & Memorial Gallery): 224 Washington Street. Residence from 1916 to 1932 of American-born artist Gari Melchers (1860-1932), best known for his portraits of the famous and wealthy, including Theodore Roosevelt, William Vanderbilt and Andrew Mellon, and as an important impressionist artist of the period. The artist's studio contains the nation's largest collection of his works. (Daily; closed on Jan. 1st, Thanksgiving, Dec. 24, 25, 31). Phone 899-4860.

Confederate Cemetery: Washington Ave between Amelia and William Streets. 2,640 Confederate Civil War soldiers are buried here, some in graves marked "unknown."

Fredericksburg Area Museum. (1814). 903 Princess Anne

St. Museum and cultural center interprets the history of Fredericksburg from its first settlers to the 20th century. Changing exhibits. Children's events. (Daily; closed Jan. 1, Thanksgiving, Dec. 25). Phone 371-3037.

Fredericksburg Masonic Lodge #4: Princess Anne and Hanover Streets. Washington was initiated into this Lodge, Nov. 4th, 1752. The building, dating from 1812, contains relics of his initiation and membership; authentic Gilbert Stuart portrait; 300-year-old Bible on which Washington took his Masonic obligation. (Daily; closed Jan. 1 , Thanksgiving, Dec. 25). Phone 373-5885.

Hugh Mercer Apothecary Shop: 1020 Caroline St. 18th century medical office and pharmacy offers exhibits on the medicine and methods of treatment used by Dr. Hugh Mercer before the Revolutionary War. Authentic herbs and period medical instruments. (Daily; closed Jan. 1 , Thanksgiving, Dec. 24, 25, 31).

James Monroe Museum: 908 Charles St. James Monroe, as a young lawyer, lived and worked in Fredericksburg from 1786 to 1789 and even served on Fredericksburg's City Council. Museum houses one of the nation's largest collections of Monroe memorabilia, articles and original documents. Included are the desk bought in France in 1794 during his years as ambassador and used in the White House for signing of the Monroe Doctrine; formal attire worn at Court of Napoleon; and more than 40 books from Monroe's library. Also garden. Site is a National Historic Landmark. Owned by Commonwealth of VA, and administered by Mary Washington College. (Daily; closed Jan. 1 , Thanksgiving, Dec. 24, 25, 31). Phone 899-4559.

Kenmore: 1201 Washington Ave: Considered one of the finest restorations in Virginia; former home (circa 1752) of Col. Fielding Lewis, commissioner of Fredericksburg gunnery, who married George Washington's only sister, Betty. On an original grant of 863 acres Lewis built a magnificent home; the rooms have full decorative molded plaster ceilings, Diorama of 18th-century Fredericksburg. (Daily; closed Jan. 1, Thanksgiving,

Dec. 24, 25, 31). Tea and gingerbread served free (with paid admission) in the colonial kitchen. Phone 373-3381.

Masonic Cemetery: George and Charles Streets. One of nation's oldest Masonic burial grounds.

Mary Washington House: 1200 Charles St. Bought by George for his mother in 1772. She lived here until her death in 1789. Here she was visited by General Lafayette. Some original furnishings. Box-wood garden. (Daily; closed Jan. 1, Thanksgiving, Dec. 24, 25, 31). Phone 373-1569.

Mary Washington Monument: Near "Meditation Rock," where Mrs. Washington often went to rest and pray, and where she is buried.

Old Slave Block: William and Charles Streets. Circular block of sandstone about three feet high, from which ladies mounted their horses, and slaves were auctioned in antebellum days.

Presbyterian Church: (1833). SW corner of Princess Anne and George Streets. Cannonballs in the front pillar and other damages inflicted in the 1862 bombardment. Pews were torn loose and made into coffins for soldiers, Clara Barton, founder of the American Red Cross, is said to have nursed wounded here. A plaque to her memory is in the churchyard. Open on request (daily exc. Sat). Phone 373-7057.

Rising Sun Tavern. (circa 1760). 1306 Caroline St. George Washington's youngest brother, Charles, built this tavern, which became a social and political center and stagecoach stop. Restored and authentically refurnished as an 18th-century tavern; costumed tavern wenches, English and American pewter collection. (Daily; closed Jan. 1, Thanksgiving, Dec. 24, 25, 31). Phone 371-1491.

St. George's Episcopal Church & Churchyard: NE corner of Princess Anne & George Streets. Patrick Henry, uncle of the orator, was the first rector. Headstones in the churchyard bear the names of illustrious Virginians. (Daily). Phone 373-4133.

St. James House: 1300 Charles St. Frame house built in 1760s; antique furnishings, porcelain and silver collections; landscaped gardens. (Open Historic Garden Week in April and first week in Oct.; other times by appointment). Phone 373-1569.

Annual Events

Historic Garden Week: Private homes open. Usually last week in April.

Market Square Fair: Entertainment, crafts demonstrations, food, mid-May.

Quilt show: Exhibits at various locations. Demonstrations and sale of old & new quilts. Sept.

Christmas Candlelight Tour: Historic homes open to the public; carriage rides; Christmas decorations and refreshments of the Colonial period. First Sunday in December.

Hotels

Best Western Johnny Appleseed Inn: 543 Warrenton Road. 703-373-0000. Cable TV. Pool. Playground. Cafe 6 a.m.-1:00 p.m. Service bar. Check-out noon. Coin laundry. Meeting rooms. Sundries. Accepts credit cards.

Best Western Thunderbird: 3000 Plank Rd.,703-786-7404. Crib $2. Cable TV. Free continental breakfast. Cafe 1:00 a.m.-1:00 p.m., Check-out noon. Accepts credit cards.

Comfort Inn-North: 557 Warrenton Rd., 703-371-8900; fax 703-372-8958. 80 rooms, 10 kitchen units. Family, weekly rates. Crib free. Cable TV. Indoor pool. Free coffee in lobby. Cafe adjacent open 24 hours. Check-out 11:00 a.m. Meeting rooms, Exercise equipment, weight machine, rowers, whirlpool. Accepts credit cards.

Days Inn North: 14 Simpson Rd., 703-373-5340. 120 rooms, crib free. Cable TV. Pool. Free continental breakfast, Cafe. Check-out noon. Accepts credit cards.

Hampton Inn: 2310 William Street., 703-371-0330; fax 703-371-1753. 166 rooms. Under 18 free; mid-week rates. Crib free. Cable TV. Pool. Free continental breakfast. Check-out noon. Coin laundry, Meeting rooms. Accepts credit cards,

Hollday Inn-North: 564 Warrenton Road. 703-371-5550; fax 703-373-3641. 150 rooms. Under 18 free. Crib free. Cable TV. Pool; wading pool. Cafe 6 a.m.-2 p.m., 5-10 p.m.. Room service. Bar 4 p.m.-2 a.m.; entertainment, dancing Friday, Saturday. Check-out noon. Coin Laundry. Meeting rooms. Valet service. Sundries. Refrigerators available. Accepts credit cards.

Ramada Inn-Spotsylvania Mall: Box 36, 22405. 703-786-8361; fax 703-786-8811. 130 rooms. Under 18 free. Crib free. Cable TV. Pool. Cafe 6 a.m.-10 p.m., Room service 11:00 a.m.-9:00 p.m. Service bar noon-10 p.m. Check-out 1:00 p.m. Meeting rooms. Valet service. Sundries. Accepts credit cards.

Sheraton Inn: 2801 Plank Rd., 703-786-8321; fax 703-786-3957. 195 rooms. Under 18 free. Crib free. Cable TV. Pool; wading pool, poolside service, lifeguard. Cafe 6:30 a.m.-10:00 p.m.. Room service. Bar 11:30-2:00 a.m.; entertainment, dancing except Sunday. Check-out noon. Meeting rooms, Bellhops. Valet service. Sundries, gift shop. Airport transportation. Tennis. 18-hole golf, low greens fee, pro, putting green, driving range, lawn games. Private patios, picnic tables. Credit cards.

Sleep Inn: 595 Warrenton Road. 703-372-6868; fax 703-899-9193. 68 rooms, shower only. April-early September. Under 18 free. Crib $5. Cable TV. Free coffee in lobby. Free continental breakfast. Cafe adjacent 7:00 a.m.-1:00 p.m.; Friday, Sat to 11:00 p.m.. Check-out 11:00 a.m. Meeting rooms. Sundries. Accepts credit cards.

Inns

Fredericksburg Colonial: 1707 Princess Anne Street. 703-371-5666; fax 703-373-7557. 30 rooms. Under 12 free. Crib free, Cable TV. Free coffee. Free continental breakfast. Check-out 11:00 a.m., check-in 2:00 p.m. Refrigerators. Built 1928; each room individually decorated with antiques. Accepts credit cards.

Kenmore: 1200 Princess Anne Street. 703-371-7622; 800-437-7622; fax 703-377-5480. 13 rooms. Crib free. TV in lounge; cable. Free coffee. Free continental breakfast. Complimentary tea. Dining room 11:30 a.m.-2:30 p.m., 5:30-9:30 p.m. Room service. Bar 11:30 am-11:00 p.m. Check-out noon, check-in 2:00 p.m. Fireplace, canopy bed in some rooms. Street parking. Structure built late 1700s; in historic district. Accepts credit cards.

Richard Johnston: 711 Caroline Street. 703-899-7606. 8 rooms, 2 suites. No room phones. Free continental breakfast. Check-out 11:00 a.m.. Some fireplaces. Built 1788; antique and period furnishings, On the Rappahannock River. Totally non-smoking. Accepts credit cards.

Restaurants

La Petit Auberge: 311 William Street. 703-371-2727. Hours: 11:30 a.m.-2:30 p.m., 5:30-10:00 p.m.; early-bird dinner Mon.-Thurs. 5:30-7:00 p.m. Closed Sunday & major holidays. Reservations accepted. French, American menu. Bar. Specializes in chateaubriand, seafood. French cafe decor. Accepts credit cards.

Olde Mudd Tavern: 1/4 mile west of Thornburg, exit 118 on I-95. 703-582-5250. Hours: 4:00-9:00 p.m.; Sun. noon-8:00 p.m. Closed Mondays and Tuesdays, January 1st, December 25, also 1st week of July. Reservations accepted. Children's meals. Specializes in fresh vegetables, seafood, steak. Own baking. Entertainment Saturday. Parking. Early American decor. Civil War pictures. Accepts credit cards.

Ristorante Renato: 422 William Street. 703-371-8228. Hours: 11:30 a.m.-2:00 p.m., 4:30-10:00 p.m.; Sat, Sun from 4:30 p.m. Closed most major holidays. Northern Italian menu. Bar. Semi-a la carte: lunch & dinner. Specializes in seafood, poultry, pasta. Parking. Antique chandeliers. Fireplace. Accepts credit cards.

Camping

Koa Fredericksburg/Washington DC: Semi-wooded sites. Southbound from junction I-95 & US-1, go 4 miles south on US-1 then 2 1/2 miles east on Hwy. 607. **Facilities:** 115 sites, 33 full hookup ($), 61 water & elect (20, 30 & 50 amp receptacles), 21 no-hookups, 49 pull-throughs, a/c allowed ($), heater allowed ($), tenting available, group sites for tents, RVs, camping cabins, RV storage, flush toilets, hot showers, sewage disposal, laundry, public phone, grocery store, RV supplies, ice, tables. **Recreation:** rec. hall, coin games, pool, 2 pedal boat rentals, pond fishing, 3 bike rentals, playground, planned group activities (weekends only), horseshoes, volleyball, local tours. Open all year. Discover/Mastercard/Visa accepted. Member of ARVC; VCA. Phone: (703) 898-7252. KOA 10% value card discount.

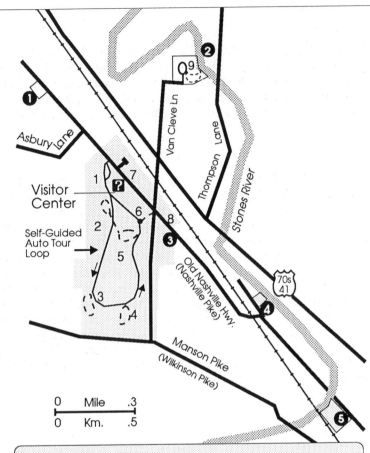

Stones River
National Battlefield
Murfreesboro, Tennessee

1 General Rosecrans Headquarters Site

2 Artillery Monument

3 Hazen Monument

4 General Bragg Headquarters Site

5 Brannon Redoubt

Chapter 8

Stones River

December, 1862 – January, 1863

The park at Stones River is located just off the Nashville Highway at Murfreesboro, Tennessee, and can best be reached from I-75 going west from Chattanooga or east from Nashville. The Visitor Center is open daily to 5 p.m. Camping facilities are available outside the park and pets are welcome so long as they are kept on a leash. Admission is $1.

The park incorporates many walks, trails, and areas of great natural beauty, and many of the main points of interest are a short walk from the roadway. You will not be restricted to the main roads and paths, so you can feel free to explore the battlefield as you wish. Be sure to take along a stout pair of walking shoes, lock your car doors when you leave, and remove any valuables, such as cameras, from view.

Stones River
National Battlefield

By mid 1862 President Lincoln and his advisors had decided the time had come to take advantage of the North's decided superiority in numbers. No less than three separate Union armies would mount a concerted effort against the Confederacy; the

Gen. Braxton Bragg.

Army of the Potomac in the east, the Army of the Tennessee and the newly formed Army of the Cumberland in the West. As Christmas approached, however, the Army of the Potomac, first under the command of General George B. McClellan and then Ambrose E. Burnside, had suffered crushing defeats at the hands of the wily commander of the Army of Northern Virginia, Robert E. Lee. The Confederate victories at Second Manassas and Fredericksburg were major setbacks for the Union campaign in the East.

In the West, Ulysses S. Grant's Federal Army of the Tennessee, after great victories at Forts Henry and Donelson and at Shiloh, was bogged down and in difficulties on its long march southward toward the Mississippi port of Vicksburg. Only General Rosecrans and the Army of the Cumberland, encamped in Nashville, Tennessee, offered the Federal president any real hope of a significant Union victory before the end of the year.

And so it was that the year 1862 ended and the year 1863 began with the battle of Stones River. Flushed with their success at Shiloh, the Union forces at forts Henry and Donelson turned their attention to General Braxton Bragg's Confederate army camped at Murfreesboro, Tennessee. Three miles away to the South of here at Murfreesboro, Confederate General Braxton Bragg had massed his Army of Tennessee, some 38,000 strong, and was preparing to mount a counter-offensive against Union Major General William Starke Rosecrans and his Army of the Cumberland.

Braxton Bragg was a controversial figure. It was claimed by many of his subordinate generals that he was an extraordinarily inept commander. Then again, by many others, he was regarded as a brilliant one; always he was cautious, almost to a fault. He was, without doubt, a brilliant organizer and a strict disciplinarian. Historians, however, still argue about his battlefield abilities.

General Rosecrans was an energetic man, often impulsive and irascible. He needed little sleep and often

Major Gen. William Starke Rosecrans.

spent the long hours before a battle wandering back and forth between the tents, or talking with his commanders until the early hours of the morning. He was not a tactful man, a trait that would eventually cost him his command.

Neither of these two had the natural military flair of Grant or Lee. Both men were competent enough commanders, but both made mistakes, more of omission and neglect than of tactics, that caused them to lose men, equipment, and territory, unnecessarily. They were a good match for each other, and would, within the year meet again at Chickamauga.

Rosecrans started his army south from Nashville on December 26th. His objective was to drive Bragg from Murfreesboro and so secure the Nashville and Chattanooga Railroad which you can see to the left and behind you. It took Rosecrans four days to move his army the 25 miles from Nashville to the Stones River. Hampered by heavy rains and an aggressive Confederate cavalry, he had to fight for every inch of the way. The Army of the Cumberland began arriving in the Stones River area on

December the 29th, hungry, tired, and very much the worse for their harrowing journey. By the evening of December 30th the two armies were confronting each other and awaiting the inevitable conflict that was to come.

General Rosecrans had deployed his forces as follows: General Crittenden commanded the Union left flank, General George H. Thomas the center, with General Alexander McDowell McCook's XIV Corps on the right flank. On the Confederate side the left flank opposing General McCook was held by General William Joseph Hardee, the center by the bishop General, Leonidas Polk, and the left flank by the one-time vice-president of the United States, General John Cabell Breckinridge.

Coincidentally, both Rosecrans and Bragg had formulated almost identical battle plans – both very simple in their conception. Each general determined to attack the other's right flank and, in a great wheeling action, to roll up the enemy line and fold it backward to destruction. Bragg intended to smash McCook's corps and drive it back to the banks of the Stones River; Rosecrans intended to smash Breckinridge's divisions and drive the entire Confederate army back toward Murfreesboro. The outcome of these two identical battle plans depended almost entirely upon the timing; he who strikes first, wins.

But then, as it almost always does, fate took a hand. Rosecrans, for all intents and purposes, outsmarted himself. Not knowing that he already held a decided superiority in numbers, he decided to even the odds a little. He would, he decided, deceive the Confederate commander into believing that it was he, Rosecrans, who had the superior force. He devised a ruse whereby he would give the impression that he was massing his forces with General McCook for an all-out attack on the Confederate right flank. The idea was to draw the Confederate brigades away from Breckinridge's position on the left thus weakening it for his intended attack there early on the morning of the 31st. Accordingly, Rosecrans issued orders for large campfires to be burned along a long line on, and away from, McCook's right. The ruse worked all too well, but not with the desired results.

When it became apparent to Bragg that Rosecrans was extending his right flank, he knew he had to counter the move. In order to do that he moved Generals McCown's and Cleburne's divisions to his own left flank and put them under the command of General Hardee. Thus Rosecrans, while achieving his advantage in numbers for his planned assault upon Breckinridge and the Confederate right flank, had inadvertently given Bragg a similar advantage against his own right flank. The timing of the attack, as already mentioned, was to be a crucial factor in the coming battle. General Bragg's orders on the evening of the 30th called for General Hardee, followed in succession by General Polk, to launch a massive assault against McCook and the Union left flank at dawn the following morning. Rosecrans' opening strategy called for General Van Cleve to cross the Stones River and move against Breckinridge at 7 a.m. Thus Rosecrans, unknowingly, handed Bragg the initiative that almost cost him, Rosecrans, the battle.

As the first streaks of dawn appeared in the sky on the morning of the 31st, Hardee moved against McCook. The full force of the reinforced Confederate advance fell upon the Union brigades of Willich and Kirk, of General Richard Johnson's division. Most of the Union troops were up and about when the Confederate tide hit the Federal positions, but they were not ready for the avalanche of death that fell upon them that morning. Confusion reigned supreme in the Union ranks and the situation was not improved when General Kirk fell mortally wounded during the first few moments of the Confederate attack and General Willich, returning from a conference with General Johnson, and whose men were still eating breakfast, was captured almost at the same time.

The Chicago Board of Trade Battery:
It was here on the morning of December 31st 1862, on the rising ground in front of you, that Union Captain James Stokes in command of the Chicago Board of Trade battery of two James rifles and four six-pounder guns, was positioned in support of Colonel James St. Morton's Pioneer brigade. The view you are looking at now has changed very little from the one Captain Stokes had that New year's Eve of 1962.

Rosecrans soon realized that his plans had gone badly wrong and immediately set about improvising a defense against what he perceived to be an impending disaster. Van Cleve's division, already on the Confederate side of the Stones River and prepared for its assault on Breckinridge and the Confederate right, was recalled back across the river and reformed, here, along the Nashville Pike, where, reinforced by General Wood's division of more than 9,000 men and a formidable array of artillery, including this Board of Trade battery commanded by Captain Stokes, they prepared to turn the advancing Confederate tide.

So, as you look toward the line of cedars before you, it's not difficult to imagine what was confronting Captain Stokes that morning. First, as the sounds of the battle raging in the distance drew closer, hundreds of fleeing Federal soldiers ran from the cedars in an uncontrolled stampede that was reminiscent of a great herd of animals running before a forest fire. They rushed headlong across the field in front of you, many without their weapons, all unheeding of their officers screaming at them to turn and reform. Captain Stokes and the other artillery commanders on this new defensive line, cannons double-loaded with canister, prepared to receive the Confederate attack.

Suddenly, as the last remnants of the fleeing Federal regiments cleared the line of cannon, a long line of charging, gay uniformed soldiers broke out of the trees and came charging across the fields to the left, right, and center.

"Fire at will!" was the order that passed down the Federal line of artillery. And, fire they did. At a rate of almost two rounds per minute, Captain Stokes and the rest of the Federal line hurled death and destruction at the charging Confederate line. On they came, great gaps opening in their ranks as round after round of double-loaded shot and shell crashed in on them. Then, the long gray line began to falter, and as they did the shouting and cheering of the gun crews in the Federal line began.

As the Confederate line began to turn, Colonel Morton ordered his Pioneer brigade to fix bayonets and charge the wavering Confederate line. It was enough. Soon the gray clad line was falling back toward the relative safety of the trees. All along the line to the left and right of where you now stand the story was the same. The Confederate advance, for the time being at least, had been stopped just short of General Bragg's objective. All along the battle line to your right, for almost four miles, Hardee and Polk had driven the Federal right flank before them like leaves in the wind, and all along that line the Confederate advance had stopped.

Abandoned cannon at Stones River battlefield.

By this time it was 10 a.m. Bragg sent orders to Breckinridge on his right flank to move his division to the left and so infuse new momentum into the slowing Confederate offensive. Breckinridge, however, thought he was facing serious problems of his own. He knew that Van Cleve had crossed the river that morning and thought he was poised to launch an attack upon him, Breckinridge. Unfortunately he was unaware that Van Cleve had been recalled back across the river and was engaged elsewhere on the Union Line. He therefore sent word to Bragg that he was unable to move, and by the time he realized that Van Cleve was no longer a danger thought it was too late for him to be of any use to Bragg.

The park today is a small one when compared to those at Chickamauga, Gettysburg, and the like. Originally the battle was fought on the grand scale over an area of more than

4,000 acres. Still, the park is an interesting one and the story of what happened here is just as important as that of any of the more well known parks.

To begin your tour of the battlefield you should leave **Stop Number 1** at the Visitor Center and proceed along the loop road until you reach **Stop Number 2**, The Cedar Glades. Leave your vehicle in the parking lot and follow the footpath for a short way through the trees until you reach the Park Service Plaque.

The Cedar Glades:
The terrain here still looks much the same as it did in 1862 so it should be easy for you to imagine what it must have been like to fight a battle in such a restricted setting as this dense woodland. The trees are Tennessee red cedar and the rocky outcrops are made of limestone. You are standing close to the position where the Confederate drive was stopped by elements of General McCook's corps at around 10 a.m. on the morning of December 31st.

Can you imagine what it must have been like for the defeated Union soldiers fleeing through these woods in confusion? Better yet, can you imagine what it must have been like to try to fight here? As you can see, the woods are so dense it's difficult to see more than 60 feet or so in any direction. Add to that the dense smoke of the cannon and musket fire and you will begin to understand how difficult it must have been for the individual company commanders to maintain control of their men, much less for the general in command of a brigade or division to maintain any sort of organized battle order. And you might try to put yourself in the shoes of the pursuing Confederates. How must it have felt to them to have been victoriously charging through these cedars one moment, and then to run straight into the mouths of the massed cannon on the new Federal line of defense?

Continue on along the loop road for about a half-mile until you reach **Stop Number 3** to your right. Once again you can park your car and make your way along the footpath into the woods where you will find Water's Alabama battery; it's a walk of about ten minutes.

Water's Alabama Battery:

The limbered cannon you see here is typical of those used throughout the Civil War. In the limbered position, as this one is, the cannon is ready for transportation. It is hooked first to the two-wheeled limber, an ammunition chest which in turn was pulled by a team of six horses. Each field piece was supported by a caisson which carried three more ammunition chests and it, too, was pulled by a team of six horses. The cannoneers walked alongside their equipment while three drivers rode the three horses on the left-hand side of the team. Four types of ammunition could be fired by the gun you see in front of you: canister, a soft metal container of round metal balls, each about an inch in diameter; it was, to all intents and purposes, a giant shotgun shell. When the gun was fired the canister would burst and deliver the balls in a wide pattern; at close range when used against massed infantry the effect was devastating. There were two types of exploding shell. These would burst into fragments, by way of a fuse, and scatter shrapnel with devastating effect. Finally, there was the traditional round-shot itself. This was used primarily for battering the target into rubble.

When you are ready, continue your tour and proceed to **Stop Number 4**, about a half-mile further along the loop road. Park your vehicle and follow the path into the trees until you arrive at the site of the wrecked cannon.

The Slaughter Pens:

You are now standing at a point very close to what was the Union center. General Negley's division was posted here with General Sheridan's division just about a half-mile away to the south and to Negley's right, just beyond the Wilkinson Pike.

As Confederate General Leonidas Polk's corps moved steadily forward at the Confederate center, General Hardee was executing the classic flanking maneuver by wheeling his corps ever inward against Union General McCook's corps on the Federal right flank. To understand what was happening you might imagine Polk's corps as the hub at the center of a giant wheel, and Hardee's corps in a long line of battle as a spoke in the wheel turning relentlessly in a clockwise motion and sweeping everything in front of it from the field.

As the Federal right flank began to crumble under the continued onslaughts of Hardee's corps, the shattered brigades of Willich and Kirk streamed through this and Sheridan's position as they fled toward the rear and safety. Having a good idea of what was to come, the two Generals, Sheridan and Negley, braced themselves and their divisions and made ready to greet the advancing Confederate hoards.

At first, Sheridan's division managed to hold its ground, but with the collapse of the entire Union right, the fighting at his position became desperate. Men and animals were mowed down by the hundreds, but, for a while at least, Sheridan managed to hold on. The Confederate advance stalled, only to be renewed with even more ferocity. Sheridan's brigades began to give way and slowly they withdrew in a fighting retreat to reform in a new defensive position just to your right and rear. General Negley now faced south toward the Confederate advance; Sheridan faced west.

The Confederate advance continued. On they came, an avalanche of gray-clad infantry: irresistible. The situation here became extremely grave. The Union defenders faced a firestorm of unbelievable proportions. So much so that the place where you now stand became known as "The Slaughter Pens." And Sheridan's new line held. Confederate attack after attack, however, slowly whittled away at his division until, eventually, realizing his position was rapidly becoming untenable, he was forced to withdraw. At the start of the battle Sheridan's division had numbered more than 4,100 men. As he made his fighting withdrawal, he left more than 1,600 officers and men on the battle field at the Slaughter Pens; and four of his brigade commanders had been killed.

But Sheridan's and Negley's efforts had not been in vain, for they had managed to buy Rosecrans enough time to build his new line of defense along the Nashville Pike. Sheridan, in recognition of his efforts that day, was later promoted to the rank of Major General.

Of the fighting on the Confederate side? One anonymous infantryman had this to say: *"The crest occupied by the Yankees was belching loud with fire and smoke and our Rebels were falling like leaves in Autumn in a hurricane. The leaden hail swept Maney's brigade from the field. . . . The brigade had fallen back about two hundred yards when General Cheatham's presence encouraged them. The impression General Frank Cheatham made upon my mind, leading the charge, I will never forget. I saw either victory or death written upon his face. Then it was I saw the power of one man, born to command, on a multitude of men. . . . Maney's brigade raised a hoot and a yell and swooped down on those Yankees like a whirling gust of woodpeckers in a hailstorm, paying the blue-coated rascals back with compound interest. The whole wing of the Yankee army was driven back. . . . The ground was covered with Blue-coat's dead. I have fought in over a dozen pitched battles and I cannot remember now ever seeing more dead men, horses, and captured cannon all jumbled together in that scene of blood and carnage."*

You can continue you tour by proceeding on along the tour route until you reach Stop Number 5, a distance of about a half-mile.

Stop Number 5:
At about 10 a.m. the Confederate attack was still moving forward in high gear, and it was at this position, at Stop Number 5, that Confederate General Daniel S. Donelson and his Tennessee brigade smashed into the brigades under the command of Union General Crittenden that were holding the line to General Negley's left, driving them back into the woods. Union Colonel Charles Cruft was holding a position here just to Negley's left. The Confederate charge broke through the first line of Union defenders and then continued on to encounter Cruft's main line here. The fighting was fierce, and, for a little while at least, Cruft was able to hang on to his position. But, inevitably, he was forced to give way before Donelson's onslaught. Soon, Cruft's

entire brigade was on the run, driven back into the woods in confusion and disorder where they became intermingled with the brigades of Negley and Sheridan, both of whom were by now fighting hard to maintain an orderly withdrawal back toward the Nashville Pike.

Thousands of Federal soldiers fled in confusion as the Confederate advance here, and all along a mile-and-a-half wide front to the west, continued to roll up the Union right flank.

Donelson's brigade pursued Cruft's brigade through the woods and into the cotton field beyond, but by that time Donelson's force, having suffered heavy casualties and by now in almost as bad a condition as the fleeing Federals, had found they could go no further. All along the line of battle the Confederate attack was beginning to run out of momentum, and soon, as did Donelson's brigade, it ran out of steam altogether and stopped. By the close of battle he had captured eleven Union cannon and more than a thousand Federal infantrymen. By the end of the day Donelson had pulled back into the woods close to this position and had made camp for the night.

At Stop Number 6, just a couple of hundred yards further along the road, you can leave your vehicle and walk to the edge of the field.

Stop Number 6:
By noon on December 31st the situation was as follows: Bragg had driven the Federal right flank back almost to the Nashville Pike. Sheridan and Negley had conducted their fighting withdrawal and the remnants the entire Union right, including Cruft's decimated brigade, were now dug in on Rosecrans' new line of defense in front of you. At the same time five Federal brigades under the commands of Generals Hazen, Grose, Hascall, Wagner and Schaefer with two batteries of artillery were holding the high ground in front of the Nashville Pike about a half-mile away to the southeast. This high ground was known as "The Round Forest," and we will be visiting it a little later at Stop Number 8.

All along the old highway thousands of Union soldiers had thrown up a temporary breastwork behind the rail fence. Thousands more were held in reserve and preparing to defend the position from the behind the protection of the railroad embankment just beyond the road. In front of you in the cotton field were eight Federal cannon, to the left on the high ground that is now the Stones River National Cemetery were 18 more, and at the position where the Visitor Center now stands were the six cannon of the Chicago Board of Trade Battery commanded by Captain Stokes. In all, 32 pieces of Union field artillery and an almost impregnable line of infantry now faced the Confederate line of battle; it was too much. The exhausted Confederate brigades drew back into the cedars and established a new line of their own, then settled down to await the Union counter attack; it never came.

Meanwhile, General Bragg, now fully aware that Hardee's drive had come to an end, decided he could still win the day if he could deliver a hammer blow to the Federal line to the east.

As you make your way to **Stop Number 8**, the site of the struggle for the Round Forest, you might like to take a little time out to visit the National Cemetery at **Stop Number 7**.

Stones River National Cemetery:
The cemetery here at Stones River was established in 1865. The bodies of Union soldiers killed not only here, but at battlefields all across the middle Tennessee area were disinterred and then reburied here. There are some 6,100 Civil War graves in the cemetery of which 2,307 are unknown. Veterans who fought in many other wars, too, are buried here: The Spanish American War, World Wars One and Two, Korea, and Viet Nam. There are no Confederate soldiers buried here, but more than two thousand were laid to rest at the Confederate Circle in the Evergreen Cemetery in Murfreesboro; they are all unknown.

Be sure to take note of the plaques along the drive. The lines of poetry are taken from "The Bivouac of the Dead" by Theodore O'Hara, written in 1847 to honor the American men who died fighting in the war with Mexico. The words written on the plaque are poignant, and entirely appropriate, for this cemetery is a very special place.

On leaving the National Cemetery you should proceed on along the road until you reach the intersection with McFadden Lane. Go straight on until you find the Park Service parking lot and park your vehicle. You have now reached Stop Number 8 on your tour.

The Round Forest:
This area of slightly higher ground, about four acres in all, was where, just before noon on December 31st, five Union brigades and two batteries made ready to receive an all-out Confederate attack. Bragg knew that if he could capture the Round Forest he would be positioned to sweep along the Nashville Pike and the railroad, rolling up the federal line in front of him. Once again he would attempt the classic flanking maneuver.

Confederate General James F. Chalmers was the first to test the metal of the defenders on the high ground here in front of you. It was at about 11 a.m. that he led his Mississippi brigade straight into what must have seemed to be the jaws of death. The massed Union infantry and the artillery on the high ground all opened fire on Chalmers' advancing brigade at the same time. The firestorm was devastating. All around him Chalmers' Mississippians were dropping like flies under the deadly hail of iron and lead. Chalmers himself was wounded in the head and had to be carried from the field, unconscious. The Mississippians, now leaderless, milled around in confusion until at last they fled from the field in disarray. And the battle for the Round Forest had barely begun.

General Bragg knew that an all-out frontal attack on the Federal positions on the Nashville Pike would be suicidal. The only way to outright victory was to attack Rosecrans down the Pike and the railroad from the southeast. If this could be done he would be attacking with his force in line-abreast against a cross-section of the Federal line less than 200 yards wide. The firepower he would be able to deliver would be irresistible, and victory would be won, almost within the hour. But first he had to win the Round Forest where the Federal defenders were guarding the gateway at the left flank of Rosecrans' new line of defense.

As soon as he got word of the destruction of General Chalmers' brigade, Bragg sent word across the Stones River to General John C. Breckinridge to cross the river with his entire division and sweep the Federals from their position. Breckinridge, however, as we already know, was the victim of false intelligence. He knew that at first light that morning Union General Van Cleve had crossed the river and formed his division in line of battle in front of him, preparing for Rosecrans' planned attack on the Confederate right flank at 7 o'clock that morning. As we know, that attack never came. However, what Breckinridge did not know was that Van Cleve had been recalled in order to support Rosecrans' main force

Then Brigadier Gen. John C. Breckenridge

against Bragg's preemptive attack. So, believing himself to be in imminent danger of attack from Van Cleve, he sent word to Bragg that he could not leave his position. But Breckinridge was wrong, and although it was not entirely his fault, it was some three hours later that he realized the truth and made ready to move. That delay probably cost Bragg the battle.

During those crucial three hours Rosecrans reinforced the defenders at the Round Forest with every spare regiment, cannon, and soldier he could lay his hands on. By the time the first of Breckinridge's brigades under the command of Daniel W. Adams had crossed the river at about 2:30 in the afternoon they were ready and waiting for him.

It was at this point that the Confederate commander made a terrible mistake. Instead of waiting for Breckinridge's entire division of four brigades, more than 6,000 men, to assemble, cross the river, and then attack the Federal position en masse, and thus overwhelm the defenders by sheer weight of numbers, he hurled the single brigade against the now mighty force assembled on the rise.

Onward, up the slope, the Confederates charged at the double-quick until they came under the massed guns of the Union artillery. Great gaps were literally blown into the advancing Confederate line, but still onward they came, never faltering under the deadly rain of canister and shrapnel. Suddenly they were within range of the muskets of the Union infantry. The firepower now turned against Adams' brigade was unimaginable. The Confederate attack faltered, stalled, and was finally beaten back in disarray; Adams himself was shot during the attack; his brigade was decimated.

Next in line was the brigade of John K. Jackson. He, too, hurled his men up the rise and he, too, was beaten back by the withering fire of the Federal defenders. More than a third of his brigade fell dead and wounded on the approaches to the Round Forest and all of his regimental commanders were either killed or wounded. And still the Union force stood fast.

Almost an hour later the last two of Breckinridge's brigades under the command of Generals William Preston and Joseph Palmer hit the slopes in front of the Round Forest. By sheer weight of numbers the Confederate force drove forward until it reached a point only 150 yards short of the Federal position, only to be driven back by a hailstorm of canister, shrapnel and minie balls.

By this time the last light of day was beginning to leave the sky, and with it the fighting dwindled until finally it stopped altogether. The first day of the battle for Stones River was over. Both armies settled down for the night and to lick their wounds. The Union army had lost a fourth of its entire number. The Confederate army had fared little better but, even though Rosecrans had not been driven from the field, the day belonged to them.

General Bragg was exultant. He retired from the field that night convinced that he had won the battle, so much so that he sent the following message to President Jefferson Davis: "God has granted us a happy New Year."

That same evening General Rosecrans, in conference with his Generals, discussed his options. General McCook who, while commanding the Union right flank, had taken almost everything General Bragg could throw at him, was convinced that the army should be put into retreat. General Stanley, the Union cavalry commander, agreed with McCook. Generals Thomas and Crittenden had very little to say except that they would support Rosecrans to the utmost of their ability no matter what he might decide to do.

Rosecrans decided to stay and fight it out. And, in accordance with his orders, the Union line on the left flank was pulled back some 250 yards to a more advantageous position. Van Cleve was sent back across the river in support of the new left flank. Rosecrans and his Army of the Cumberland settled down to await the New Year and the expected Confederate attack.

It was New Years Eve at Stones River, but there was little celebrating done that night. No champagne corks popped and there was little singing to be heard. Only the howl of the winter wind and the rattle of the rain on the tents broke the silence of the night as the two badly mauled armies huddled on the battlefield and waited for whatever morning and the New Year might bring.

If you will walk just a little way along the path to the cemetery you will find the Hazen Monument. This is the oldest Civil War monument in the United States. It was erected by the survivors of General William B. Hazen's brigade to the memory of their fallen comrades. The remains of the fallen officers are interred beneath the monument with the graves of 55 of Hazen's soldiers around them.

Engraving from Frank Leslie's Illustrated Newspaper, *based on a sketch by Fred B. Schell of the battle at Stones River.*

On the morning of January 1st, 1863, dawn came and went without event. It was a cold, wet, dreary day. As the morning wore on the two major players each awaited some sort of action from the other. Bragg, clearly surprised that Rosecrans was still on the field, seemed to be at a loss as to what to do next; he decided to do nothing. Instead he waited, convinced that it was only a matter of time before his adversary's nerve would break and he would retreat, leaving him, Bragg, in sole possession on the field. All day long the Confederate cavalry harried, this way and that, behind the Federal lines, capturing and destroying Union supplies, but still Rosecrans held his ground; and still Bragg waited.

January 1st turned into January 2nd and for most of the day things continued much as they had the day before. By noon, however, events had been set in motion that would bring the impasse to a climactic conclusion.

On January 1st Union General Samuel Beatty moved his division across the Stones River and deployed it on a ridge about a half-mile from the river on the Union left flank, facing General Breckinridge on Bragg's right flank. Bragg, on being informed of Beatty's new position, assessed the situation and realized that not only was Beatty in a position to threaten his left flank, his artillery could threaten General Polk's corps at the Confederate center, as well. The only solution to the problem was to drive Beatty from the ridge; Breckinridge was elected to do the job.

When you are ready to continue your tour you will need to go to the Artillery Monument at **Stop Number 9**. Leave here and go back to the intersection with McFadden Lane and turn right. Follow the road across the railroad and Highway 41 until you reach the Park Service parking lot at Stop Number 9. Be careful as you cross the highway. The traffic is always heavy.

As you cross the railroad tracks look to your left and you will see a sign telling you that: "Garesche (pronounced GAR-SHAY) fell here." The story of Union Lt. Colonel Julius P. Garesche is an interesting one. As early as 21 years before the battle of Stones River, Garesche had an overpowering premonition of his own violent death. He graduated from West Point in 1841, 30th in a class of 52. It was at West Point that he became a close friend of William Rosecrans. It was a friendship the two men maintained until Garesche's death at Stones River. On September 14th 1861, Garesche's brother, Frederick, a Roman Catholic priest, told him that he had received a heavenly commission to reveal to Julius that he would be killed during his first battle. At first Garesche did not believe his brother's prophecy. After all, Garesche was an officer on the General Staff, and as such he would never see combat service. But Garesche was a very pious man, and because of this many of his compatriots believe that he felt he would thwarting God's divine plan for him if he continued to avoid his destiny. At any rate, in April of 1862 he

Lt. Col. Julius Peter Garesche.

began to actively seek a field commission. His opportunity came when his friend, General Rosecrans, was appointed to the command of the Army of the Cumberland. It was a natural course of action for Rosecrans to appoint Garesche his Chief of Staff.

In the early hours of the morning of December 31st, 1862, just before the battle for Stones River was to begin, Garesche was observed on his knees in a glade of cedars reading his prayer book. A few moments later he rejoined Rosecrans and the two of them in the company of several other officers left camp to review the Union lines. It was sometime during this review that a solid round-shot from a Confederate cannon hit Garesche in the head, decapitating him. For several seconds his headless body continued to ride its horse until, eventually, it bucked and threw his body to the ground. Frederick's prophecy had come to pass 15 months and 17 days after it had been made.

Generals Breckinridge and Bragg were not on the best of terms. In fact, at times, there was open hostility between them. When Breckinridge received Bragg's order to attack Beatty's well defended position he protested to Bragg in the strongest terms,

claiming that such an offensive action against the Union forces
on the ridge would be suicidal. Even Polk said that Beatty
offered no real threat. But Bragg was adamant and at 4 p.m.
Breckinridge put his brigades into battle formation. Two of his
brigades would attack Beatty line-abreast with the remaining
two brigades following in close support.

Beatty's brigade prepares to meet the Confederate charge.

Meanwhile, Union General Crittenden was conducting an inspection of his own brigades deployed along the Nashville Pike.
As he did so he noticed the new movements in the Confederate
positions across the river at Breckinridge's position. Realizing
that something serious was about to happen he ordered his
Chief of Artillery, Major John Mendenhall, to gather together
every piece of artillery he could lay his hands on and to assemble
them here on the high ground on the west bank of the river at
McFadden's Ford, close to the monument at Stop Number 9.
Here on the small hill in front of you Mendenhall assembled 45
assorted cannon. These were supported by 12 more on the high
ground at what is now the National Cemetery, bringing the
total to 57 – a bristling array of weaponry that entirely dominated the ground on the far side of the river.

At 4 p.m. General Polk opened up a massive diversionary bombardment all along his front line; at the same time Breckinridge launched his first two brigades at Beatty's defenders on the ridge. This time there was no Confederate surprise. The Union soldiers were outnumbered by Breckinridge's division almost two to one. They gritted their teeth, gripped their muskets, and gazed down at the advancing Confederate tide. Then, Beatty's men let fly with everything they had, but it was to no avail. On they came, Breckinridge's gray-coated brigades. Then at a distance of about 150 yards General Roger Hanson's Orphan Brigade of Kentuckians fired a single volley into the Union line, leveled their bayonets, and screaming the rebel yell at the top of their lungs, charged up the slope into the Federal position; it was too much. Beatty's ranks crumbled, then disintegrated before the Confederate hoard, his men fleeing in confusion. The ridge belonged to Breckinridge. Unfortunately his men were not satisfied and, instead of consolidating their new position, they streamed over the ridge and down the hill toward McFadden's Ford in pursuit of Beatty's brigades. It could not have happened better for the waiting gunners had they planned it themselves. They waited patiently until the main force of Breckinridge's division was well within range of the massed guns here on the high ground in front of you. And then they opened fire. The carnage they wrought upon the charging Confederates must have been terrible to behold. Regiment after regiment was blown to shreds in front of the Federal cannon as the gunners fired, loaded, fired, and loaded, again and again. Breckinridge's division was decimated. By the time the remnants of the retreating Confederate brigades had cleared the field, almost a third of the division, 1,700 of the 4,500 men, lay dead, dying or wounded upon the battlefield; the battle for Stones River was over.

Both General Bragg and General Rosecrans claimed victory, but the truth is that there were no winners here at Stones River. It's true that after Breckinridge's suicidal attack and subsequent defeat Bragg turned his army and withdrew southward toward Chattanooga. That left Rosecrans in possession of the battlefield and, technically at least, the victor. But Rosecrans was in no better shape himself, and it took almost six months for his army to recover to a point where they could operate effectively once again. The two generals had fought themselves to a standstill. The combined losses of the two armies at the battle of Stones River totaled more than 23,000.

You will find the banks of the river and McFadden's Ford just a short walk down the hill to your left. It is a very beautiful and peaceful place, where you might like to sit for a moment or two and reflect, as you

The banks of the Stones River at McFadden's Ford.

watch the river flowing gently through the trees, on the great events and the heroic deeds that took place here early in 1863. Today it seems difficult to envisage the carnage that littered the countryside all around you, but it's not too difficult to imagine that perhaps each January 2nd, on the anniversary of Breckinridge's fatal charge, the ghosts of General Hanson's Orphan Brigade of Kentuckians lead the way up the ridge on the other side of the river. Do their rebel yells still echo across the countryside as they charge into the teeth of the ghostly artillery on the hill behind you? Probably not. It doesn't really matter, does it? The Artillery Monument on the hill today honors all those who died here at Stones River, Union or Confederate.

Where to Stay, What to Do in Murfreesboro TN

Attractions

Oaklands: 900 N Maney Ave, 2 miles N of I-24. This 19th-century mansion, an architectural blend of four different periods, was a social center before the Civil War and command headquarters for Union Colonel W.W. Duffield, who surrendered Murfreesboro to Confederate General Nathan Bedford Forrest at the house. Rooms restored and furnished with items appropriate to the Civil War period. Medical collection. Grounds landscaped in period style. (Daily exc. Mon.; closed major holidays). Sr. citizen rate. Phone 893-0022.

Stones River National Battlefield: On US 41/70 S. Park covering approx. 400 acres preserves the site of the Battle of Stones River (Dec. 31, 1862-Jan. 2, 1863), a bitter clash resulting in 10,000 Confederate and 13,000 Union casualties. The Confederates failed in this attempt to halt the Union advance on Chattanooga. The park includes the Hazen Monument (1863), one of the oldest memorials of the Civil War, and the National Cemetery, with 7,000 graves, tablets and markers. Self-guided tours; auto tape tour (1 1/4 hr) at Visitor Center. Living history demonstrations on summer weekends. Visitor Center has battlefield museum, films (daily). Battlefield and National Cemetery (daily; closed Dec. 25). Contact the Superintendent, 3501 Old Nashville Hwy., 37129; 893-9501. Free.

(For further information contact the Rutherford County Chamber of Commerce, PO Box 864, 37133; 893-6565-6565.)

Annual Events

Street Festival & Folkfest: International dancers, arts & crafts. May.

International Grand Championship Walking Horse Show: Early Aug.

Hotels

Days Inn: 1855 S. Church Street. 615-896-5080; fax 615-896-5080. 81 rooms. Crib free. Cable TV. Pool. Cafe 6-10:30 a.m. & 4-8 p.m. Room service. Bar 4 p.m.-1 a.m. Check-out noon. Meeting room., Accepts credit cards.

Garden Plaza: 1850 Old Fort Pkwy. 615-895-5555. 170 rooms. Under 12 free. Crib free. Cable TV. Indoor pool; whirlpool, poolside service. Cafe adjacent 6:30 a.m.-11 p.m., bar 4 p.m.-midnight. Room service. Check-out noon. Meeting rooms. Bellhops. Valet service. Health club privileges. Refrigerators; some wet bars. Accepts credit cards.

Hampton Inn: 2230 Old Fort Pkwy. 615-896-1172. 119 rooms. Under 18 free. Crib free. Cable TV. Pool. Free coffee in lobby. Free continental breakfast. Cafe adjacent, open 24 hours. Check-out noon. Meeting room. Accepts credit cards.

HoJo Inn: 2424 S. Church Street at junction with US 231 & I-24; 615-896-5522. Under 12 free. Crib free. Cable TV. Pool. Check-out noon. Coin laundry. Meeting room. Game room. Accepts credit cards.

Holiday Inn: 2227 Old Fort Pkwy. 615-896-2420. 180 rooms. Crib free. Cable TV. Indoor pool; wading pool. Cafe 6 a.m.-2 p.m., 5 p.m.-10 p.m. Room service. Bar 4:30 p.m.-2 a.m.; dancing exc. Sun. Check-out noon. Coin laundry, meeting rooms, bellhops. Valet service. Exercise equipment; weights, bicycles, whirlpool, sauna. Holidome game room. Accepts credit cards.

Shoney's Inn: 1954 S. Church Street. 675-896-6030; fax 615-896-6037. Reservations 800-222-2222. 125 rooms. Under 18 free. Crib free. Cable TV. Pool. Free coffee in lobby. Cafe adjacent 6 a.m.-11 p.m. Bar 4 p.m.-midnight, closed Sun. Check-out noon. Meeting rooms. Valet service. Sundries, Health club privileges. Some refrigerators. Accepts credit cards.

Wayside Inn: 2225 S. Church Street at the junction with US 231 & I-24. 615-896-2320. 103 rooms. Under 18 free. Crib free. Cable TV. Pool. Cafe 6 a.m.-9 p.m. Room service. Check-out 11 a.m. Meeting room. Some bathroom phones, refrigerators, wet bars. Whirlpool in suites. Accepts credit cards.

Restaurant

Ming Garden: 1433 Memorial Blvd. 615-895-1600. Hours: 11 a.m.-l0 p.m. Closed Thanksgiving. Reservations accepted Fri. & Sat. Chinese menu. Bar. Semi-a la carte. Specializes in pork, beef, seafood. Parking. Oriental decor; original artwork. Accepts credit cards.

Chapter 9

Chancellorsville

May, 1863

The Chancellorsville National Battlefield Park is ten miles to the west of Fredericksburg VA on US 3. The Visitor Center offers full facilities for the handicapped and is completely accessible to wheelchairs. Picnicking is allowed only in the designated areas and tables are provided for that purpose. Phone 540-323-4510.

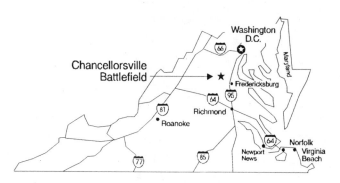

For almost five months after the Confederate victory at Fredericksburg in December 1862 the two great armies were content to wait one upon the other in the very same positions they had occupied before the battle. The Union Army of the Potomac, now more than 130,000 strong, occupied a vast area on the eastern side of the Rappahannock river. The Confederate Army of Northern Virginia occupied the ridges just to west of the city. Both armies were well within sight of one another.

General Ambrose E. Burnside had been replaced as commander of the Army of the Potomac by General Joseph "Fighting Joe" Hooker, a brave but boastful and arrogant man. His first task

Major Gen. Joseph Hooker.

as commander was to break up the huge, unwieldy Grand Divisions of General Burnside's command and re-institute the more manageable corps structure. It now became, in Hooker's own words, *"the finest army on the planet."* President Lincoln visited General Hooker during the early part of April, 1863, *"to get away from Washington and the politicians,"* as he put it. But more than that, to check on the moral of the army and to find out exactly what General Hooker planned to do with this "finest army on the planet" now that spring was approaching.

"My plans are perfect," Hooker bragged to Lincoln. *"May God have mercy on General Lee for I will have none."*

Braggart though General Hooker might have been he was also a good soldier. He was, however, inflicted with the same disease as all of his predecessors. He, too, was obsessed by the northern cry, *"on to Richmond."* And civilian though he was, Lincoln was aware, as most of his generals were not, that it was not Richmond that was their objective but the Confederate army. And so Lincoln left Hooker with a few kind words, some sound advice –

"in your next fight, gentlemen, put in all your men" – and then, with a premonition of impending disaster, he returned to Washington.

Hooker's plan was an excellent one. It was a plan of dash, daring, and more imagination than any of his predecessors' had shown before. He would, by the end of April, take three army corps up the eastern bank of the Rappahannock river to Kelly's Ford some 25 miles northwest of Fredericksburg. There he would cross both the Rappahannock and Rapidan rivers, and by so doing get on Lee's left and rear flanks. Of the three army corps he would leave behind, two would create a diversion and thus keep the Confederate army in their defensive positions, while the third would hold itself in reserve ready to move in whatever direction might afford it the best opportunity.

Essential to the success of his plan, or so Hooker thought, was the part to be played by General Stoneman, his cavalry commander. Stoneman was to leave camp some two weeks before the main body of the flanking army, cross the river to the north of Fredericksburg, and sweep down upon Lee's lines of communication to Richmond, cutting off his supplies. If this could be done, Hooker believed, Lee would rapidly run out of food and ammunition and, with Hooker's three corps on his left and rear, and with three more in front of him, Lee's army must either be destroyed or forced to retreat. Hooker would be doing the unthinkable by splitting his army, but the rewards were, he felt, well worth the risk.

On the morning of April 13th General Stoneman, at the head of a column of cavalry some 10,000 strong, and with General Hooker's words, *"let your watchword be fight, fight, fight,"* ringing in his ears, moved out and headed northward to Warrenton Junction on the Orange and Alexandria Railroad; almost immediately things began to go wrong. After only two hours of marching the skies opened and for 36 hours it poured with rain, preventing Stoneman from crossing the river. As the rain continued on and off for several days the river continued to rise and it remained impassable until April 28th. Stoneman was so long delayed he was unable to offer any effective help to Hooker until

Major Gen. Daniel E. Sickles.

after the impending battle was over. Hooker decided he couldn't wait until his erstwhile cavalry commander was able to carry out his part of the plan and so, on April 27th, with the 5th, 11th, and 12th Corps under the commands of Generals George Meade, Oliver O. Howard, and Henry W. Slocum, he moved northward up the east bank of the Rappahannock, well screened from the eyes of the watching Confederate observers on the heights overlooking Fredericksburg to the west.

At dawn the next day General French moved his division to Banks' Ford to begin a diversion there. General Sickles' 3rd Corps moved south of Fredericksburg to join the 1st and 6th Corps of Generals Reynolds and Sedgewick where they would begin their diversionary actions and then continue them until Hooker was able to cross the river and turn southward.

By the evening of the 29th Hooker and his three corps had successfully crossed the Rappahannock at Kelly's Ford. Slocum and Howard then moved southwest to cross the Rapidan at Germanna Ford while Meade moved further to the south and crossed the river at Ely's Ford. By the evening of April 30th all three corps were encamped around a lonely farmhouse known as Chancellorsville, just ten miles to the west of Fredericksburg. Chancellorsville was not a town. It was merely a crossroads in a densely wooded area known then as The Wilderness.

In the meantime General Sickles had thrown two bridges across the Rappahannock south of Fredericksburg hoping to draw the Confederates down from the heights, but they had ignored him. Hooker ordered Sickles and his 3rd Corps to march at all speed and join him at Chancellorsville, which he did the next morning. Hooker's plan, to this point at least, had been carried out brilliantly. He had successfully outflanked the South's finest general and was now in position to destroy the entire Confederate army. Hooker's wing of the Army of the Potomac was infused with a confidence they had not felt for a long time. Spirits in the ranks rose and the rigours of the past several days of hard marching were forgotten. Orders were carried out by the officers and men with a cheerfulness hither too unknown in the ranks. Major General Schurz was heard to say, *"I have never known my command to be in a more excellent condition."* All Hooker had to do now, so it seemed, was to fall upon Lee from the rear and destroy him. He was heard to boast: *"I have Lee in one hand and Richmond in the other."*

But General Hooker wasn't dealing with just anyone. His adversary was arguably the finest battlefield tactician the world had ever seen, and he had plans of his own. Robert E. Lee was not fooled by the diversions of the Federals left behind at Fredericksburg, and he was not about to do what Hooker hoped he would do.

In the late morning of April 29th Confederate cavalry commander General J.E.B. Stuart, Lee's "eyes and ears," reported that a large Federal Force was crossing the river at Kelly's Ford. A few hours later he reported that his men had captured soldiers belonging to the Union's 5th, 11th, and 12th Corps, and that the enemy was already crossing the Rapidan River in force at Germanna and Ely's Fords. Lee realized he had better do something to protect his flank, and he'd better do it fast. His maps indicated that Hooker's early objective must be the crossroads at Chancellorsville. He immediately ordered General Richard H. Anderson's brigade to Chancellorsville to cover the roads there, and then ordered General Lafayette McLaws to stand in readiness to move to Anderson's aid should it become necessary to do so.

General Lee spent the morning of April 30th in conference with General Stonewall Jackson trying to decide what to do next. As he saw it, the Army of Northern Virginia had but two options.

Major Gen. Lafayette McLaws.

One of those was to retreat southward, the other to attack the Federal Army at Chancellorsville. Lee knew that retreat was what Hooker expected him to do; it was, after all, the easiest solution to his predicament. Lee, however, was not about to do the expected. He decided as follows: *"It was, therefore, determined to leave sufficient troops to hold our lines, and with the main body of the army to give battle to the approaching column. Early's division of Jackson's corps, and Barksdale's brigade of McLaws' division, with part of the Reserve Artillery, under General Pendleton, were entrusted with the defense of our position at Fredericksburg, and, at midnight on the 30th, General McLaws marched with the rest of his command toward Chancellorsville. General Jackson followed at dawn the next morning with the remaining divisions of his corps."*

On the morning of May 1st the generals commanding the Federal forces at Chancellorsville were waiting impatiently for orders to begin their advance; General Stonewall Jackson had joined Generals Anderson and McLaws. The stage was set. Lee would face Hooker's four corps, almost 80,000 men, with a force that numbered less than 44,000. Lee was outnumbered almost two-to-one.

To begin your tour of the Chancellorsville National Battle-field, leave the parking area at the Visitor Center by the exit closest to the building and turn right. Proceed along the road for eight-tenths of a mile and then turn right again. Continue on for about a half-mile to the parking area on your right at **Stop Number 1**.

Leave your car in the parking area and walk across the field to the four-lane highway and stand close to the intersection, facing the highway in front of you.

Chancellorsville:
In 1862 this was part of a large tract of undeveloped land known locally as "The Wilderness." It was a wild and remote area covered in dense woodlands, swamps and underbrush. It was, in many areas, almost impassable. But here, in the heart of the Wilderness, three major roads came together. The highway in front of you is the old Orange Turnpike. In 1863 this road carried goods between the port city of Fredericksburg, some ten miles away to the east, and Orange, Virginia. Ely's Ford Road to your left ran northward to the Rapidan River just five miles away.

The third road, the one across the turnpike, is the Orange Plank Road. It, too, was a major route between Fredericksburg and Orange. The road was partially covered with wooden planks to provide a hard surface capable of carrying heavy wagons when the road was wet and muddy, hence the name. The foundations you see behind you belong to the house from which the battle here took its name. It was opened in 1816 as an inn, but at the time of the battle it was the home of Mrs. Sandford Chancellor and her six daughters.

At 11:00 a.m. on the morning of May 1st the Union troops moved out into the Wilderness from their encampment here at the Chancellor home, full of enthusiasm and dreams of glory. They were confident of victory over the Confederate forces.

When you are ready to continue your tour, leave the parking area, go to the intersection and turn left onto the Orange

Turnpike now known as US Route 3. Continue along the road for about a mile until you reach a large sign indicating McLaws Drive, the old Furnace Road. Turn right there and proceed to the first large historical sign you see; its about 200 yards further on along the road to your right. Park your car, leave it, and stand with your back to the sign.

McLaws Drive:

As we already know, the Union troops left their encampment at the Chancellor home on the morning of May 1st and began the ten-mile march toward Fredericksburg and the Confederate rear. As two divisions of Major General George Meade's 5th corps moved eastward along the river road to the north of here, his third division, Sykes', was moving along the Orange Turnpike, past this point, and on toward Zoan Church about a mile and a half away to the east where they would run head on into Mahone's brigade, the advance guard of General Anderson's advancing Confederate column.

Major Gen. Henry W. Slocum.

At the same time, General Henry Slocum's 12th Corps was advancing eastward along the Orange Plank Road just to the south of here. General Sykes soon found himself overwhelmed by the advancing Confederate army and began to fall back. When he reached this position he prepared to make a stand on the ridge and sent a courier to General Hooker with an urgent call for reinforcements. The courier returned a little while later carrying, not news that the requested reinforcements were on the way, but orders that all troops, including General Slocum's entire 12th Corps, should fall back on Chancellorsville and take

up defensive positions there. General Hooker, for all his brag-
ging, seemed to be giving up without a fight. Generals Meade
and Slocum were astounded. *"If he can't hold the top of a hill,"*
Meade wondered, *"how does he expect to hold the bottom of it?"*
By the evening of May 1st the entire Union army was, once
again, encamped around Chancellorsville; the Confederate
army was entrenched here, along the ridge.

To continue your tour, proceed on along McLaws Drive for
about a half-mile to the intersection with the Orange Plank
Road, now US Route 610, and park in the pull-off to your
right, just before the intersection.

The Furnace Road-Orange Plank Road:
On the morning of May 1st, Union General Henry Slocum's 12th
Corps advanced eastward along the Orange Plank Road in front
of you. Just as General Sykes' division had run into General
Anderson's brigades advancing westward, so Slocum's corps ran
head-on into Stonewall Jackson's 2nd Confederate Corps about
a mile away beyond the Catharpin Road. And, just like Sykes,
Slocum was ordered to fall back to Chancellorsville.

Continue on across the intersection and park in the pull-off
there, then walk to the sign furthest to your right where you
will find a map showing the dispositions of the combatants
as of the evening of May 1st. When you have finished at the
map turn around and face the Furnace Road.

The Lee/Jackson Bivouac:
After the engagements of the early afternoon of May 1st. The
Confederate forces under the command of General's Jackson
and Lafayette McLaws pursued the retreating Federal forces
back toward Chancellorsville. If General Hooker didn't recognize the advantages of the strong defensive positions offered by
the high ground along the ridge, Generals Lee and Jackson
certainly did. By the close of day the divisions of McLaws and
Anderson were firmly entrenched here along the Furnace Road,
while General Jackson's divisions were being held in reserve
along the Orange Plank Road. During the evening of May 1st
the two Generals, Lee and Jackson, sat down in the woods on

Lee and Jackson in the "cracker box" council on the night of Friday, May 1.

empty cracker boxes to discuss the strategy they would adopt the following morning. It was an historic meeting made famous by the wonderful picture shown on the previous page and drawn by battlefield artist, W.L. Sheppard.

After Hooker's unexpected withdrawal back to Chancellorsville Lee was puzzled as to exactly what had happened. He, like Meade and Slocum, knew that the Union forces had vacated some very strong and defensible positions. What was Hooker up to? Was his left flank weak, and should it be attacked? Reconnaissance told Lee this what not the case. The Federal left had taken a position of great natural strength anchored on the banks of the river behind a system of log breastworks and was surrounded by dense woods and virtually impenetrable undergrowth. Lee knew that a frontal attack against the superior and well entrenched enemy would be suicide. And if the enemy right flank was anchored as well as the left flank, then he, Lee, was in for a difficult and bloody fight the following morning.

Fortunately Lee's "eyes and ears," Jeb Stuart's cavalry, had been reconnoitering out on the western perimeter of the Union line. He had found that far from being tightly anchored on high, easily defended ground as it should have been, the Federal right flank was in an extremely weak position, and ill-prepared for a surprise attack. *"It was, therefore, resolved,"* Lee reported, *"to endeavor to turn his right flank and gain his rear, leaving a force in front to hold him in check and conceal the movement."*

The plan was a risky one. The flanking force would somehow have to make a forced march through the Wilderness, around the Federal positions, far enough away from them for the maneuver to remain undetected. It was estimated that it would be a march of some 12 miles or more. It was a bold and desperate plan, but what were the alternatives? Lee wrote to President Davis: *"It is plain that if the enemy is too strong for me here, I shall have to fall back, and Fredericksburg must be abandoned. If successful here, Fredericksburg will be saved and our communications retained. I may be forced back to the Orange and Alexandria or the Virginia Central road, but in either case I will be in a position to contest the enemy's advance upon Richmond. I am now swinging around to my left to come up in his rear."*

It was decided that General Jackson and his entire 2nd Corps, some 32,000 men, would make the flanking movement. At 7:30 in the morning the leading elements of the corps moved out past the crossroads here toward the southwest. By the time the column had cleared the crossroads it was more than six miles long. Lee was left in position with only the division of Anderson and McLaws to defend the Confederate positions.

> Return to your car and proceed on along the Furnace Road for about a mile until you reach a Park Service sign to your right near a clearing in the woods. You can pull off the road there and leave your car in the parking area.

The View to Hazel Grove:
Obviously, if the Confederate plan was to succeed, secrecy was essential. If Hooker were to learn of the flanking movement, all he would have to do was strengthen his left flank, then fall upon

his enemy's divided army to the front and rear and destroy him. Alas, almost before Jackson's march had gotten properly under way, the Union scouts in the treetops at Hazel Grove about a

Major Gen. Oliver O. Howard.

mile away to the northwest spotted Jackson's column as it moved past this clearing in the Wilderness. At about 9:30 a.m. a Federal battery at Hazel Grove opened fire on the Confederate column, causing some confusion.

General Hooker was informed of the unexpected enemy movements and immediately realized that Lee was trying to flank him. He sent a dispatch to General Howard on the right flank warning him of the Confederate intentions.

Continue on along the Furnace Road for about a half mile until you reach a fork in the road and then turn to your left and park opposite the remains of the Catharine Furnace.

The Catharine Furnace:
The furnace was built in 1836. It was an iron foundry and was in operation until 1846 when it was closed due to falling iron prices. It was opened again by the Confederacy to support the Southern war effort and continued in production until it was destroyed by Union General George Custer in the spring of 1864.

If you will stand with your back to the Park Service sign and face the road you will be facing the route taken by General Jackson on the morning of May 2nd. His column moved past this point from your left to right. General Jackson posted the 23rd regiment of Georgians here to act as a rearguard against any enemy attack to his rear. And it's just as well that he did because, for some inexplicable reason, General Hooker had changed his mind and had decided that the Confederate army was not trying to flank him after all; Lee and his entire army, Hooker decided, was in full retreat. With that, he abandoned any idea of defending his right flank and, instead, detached General Birney's division of Sickle's 3rd Corps from its position at Hazel Grove and sent it to attack Jackson's column from the rear, thus leaving General Howard's 11th Corps isolated on the Union right flank.

The tiny force of Georgians met Birney's division close to this position and fought them to a standstill in the woods to your left. They were able to delay Birney long enough for Jackson's entire force to clear the area. Then, heavily outnumbered, they were forced to fall back to the unfinished railroad embankments about half a mile away to your right. There they fought on until, eventually, they were overwhelmed and captured.

In the meantime General Lee had sent two brigades to protect Jackson's rear to your left, and Jackson himself had detached two more and sent them back to contain the Federal attack here and to your right. Faced by what had now become a superior force, General Birney halted his attack and waited for reinforcements to arrive. By the close of day more than 20,000 Federal troops had been sent to this position, all of them taken from the center of the Union line, leaving General Howard on the Union right flank totally isolated, and totally exposed. By the time Jackson arrived in position there was a gap in the Federal line between Howard and the nearest supporting unit of more than a mile and a half.

Continue on along the gravel road, now called Jackson Trail East, to Stop Number 7. The road, though today it bears no resemblance to the trail through the woods that it was in 1863, is the one that Jackson took on his march around the Union army. You will need to drive for almost three miles to the intersection with Brock Road where you can park.

Stops 7 and 8, The Brock Road:
For more than two hours Stonewall Jackson and the Confeder-

*Generals Francis C. Barlow, David B. Birney, John Gibbon
(standing l to r) and W. S. Hancock (seated). All fought at
Chancellorsville.*

ate 2nd Corps marched along this trail until finally they arrived
at the junction here at Brock Road. Jackson's guide had informed him that the most direct route to his objective lay up the
Brock road to his right. Jackson, however, realizing that his
movement had been discovered, and that his plans for an attack
on the Union right might now be in jeopardy, decided to take a

longer way around by turning left here and proceeding in the opposite direction and away from the enemy's right flank, thus reinforcing the impression that he was indeed in full retreat. Once again, when he was out of sight of the enemy observers, Jackson turned his corps northward and proceeded again toward the enemy right flank.

Steadily the six-mile-long column of marching men made their way toward the enemy flank. The march was made according regulations with a ten-minute rest every hour. Jackson and his officers constantly were riding back and forth along the entire length of the column keeping the stragglers in line and maintaining absolute silence in the ranks.

To follow the route of Jackson's march turn left here and proceed along the Brock Road for about a quarter of a mile and then turn right onto Jackson Trail West. Follow the trail for about two and a half miles until you reach its end and then stop at the intersection with Brock Road. Turn left onto the Brock Road at Stop Number 8 and go for about a mile until you reach the intersection with the Orange Plank Road and turn left, then immediately turn left again into the parking area at **Stop Number 9**. Ignore the Park Service signs here; they refer to the Battle of the Wilderness fought in 1864. Leave your vehicle in the parking area, walk to the intersection and stand facing the Orange Plank Road with the Brock Road to your right.

The Orange Plank Road:
It must have quite a sight to see the head of the Confederate column as it slowly appeared in the distance to your right at about one o'clock on the afternoon of May 2nd. To give you an idea of the size of this movement, follow the route you have just driven all the way back, via your imagination, to Stop Number 6 at the Catharine Furnace some ten miles away. Can you believe, as the first brigades of Jackson's column passed this point here at the Orange Plank Road, the last brigade were just making the left turn there onto Jackson Trail East? Jackson's original plan was to turn right here and fall upon the enemy at a point just a little to the east of the Wilderness Church. When

he arrived here, however, he was met by Cavalry General Fitz
Hugh Lee. Lee requested that Jackson and one other officer
accompany him along the Plank Road to your right to view the
enemy positions. When the three officers arrived at the Buton
Farm they dismounted and crept forward to the top of a small
hill and looked down upon the enemy. It was an awe-inspiring
sight. The entire Union 11th Corps was spread out before them,
at ease, and unsuspecting of the horrors that soon would fall
upon them. It was about two o'clock in the afternoon. Jackson
smiled, uttered a silent prayer of thanks, and then, five minutes
later, turned and rode back along the Plank Road to his waiting
troops.

Jackson was elated that his flanking movement had been successful but, after having observed the positions occupied by the
Union 11th Corps, he knew that he would be unable to successfully attack them along the Orange Plank Road. An attack there
would not turn the enemy flank. To do that he must continue
further on up the Brock Road to the north and make the turn
where the Brock Road joined the Orange Plank Road. The new
plan meant that his men must march onward for several more
hours. Could his tired troops withstand the extra march and
arrive in position in time to make a decisive strike against the
enemy right? And would they be in condition do so? Jackson
didn't hesitate. He sent a report of the change of plan to General
Lee and gave the order to march northward along the Brock
Road toward the intersect and the unsuspecting Union 11th
Corps.

> Return to your car and turn left at the intersection onto
> Brock and proceed for about a mile and a half to the inter-
> section with the Orange Plank Road and then turn right, get
> into the left-hand lane and continue on for about a mile and
> a quarter until you reach the Laurel Hill Memorial Park on
> the left. Turn into the park and drive to the top of the hill,
> leaving your car in the parking area. Walk on over to the
> statue with three figures and stand facing the highway.

The Laurel Hill Memorial Park:
This position was, at the time of the battle, just inside the Union

line. The men of General Oliver Otis Howard's 11th Corps were in a line of battle along the Orange Turnpike in front of you, dug in behind log breastworks and shallow trenches. The line stretched eastward for about a mile and a half. The extreme right flank of Howard's line, two regiments of Colonel Leopold Von Gilsa's brigade, of General Charles Devens' division, was anchored close to where the houses now stand just a short distance to your right. They were facing west and were the only Federal troops in position facing the direction from which Jackson's onslaught was about come. The rest of the Devens' division, and the divisions of Schurz and Steinwehr, all were facing south in a long line in front of you: Schurz held the center and Steinwehr the extreme left. Beyond that lay a huge gap in the Union line of more than a mile. The 11th Corps would face Jackson's more than 30,000 men alone and unprepared.

All afternoon the Union scouts reported back to Hooker, Howard, and Devens, that large concentrations of enemy troops were moving westward. Hooker warned Howard and told him to make preparations to receive the enemy. Howard did nothing more than warn his division commander, General Devens. Devens also was receiving information from the field that the enemy was en route toward his right flank. Devens again ignored the intelligence, putting it down to nervousness on the part of inexperienced observers who might have seen a few wandering horsemen cut off from the rest of the Confederate army: the enemy was, after all, in full retreat. Wasn't it? And as if to reinforce his opinions he received an order from General Hooker at about four o'clock that afternoon to detach General Barlow's Brigade of 2,500 men, the largest in the 11th Corps, and send it southward to shore up General Birney's attack on the retreating Confederate column. All was well on the Federal right flank; at least that's what everyone thought. So secure did Howard feel he accompanied Barlow and his brigade southward to join Birney.

Meanwhile General Jackson already was forming his corps in line of battle ready to fall upon the Union flank. He formed his corps in three great ranks, more than a mile wide, that faced across the end of the Federal line. General Robert Rodes' divi-

Brig. Gen. Robert E. Rodes.

sion was in the front rank, General Raleigh Colston's division in the second rank, and General Ambrose Powell Hill's division, whose brigades were still marching along the Brock Road to join him, in the third rank.

It was now close to 5 p.m. Most of the 11th Corps had stacked their arms and were preparing supper. The smoke of the cookfires was drifting lazily upward into clear, blue sky when suddenly the woods around them exploded – echoing with the sounds of half a hundred bugles and the fearsome screaming of the Rebel yell as thousands upon thousands of gray-clad soldiers crashed, whooping and firing, from the woods.

Colonel Von Gilsa's two regiments were smashed to pieces in the very first moments of the attack. The rest of Devens' division was taken in the flank and driven back in total disorder upon Schurz' division, which in turn fell back in total confusion, panic-stricken, upon General Steinwehr's division. In only a few moments General Howard's entire corps was fleeing eastward down the turnpike and through the woods from your right to left towards Chancellorsville; in less than two hours the Federals on the right flank would be driven from the field. General Howard, now returned from his foray southward, said: *"The noise and smoke filled the air with excitement and, more quickly than it could be told, with all the fury of the wildest hailstorm, everything, every sort of organization that lay in the path of the mad current of panic-stricken men, had to give way and be broken into fragments."*

General Schurz in his report said: *"The officers had hardly time to give a command when almost the whole of General McLean's*

Confederate surprise attack on the 11th Corps.

brigade, mixed up with a number of Von Gilsa's men, came rushing down the road from General Devens' headquarters in wild confusion, and worse than that, the battery of the First Division broke in upon my right at full run. This confused mass of guns, caissons, horses, and men broke lengthwise through the ranks of my regiments deployed in line on the road. The whole line on the old Turnpike facing south, was rolled up and swept away in a moment."

Federal Colonel Charles Fessendon Morse of the 2nd Massachusetts was with General Sickles' troops fighting the Jackson's rearguard at Catharine Furnace when the pandemonium on the Federal right flank broke out. He describes the action: *"The Third Corps, General Sickles, was removed out to the right of the Twelfth and advanced toward Fredericksburg. The order then came to General Slocum that the enemy was in full retreat, and to advance his whole line to capture all he could of prisoners, wagons, etc. Our right, General Williams, advanced without much trouble, driving the enemy before it, but the Second Division had hardly got out of the trenches before it was attacked with great determination, yet it steadily retained its position. At about five p.m. a tremendous and unceasing musketry fire began in the direction of the Eleventh Corps. As it was necessary to*

*Gen. Howard tries to rally his troops during the rout of the
11th Corps by Jackson's forces.*

*know what was going on there in order to regulate the movements
of the Twelfth Corps, General Slocum and the rest of us rode for
our lives toward this new scene of action. What was our surprise*

The 29th Pennsylvania (Union 12th Corps) under artillery fire.

when we found that instead of a fight, it was a complete Bull Run rout. Men, horses, mules, rebel prisoners, wagons, guns, etc., etc., were coming down the road in terrible confusion, behind them an unceasing roar of musketry. We rode until we got into a mighty hot fire, and found that no one was attempting to make a stand, but everyone was running for his life. Then General Slocum dispatched me to General Hooker to explain the state of affairs, and three other staff officers to find General Williams and order him back to his trenches with all haste.

"I found General Hooker sitting alone on his horse in front of the Chancellor house, and delivered my message; he merely said, "Very Good, Sir." I rode back and found the Eleventh Corps still surging up the road and still this terrible roar behind them." (James Murfin, *Battlefields of the Civil War*, Colour Library Books Ltd., (UK) Surrey, England, 1988).

Return to your car and go back to the highway, then turn left and go for two miles until you see a sign directing you to the visitors center. Instead of following the sign to the Visitor Center turn right, in the opposite direction, onto Stuart Drive. You will find a parking area on your left just a few yards along the road close to a large Park Service sign. Leave your car there and stand facing the Park Service sign.

Stuart Drive:

By 7:15 in the early evening of May 2nd the remnants of the Union 11th Corps had fled the field and were taking up a defensive position on the Orange Turnpike around Chancellorsville. The divisions of the 12th Corps, as you know, had been sent east and south and were in position on the Federal right from Chancellorsville to Catharine Furnace. This put Jackson's corps, more than 30,000 men, squarely at the Union rear. General Lee, with the divisions of Generals Anderson and McLaws, was holding the ground on the Orange Turnpike and the Orange Plank Road in front of Hooker to the east. The Federal army was the meat in a giant sandwich, caught between the two Confederate wings.

Jackson knew that he held the advantage and he had no intention of stopping now. He halted his advance to reform his corps and then ordered General A.P. Hill's division forward to relieve General Rodes and to prepare for a night attack. *"Press them; cut them off from United States Ford, Hill; press them."* And then he rode off with several of his aids, along the turnpike, into the darkness, to assess the situation for himself. It was close to this position that General Jackson found General Lane's North Carolina brigade in line of battle close to the Confederate center and at the head of General Hill's division. Jackson and his aids rode on into the no-man's land between his own and the Federal lines.

Then, through the still of the night, the party could hear the sounds of men hard at work, harsh words of command, the sounds of digging and of falling trees. The enemy was entrenching. The Confederate attack must be continued without delay. Jackson and his men wheeled their horses and made their way quickly back toward the Confederate line. Then, as the party approached the position held by 18th North Carolina Regiment of Pender's brigade, the nervous pickets began to shoot at the approaching Confederate officers. Several of the party were hit by the large caliber minie balls and Jackson himself was hit three times. Jackson's aide-de-camp describes what happened: *"As he rode near to the Confederate troops, just placed in position and ignorant that he was in front, the left company began firing to the front, and two officers fell from their saddles dead – Captain Boswell, of the Engineers, and Sergeant Cunliffe, of the Signal Corps. Spurring his horse across the road to his right, he [Jackson] was met by a second volley from the right company of Pender's North Carolina brigade. Under this volley, when not two rods from the troops, the general received three balls at the same instant. One penetrated the palm of his right hand. A second passed around the wrist of his left arm and out through his left hand. A third ball passed through the left arm half-way from shoulder to elbow. The large bone of the upper arm was splintered to the elbow joint and the wound bled freely. His horse turned quickly from the fire, through the thick bushes which swept the cap from the general's head, and scratched his forehead, leaving drops of blood to stain his face. As he lost hold upon the bridle-rein, he reeled from the saddle, and was caught by the arms of Captain Wilbourn, of the Signal Corps."*

Jackson was removed from the field and carried out to the turnpike and at once came under Union cannon fire. When the enemy fire died away Jackson was removed to the Wilderness tavern, three miles to the rear, where Confederate surgeons removed his left arm. Lee wrote him: *"You have lost your left arm. I have lost my right."* Jackson died several days later.

Return to your car and continue on along the Stuart Drive for about a half-mile to the Confederate artillery position at Hazel Grove and park in front of the painting.

Hazel Grove:
With the demise of General Jackson the command of his corps fell to General Hill. Unfortunately, General Hill was seriously wounded almost at the same time as was Jackson. Next in line for command was General Robert Rodes, but Rodes, newly appointed to high command, was lacking experience even as a division commander, and could not be expected to manage an entire corps. The command of Jackson's corps fell then to the only person with experience enough to handle it, cavalry com-

mander J.E.B. (Jeb) Stuart. Stuart was unfamiliar with the men of the Confederate 2nd Corps and even less familiar with Jackson's plan of battle. Stuart decided that it would be a mistake to try to push on that night. Instead, realizing the importance of this position where you now stand, he ordered General Archer to attack and take it at dawn the following morning, May 3rd.

Archer's men moved out at first light up the western side of the ridge to your right. At the double-quick the Confederate brigade charged toward the crest of the hill, only to find it abandoned; General Hooker had given up this strong defensive position without a fight.

> Continue on along Stuart Drive to a point where the road divides. Take the left-hand fork and follow the road for about a half a mile to its end and park there.

Fairview:
The open fields here were, at the time of the battle, part of a small farm. The map on the sign shows the positions of the Union and Confederate armies at 10 a.m. on the morning of May 3rd. The Union troops that had held the high ground at Hazel Grove had fallen back to this position. General Hooker was, at this point, reduced to a "semi-stupor" and had ceased to function. The Union army was, in effect, leaderless.

> If you have the time you might like to take a short walk over to the Union artillery position you see in the distance.

During the battle the clearing was held by 42 massed cannon under the command of Union artillery Captain C. Best. You can see the earthworks that protected Captain Best's position at the line of woods to your right. General Stuart, now re-united with General Lee, massed 32 guns on the heights of Hazel Grove; you can see that position through the clearing. Those guns, along with others in position on either side of Hazel Grove, bombarded Captain Best's position in a devastating, three-way cross-fire. His position became untenable and he, along with the rest of the Union army, began the retreat toward the river.

Return to your car and follow the Park Service directions to Chancellorsville, leave your vehicle in the parking area, and walk on over to the cannon, and then stand and face the Orange Turnpike, modern Route 3.

The Chancellor House:
It was from here at the Chancellor house that General Hooker had made his headquarters and it was from here he directed the course of the battle. The first hint of Hooker's impending doom came at 7:00 p.m. on the afternoon of May 2nd when the remnants of General Howard's 11th Corps came streaming down the turnpike to your right. There was no stopping the panic stricken troops as they headed for safety. Upon reaching the crossroads on your left, the fleeing Federals turned northward toward the river. It was obvious to all that this was the beginning of the end for General Hooker's grand design; his perfect plan.

Captain Best withdrew his guns from Fairview and placed them in position here at Chancellorsville. The Confederate artillery took over the position at Fairview and pounded away at Union positions here, battering the walls of the house, now on fire,

Panicked 11th Corps fleeing their position on the Plank Road.

while Mrs. Chancellor and her daughters sought safety behind the Union lines.

With the house falling down around him, General Hooker remained on the porch and tried in vain to regain some sort of control over himself and his fleeing army. As he leaned in despair against one of the supports on the porch a Confederate shell struck the post just above his head and threw him to the ground. Leadership of the Union army now fell temporarily to General Couch; the Union retreat continued toward a new defensive line at Ely's Ford about a mile to the north behind you.

The battle of Chancellorsville was all but over. As the first Confederate troops passed this point in pursuit of the fleeing Federals the Chancellor house was all but consumed by the flames. General Lee rode in to take the head of his troops. The cheering that arose from the victorious Confederates must have been something to hear. By nightfall on May 6th the retreating Union army had re-crossed the river to the north of Fredericksburg. After five days of fighting the battle of Chancellorsville was over. General Hooker's "finest army on the planet" had suffered more than 17,000 casualties. The Confederate Army of Northern Virginia had suffered almost 13,000. It had been General Lee's finest hour, marred only by the death of best friend and his finest general, Stonewall Jackson. It was the beginning of the end for Fighting Joe Hooker. He was relieved of his command some few weeks later during the Gettysburg campaign and served out the rest of the war under the command of General Sherman. Hooker died in 1879 at the age of 65 as a result, so they say, of the injury he received on the porch at Chancellorsville.

Where to Stay, Things to Do

There is no town or city at Chancellorsville. The closest community to the battlefield is Fredericksburg VA just ten miles away along US Route 3. The attractions, hotels, and restaurants there are listed on page 147.

Chapter 10

Gettysburg

July, 1863

Gettysburg National Military Park is 35 miles south of Harrisburg PA on Interstate 15. The address is Gettysburg PA 17325. As you tour the battlefield stay within the speed limit and exercise extreme caution. The roads are busy and often shared by bikers and pedestrians. Pets must be kept on a leash. Please observe the rules of the countryside: take nothing and leave only footprints. Phone 717-334-1124.

Gettysburg National
Military Park

For almost a year after General Lee's miraculous escape after the battle of Antietam it seemed that he could do no wrong. The stunning Confederate victories at Fredericksburg and Chancellorsville had spread an air of gloom and despondency among the Union leaders in Washington, and the indecisive outcome of the Battle of Stones River in Tennessee had, if anything, only reinforced the feeling that the Confederate star was on the rise.

In the west General Grant was still bogged down in the swamps and bayous of Mississippi, while General Rosecrans' Army of

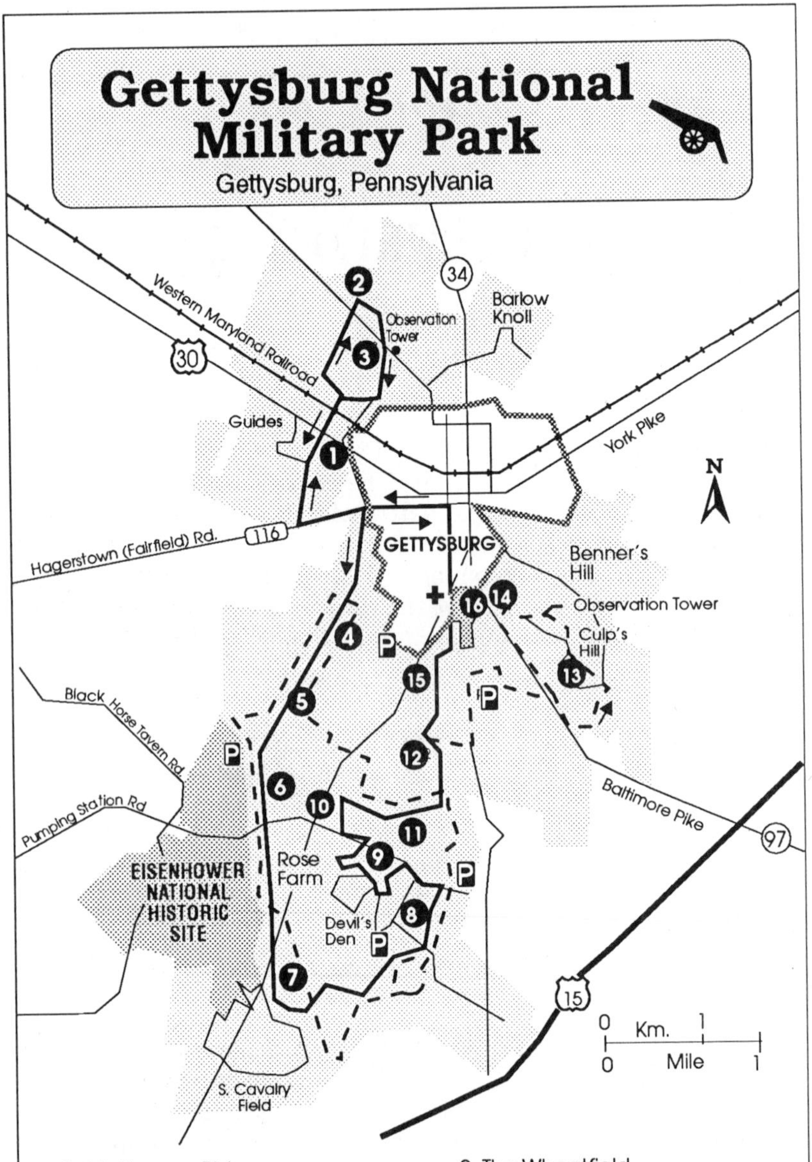

Gettysburg National Military Park

Gettysburg, Pennsylvania

N

Western Maryland Railroad

30

Guides

Hagerstown (Fairfield) Rd. 116

GETTYSBURG

34

Observation Tower

Barlow Knoll

York Pike

Benner's Hill

Observation Tower

Culp's Hill

Black Horse Tavern Rd.

Pumping Station Rd.

EISENHOWER NATIONAL HISTORIC SITE

Rose Farm

Devil's Den

Baltimore Pike

97

15

S. Cavalry Field

| 0 | Km. | 1 |
| 0 | Mile | 1 |

1. McPherson Ridge
2. Eternal Light Peace Memorial
3. Oak Ridge
4. North Carolina Memorial
5. Virginia Memorial
6. Pitzer Woods
7. Warfield Ridge
8. Little Round Top
9. The Wheatfield
10. The Peach Orchard
11. Plum Run
12. Pennsylvania Memorial
13. Spangler's Spring
14. East Cemetery Hill
15. High Water Mark
16. National Cemetery

the Cumberland had been
so badly mauled by Brax-
ton Bragg's Army of Ten-
nessee it would be more
than six months before it
could once again become
an effective force. In the
meantime, General Lee,
so it seemed, was at lib-
erty to range across
Northern Virginia as he
pleased. It was inevitable,
then, that he would once
again determine to take
the war into Union terri-
tory.

Just before dawn on July
1st, 1863, the advance elements of Lt. General A.P.
Hill's Confederate corps of

Gen. Robert E. Lee.

General Robert E. Lee's Army of Northern Virginia were marching steadily along the road toward the tiny Pennsylvania town
of Gettysburg. Dawn broke at about 4:45 that morning and, as
the first light of day turned the trees on the high ground to the
east into stark black outlines against the sky, a lone Union
picket posted to the west of McPherson's ridge close to the
Chambersburg Pike heard something moving in the distance.
He moved closer for a better look and saw a long line of gray-clad
men swinging quietly along the road toward him. Little did he
realize that what he was observing would soon turn into a
momentous series of events over the next three days the mag-
nitude of which would change the face of a continent. The
repercussions of the battle that was about to begin would echo
around the world.

Early in 1863 General Lee, after his abortive invasion of Northern territory in 1862, decided to try again. The advantages of
such an invasion were several fold. First he knew that any
movement northward on his part must lure Major General

Gen. George Gordon Meade.

Joseph Hooker after him and so remove the Union threat against the Confederate Capitol, Richmond. Second, a major victory in the north might alleviate the pressure on the Confederate Army of Tennessee in the west. Third, Lee would be in a position where he could threaten, or even capture, the Pennsylvanian capitol of Harrisburg and then strike east toward Philadelphia and Baltimore. Diplomatically, then, Lee had everything to gain, for such a victory could bring European recognition of the Confederacy and perhaps even a negotiated peace with the Union. The new Southern nation would then become a reality in the eyes of the world.

Before you begin your tour of the battlefield you might like to familiarize yourself with what you are about to experience by spending a few moments in the Visitor Center. Of special interest is the electric map. It will provide you with a graphic overview of the park and you can use it to pinpoint any or all of the main points of interest on the battlefield. The bronze plaques you will see as you tour the battlefield honor the soldiers of both armies. Those mounted on round bases honor the Confederate soldiers, those on square bases the Union soldiers.

The tour route itself is marked by a series of easy to follow signs. The first stop on the tour is about two miles from the Visitor Center. Leave the parking lot and turn onto Route 15. Proceed north, through the town of Gettysburg, until you reach the traffic circle. Make your way around the circle, follow the tour signs onto Route 30 and head west.

At the time of the Civil War Gettysburg was a small rural town with a population of about 2,500 people. It was a college town, the home of the Pennsylvania college – now called the Gettysburg College – and the Lutheran Seminary. Both institutions are still here today. Today more than a million visitors make the pilgrimage to Gettysburg to visit the famous battlefield. Many of the houses you see as you travel through the town were here at the time of the conflict. You can identify them by the small bronze plates fixed to the outside of the houses. Some you will see still show the scars they received during the battle.

The large three-story brick house on the right as you approach the traffic circle was the home of attorney David Wills. It was in this house on the evening of November 18th, 1863, that President Abraham Lincoln stayed during his famous visit to the dedication of the National Cemetery at Gettysburg battlefield. It was in this house, too, that he put the finishing touches to the speech he would make the following day: the famous Gettysburg Address.

As you make your way out of town toward the first stop you will follow Route 30 up a hill called Seminary Ridge. At the top of the hill on the right you will see the Lutheran Seminary. Three of the buildings are of original Civil War vintage, including the one with the small cupola on the top which was used as an observation post during the battle. On the left side of the road you will see an upright cannon that marks the position of one of General Lee's battlefield headquarters.

Continue along Route 30 for about a half-mile further until you come to an avenue on your left. Continue past it until you see a second avenue on your left with a small stone building nearby. Turn left there. Be careful. The turn is a dangerous one. You are now on what was, at the time of the battle, McPherson's farm.

As you make the turn, notice the two statues opposite. The equestrian statue, the officer on horseback, is Union Major

General John F. Reynolds the commander of the Federal 1st army corps. Reynolds was killed only 15 minutes after reaching the battlefield. He was the highest ranking Union officer killed in the battle. The second statue is of Union General John Buford. Buford was commander of the Federal cavalry. His men were responsible for firing the opening shots of the battle. It is interesting to know that Buford, a native of Kentucky, had a brother serving in the Confederate army.

A little way along the avenue, after you've made the left turn, you'll see another statue and a parking area. You are now on McPherson Ridge at the John Burns Statue, **Stop Number 1** on your tour. You can leave you car in the parking area while you enjoy the view and get to know this section of the battlefield.

McPherson Ridge & The John Burns Statue:

If you look behind you and to the left you can see McPherson's barn. It's all that's left of the original farm buildings. A little further to the left you can see the buildings of the Lutheran Seminary, including the one with the cupola on the top. To the right you will see the fields where the Confederates began to take position during the early hours of the morning of July 1st; the first day of the battle of Gettysburg.

By June 28th General Lee was already in the vicinity of Gettysburg. The Army of the Potomac, now under the command of General George G. Meade, had moved northward and the army was spread over a 15-mile front from the north to the south of Gettysburg.

By June 30th scouting parties from both armies had been into the town and, although General Lee knew there were some Union troops already in Gettysburg, he was unaware that a large force of Federal cavalry already occupied the town and was anticipating no serious opposition to General Heth's division of A.P. Hill's corps as it marched toward Gettysburg in search of supplies. Nor did he know that the left wing of General Meade's

Army of the Potomac was already approaching the town from the southeast.

Brig. Gen. Henry Heth.

Neither of the two army commanders intended that Gettysburg was to be a major confrontation. Neither one had sufficient information about the strength of the other's force. Lee was without his "eyes and ears," General J.E.B. Stuart, his cavalry commander. Stuart was away to the east about other business. General Meade, on the other hand, newly appointed as he was, was exercising due caution. Both commanders, according to their separate actions and orders, seemed to be intent on gathering together their wide-spread forces for the conflict both knew to be inevitable. That conflict, however, was not planned for Gettysburg. It started only as an unplanned clash between advance parties from both armies, Heth on the one hand and Buford on the other, and then rapidly escalated into a major, three-day confrontation.

By eight o'clock on the morning of July 1st the skirmishers of both armies had clashed and General Buford's cavalry division was fighting hard to hold its positions here on McPherson Ridge. Slowly, however, as General Heth fed more and more troops into the action they began to give way and the cavalrymen were driven backward past the McPherson farm.

John Burns, whose statue you see here, was a local resident. At the time of the battle he was some 70 years old, but that didn't stop him from joining the fight on the Union side. With his antique muzzle-loading musket and powder horn he fought all the morning long and was wounded several times; one of the true heroes of Gettysburg.

General John F. Reynolds, in response to the sounds of the battle, came up from the rear and quickly assessing the situation called for reinforcements; by 10:00 a.m. the brigades of Union General Abner Doubleday's 1st Corps began arriving on the field to relieve the beleaguered Buford.

When you are ready to continue your tour leave the parking area and continue along the road, following the Park Service signs, until you reach the stop sign and then turn left onto Reynolds avenue and continue along the road to Stop Number 2.

The Eternal Peace Light Memorial; Oak Ridge:
The markers you see on the hill as you drive toward the next stop on your tour are all Confederate with the exception of the Eternal Peace Light Memorial, the one with flame burning at the top. The memorial is dedicated to the soldiers of both armies who gave their lives during the battle of Gettysburg. Its flame burns constantly though the years as a symbol of man's struggle against the darkness of war, and his hope for everlasting peace. It was dedicated 75 years after the battle on July 3rd, 1938. The dedication was attended by some 1,800 Civil War veterans; the average age of those old soldiers was 94.

The next stop is the Oak Ridge observation tower; it's just a little further on along the road on the left. The tower was built in 1895. As you look to your right you can see the town of Gettysburg, the railroad is immediately below, and just beyond the road in front of you. In the distance you can see the open fields where, by 2:00 p.m., the Union brigades of General Oliver O. Howard's 11th Army Corps had taken up position and were preparing to meet the Confederate attack.

The Oak Ridge Observation Tower:
At a little after 2:00 p.m. the Confederate divisions moved out of the woods on the far side of the open fields and attacked the

Federal positions. At the same time the Confederate batteries
of Carter's artillery battalion posted on the hill near the site of
the Peace Light Memorial opened fire on the Union positions,
and Confederate General A.P. Hill's divisions were pounding
away at General Doubleday's (Reynolds) 1st Corps at McPherson's farm. At 2:30 Confederate General Jubal Early's division
arrived on the field and made a slashing attack from the northeast against Oliver Howard's right flank to the north of Gettysburg. By mid-afternoon
more than 40,000 men on
both sides were locked in a
major battle that extended
over a two-mile front. The
carnage in the fields in front
of you must have been in-
credible. It seemed the entire hillside had exploded in
a holocaust of flame, lead,
and iron. The noise of cannon fire from all direction
echoed across the fields like
a thunder storm of monu-
mental proportions, and the
smoke of battle hung like a
great gray blanket over the
battlefield.

Maj. Gen. Abner Doubleday.

August Bell was a cannoneer with the 1st Corps of the Union
Army of the Potomac and he described some of the action here
around Oak Ridge. As you stand here and look out over the
battlefield you should be able to follow his description of the
action. *". . . our infantry out in the field toward the creek was
being slowly but surely overpowered, and our lines were being
forced back toward the Seminary. It was now considerably past
noon. In addition to the struggle going on in our immediate front,
the sounds of a heavy attack from the north side were heard, and
way out beyond the creek, to the south, a strong force could be
seen advancing and overlapping our left. The enemy was coming
nearer; both in front and on the north, and stray balls began to
zip and whistle around our ears with unpleasant frequency. . . .*

Lt. Bayard Wilkeson, commanding Battery G, 4th U.S. Artillery, a hero of the battle, who was killed the first day.

The enemy did not press very closely but halted to reform his lines. At last he made his appearance in grand shape. His line stretched from the railroad grading across the Cashtown Pike, and through the fields south of it half way to the Fairfield Road.

"First we could see the tips of the color staffs coming up the little ridge and then the points of their bayonets, and the Johnnies themselves coming on with a steady tramp, tramp, and with loud yells. It was now apparent that the old Battery's turn had come again, and the embattled boys who stood so grimly at their posts felt that another page must be added to the record of Buena Vista

and Antietam. The term "boys" is literally true, because of our detachment alone, consisting of a sergeant, two corporals, seven cannoneers, and six drivers, only four had hair on their faces, while the other twelve were beardless boys whose ages would not average 19 years. As the day was hot many of the boys had taken their jackets off, some with sleeves rolled up, and they exchanged little words of cheer with each other as the gray line came on. In quick, sharp tones, like the successive reports from a repeating rifle, came Davidson's orders: "Load – Canister – double." There was a busting of cannoneers, a few thumps of the rammer-heads, and then: "Ready ! – By piece! – At will! – Fire!!"

"Holding the Line" by Gilbert Gaul shows the kind of desperate combat that occurred in the first two days at Gettysburg.

"Directly in our front – that is to say, on both sides of the pike – the rebel infantry, whose left lapped the north side of the pike quite up to the line of the railway grading, had been forced to halt and lie down by the tornado of canister that we had given from the moment they came in sight, but the regiments in the fields to their right of the pike kept on, and kept swinging their right flanks forward as if to take us in the reverse and cut us off from the rest of our troops near the Seminary. At this moment David-son, bleeding from two desperate wounds, and so weak that one of the men had to hold him up on his feet (one ankle being totally shattered by a bullet) ordered us to form the half-battery, by *wheeling on the left gun as a pivot. . . ."*

A.P. Hill's divisions were driving the Union 1st Corps backward from Seminary Ridge. By the close of battle that day the entire Union army had been driven from the field and were taking refuge on the heights of Cemetery Ridge to the east. Look to your right and you can see Cemetery Ridge in the distance. It has a light colored water tower near the top of the hill.

Meanwhile Howard's line also had began to crumble and as a result the 11th Corps was thrown into confusion; a condition that rapidly deteriorated into a complete and disorderly rout with Howard's men streaming away from the field and on through the town of Gettysburg with Early's division after them in hot pursuit.

The first day of battle ended with a total victory for the Confederate army. The Union army had suffered more than 10,000 casualties to the Confederate's 7,000. But all was not yet over. All that day the 1st of July long columns of soldiers, both blue and gray, had been converging from all directions on the little Pennsylvania township. By nightfall on the 1st Lee had more than 35,000 troops in the vicinity, outnumbering Meade by more than 10,000. By first light the following morning the numbers had grown on the Union side to more than 65,000 and on the Confederate to 60,000. By 4:00 p.m. on the afternoon of the 2nd Meade's strength had risen to 97,000 men against Lee's combined Confederate force of 75,000. It was inevitable, then, that the battle must escalate to monumental proportions.

To get to the next stop on your tour leave the parking area continue along the road and follow the battlefield tour signs. When you reach the stop sign, turn left and proceed for about a half-mile until you reach a traffic light. Turn right at the light onto West Confederate Avenue, Seminary Ridge, and continue straight on along the road until you reach the North Carolina Monument.

The North Carolina Monument:
This is probably the most famous monument on the battle-

field. It was carved by Gutzon Borglum, the creator of the images on Mount Rushmore in South Dakota. The monument here is dedicated to the soldiers of North Carolina who died during the infamous Pickett's Charge. It's an interesting, if chilling, fact that almost one of every four Confederate casualties on the battlefield at Gettysburg was a North Carolinian.

By the end of the first day of battle the Confederate army occupied a long, concave line that ran from Seminary Ridge on the right, along the unfinished railroad, and onward through the town of Gettysburg. It was a position that offered General Lee several options for battle the following day. However, it also posed many problems; problems of communication and coordination among others.

By the morning of July 2nd General Lee had decided to make an early morning attack on the Union right flank. It was a decision that was not popular with his corps commanders, Generals James Longstreet and Richard S. Ewell. Longstreet was convinced that his own plan, a defensive ac-

Lt. Gen. Richard S. Ewell.

tion that would invite Meade to attack them in well defended positions on Seminary Ridge, would be more effective than a strike against the Union right. Lee decided, in view of his generals' reluctance to take the initiative, to attack the enemy on both the right and left flanks: Longstreet to the south and

Ewell to the north. General A.P. Hill was to hammer away at the Union center with artillery fire.

Nothing went as planned. Delay followed delay. Longstreet was surly and uncooperative and never seemed ready to move. Ewell's attitude was no better. The morning hours of July 2nd passed away with little action on either side. In the early afternoon Union General Daniel Sickles caused further disruption to the Confederate program by moving his 3rd Corps, without Meade's knowledge, from the heights of Little Round Top to what he thought was a more advantageous position in the Peach Orchard, leaving Little Round Top undefended.

When you are ready to continue your tour leave the parking area and drive straight ahead for about three quarters of a mile to **Stop Number 5** and pull off the road into the parking area.

The Virginia Memorial:
This statue of General Robert E. Lee and his horse Traveler is claimed to be the finest likeness of the famous general to be found anywhere. Note how lifelike, even dignified, Traveler appears to be. Unlike most equestrian sculptures of the period this one faithfully adheres to lifelike proportions rather than the demon-like effigies so popular in other works. The Monument was unveiled on June 8th, 1917 by Miss Virginia Carter, General Lee's niece. It is the only statue of a Confederate general on the entire battlefield. It was from this position here that General Lee watched the doomed attack of July 3rd, now known as Pickett's Charge, and then the retreat of Pickett's decimated brigades.

Stop Number 6 in just a little further on along the road. Drive on for about a mile and pull off the road into the parking area at the Eisenhower Observation Tower.

The Eisenhower Observation Tower:
The famous general and one-time president of the United States loved this little Pennsylvania town of Gettysburg. If you can, you really should climb to the top of the 75-foot

observation tower. If you do you will enjoy a magnificent view of the Eisenhower farm, the surrounding countryside, and both Round Tops. Eisenhower lived for most of his early life in the vicinity of the park. His family home is not far away near Harrisburg, the capitol city of Pennsylvania. He purchased the farm as a retirement home in 1951 and, as everyone knows, he visited the farm as often as he could. General and Mrs. Eisenhower gave the farm as a gift to the United States, and today it is administered by the National Park Service as the Eisenhower National Historic Site, and is open to the public. If you would like to visit the farm you can check with the Park Service at the Visitor Center.

To continue to the next stop on your tour leave the parking area here at the tower and continue straight ahead along the road for about a mile until you reach the Alabama Memorial on Warfield Ridge. The stone walls that border the road along the way, and the avenue itself, were not here at the time of the battle. There were, however, similar stone walls built by the local farmers of the day all over the battlefield. The fighting men of both sides used them as refuge and shelter from the deadly firestorms of cannon and musket fire.

Also along the way to the next stop you will see several historic farms, all restored by the National Park Service to their authentic Civil Wartime condition. The first is on your left, a two-story log house complete with outhouse, that was owned at the time of the battle by the Snyder family. The stone house a little further on to the left was owned by the Bushman family.

When you reach the Alabama Monument pull of the road and leave your vehicle in the parking area on your right.

Warfield Ridge:
The Alabama Monument stands on Warfield Ridge at a point where the extreme right flank of the Confederate army was anchored on July 2nd, the second day of the battle. As you stand here and look to the east you will have a good view of the two

hills that were the objectives of the Confederate attack that afternoon. The larger hill to the right is Big Round Top, the one to the left is Little Round Top. Of the two hills, because of its easy accessibility, it was Little Round Top that offered the battlefield advantage to whomever might occupy it. On July 2nd it marked the extreme left flank of the Union Army. Confederate General Longstreet occupied the high ground here on Warfield Ridge. General Hood's division was at his extreme right flank with General Lafayette McLaws' division to Hood's left. It's from here that General Longstreet eventually launched his attack against the Federal positions on Little Round Top at about 4:00 p.m. on the afternoon of the second day of battle.

When you are ready to continue your tour leave the parking area and follow the battlefield tour signs to Stop Number 8 on Little Round Top. If you have the time you might like to take a walk along the nature trail to the summit of Big Round Top. It's an area of outstanding natural beauty and well worth the effort. You will find the parking area for the trail on your left, just along the way to the next stop. If you do decide to take the walking tour please take care to not disturb the environment and, please, take your litter home with you.

When you reach **Stop Number 8** leave your car in the parking area and make the short walk up the hill to the top. There you will have a magnificent view of the battlefield and you will find a taped Park Service message that describes the action here as it took place.

Little Round Top:

This is the position left unoccupied by Union General Daniel Sickle's 3rd Army Corps on the afternoon of the second day. You will remember that he decided to occupy what he thought was a much more strategically advantageous position to the northwest in the Peach Orchard. By 4:30 p.m., however, Sickle's 3rd Corps had fallen under the direct assault of General Longstreet and the Confederate First Corps as they moved toward Little Round Top. Sickles' corps was decimated and Little Round Top would undoubtedly have fallen to the Confederate attack had it not been for the efforts of Union Brigadier General G.K. Warren.

General Warren, the chief engineer of the Army of the Potomac, had been sent by General Meade to inspect the condition of the defenses in this area of the battlefield. When he arrived on the summit of Little Round Top he was able to see the battle raging away in the Peach Orchard to the northwest and knew it was only a matter of minutes before Sickles would be over-run and that the Confederate divisions would soon be rushing up Little Round Top toward the undefended positions at the top. Without a second thought Warren immediately began bringing in troops to defend the hill. His effort was just in time, for no sooner had he got his men into position than the Confederates came streaming up the hill yelling and screaming, flushed with victory in the Peach Orchard. The battle for Little Round Top raged on until nightfall and by close of battle on the second day, thanks to General Warren, the Union line here was still intact.

The large monument at the southern end of the hill is dedicated to Union soldiers of the 44th New York Infantry.

Little Round Top, seen from the Wheatfield.

Inside the monument you will find a likeness of General Butterfield, General Meade's Chief of Staff and composer of the haunting tune that signals the setting of the sun, the end of the military day – Taps.

When you are ready to continue leave the parking lot and follow the road and Park Service signs to the intersection of Wheatfield Road. Turn left there and continue to follow the signs to Stop Number 9, it's about a mile away from here.

The Wheatfield:
As we have already mentioned, General Sickles vacated his position on Little Round Top and moved to a new position at the Peach Orchard. As he bore the brunt of the Confederate attack the fighting there spread into the Wheatfield, and to the south into Devil's Den as he was pushed backward. This area saw some of the most concentrated fighting of the entire battle. For more than four hours the battle raged on across the Wheatfield, to the Peach Orchard, to Devil's Den, to Plum Run, to the slopes of Little Round Top until, by the end of the day, when one attack after another had been followed by counter-attack after counter-attack, the casualties on this section of the battlefield alone had mounted to more than 6,000 on both sides. Sickles himself had been badly wounded in the battle for the Peach Orchard and would lose a leg because of it.

From here follow the Park Service signs for a mile to Stop Number 10: the Trostle Farm and the Peach Orchard. Keep a lookout to the left along the way for the Irish Brigade Monument. You will recognize it by the Irish Wolfhound and the Celtic cross. Another interesting monument on the way is that of the 116th Pennsylvania. It was inspired by 116th's commanding officer who remembered the scene you see here. The monument depicts a fallen soldier by a stone wall. When you reach the stop sign and prepare to turn left you will see the Trostle farm and **Stop Number 10** ahead of you. Turn left, then right, then right again onto United States Avenue. Follow the Park Service signs.

The Trostle Farm & The Peach Orchard:
This area is close to the center of General Sickles battle for the Peach Orchard. The fighting here raged back and forth across the Emmitsburg Road to the west and all across these fields to the Devil's Den in the south and on to the slopes of Little Round Top in the east.

The buildings here belonged, at the time of the battle, to a farmer of German descent by the name of Abraham Trostle. As always, they have been restored by the Park Service to their original 1863 condition. The barn is a fine and interesting example of a German Pennsylvania Bank Barn. These barns were constructed so that a bank of earth allowed the farmer easy access to the upper floor of the building from ground level. As you can see from the scars in the upper brickwork, this one suffered damage from artillery fire during the battle.

44th New York Infantry Memorial.

To the right you will see an upright cannon that marks the field headquarters of General Dan Sickles. It is interesting to know that, even though Sickles was badly wounded here, he outlived every other general officer who fought at Gettysburg. And it was largely due to him that Congress passed what became known as the Sickles Bill in 1895 that created Gettysburg National Park. Dan Sickles died some 51 years after the battle in 1914.

When you are ready to continue your tour, leave the parking area and drive straight ahead until you come to a stop sign. Turn left there onto Hancock Avenue and proceed for about a mile to the Pennsylvania Memorial.

The Pennsylvania Memorial:

The Pennsylvania Memorial is the largest monument on the battlefield. On it are engraved, in alphabetical order by regiment, all of the names of the more than 34,000 soldiers and officers of Pennsylvania who fought here during the battle of Gettysburg – roughly a third of the entire Union army.

As the battle continued, and while Longstreet and the Confederate First Corps were engaging the enemy in a desperate struggle at the southern end of the battlefield, away to the north the Confederate forces under General Ewell were pressing home their attack against the Union left flank on Culp's Hill. The fighting here to the south ended at about 7:00 p.m., but the fighting on the Union left flank continued on well into the evening until it finally died away in the gathering darkness.

The second day had been an expensive one for both sides. Casualties totaled almost 17,000 men and officers, and although the Confederates occupied almost all of the ground in front of Little Round Top, the Union line still held intact along the entire length of Cemetery Ridge. It seemed as if the two great armies had fought themselves to a standstill.

When you have finished your visit to the Pennsylvania Memorial you can resume your tour of the battlefield by leaving the parking area and driving northward along Hancock Avenue to the Angle; it's just beyond the group of trees on the left and is surrounded by an iron fence. Turn into the narrow avenue to the side and park your vehicle. The Angle is **Stop Number 11** on our tour and Number 15 of the Park Service brochure.

The Angle, The High Watermark of the Confederacy:

The Angle, here on the top of Cemetery Ridge, was the scene of the last major conflict of the battle of Gettysburg. It was also a scene of extraordinary mass heroism and devotion to cause and country the like of which has seldom, if ever, been seen since.

On the evening of July 2nd, after the fighting of the second day had finished, the generals of both armies met in council of war. General Meade and his senior officers decided that rather than go onto the offensive they would maintain their defensive posture on the Ridge. Meade also determined that Lee, having failed to gain his objectives to the south and to the north of the Union line, would concentrate his efforts against the Union center; he was right.

Lee, even though he realized that his commanders had failed to take advantage of the favorable situation of both the 1st and 2nd of July, remained confident and was determined to push the battle to its conclusion and, for the first time in the war, he made the mistake of underestimating his adversary. He felt his enemy's morale must be at an all-time low and he would, as had all the others during the past two years, find a way to discontinue the battle and leave Lee the victor and in charge of the field.

But the Union morale was far from low. If anything it was at its highest of the entire battle, and despite heavy losses Meade had a numerical advantage over the Confederates by some 20,000 officers and men. And then, to compound his mistake, Lee did exactly as Meade had expected him to do.

The previous day Lee had failed first to turn the Union right flank and then the left. Knowing that his enemy had suffered enormous losses he believed he must be weak somewhere – the Union center. With that in mind he decided upon what he felt must be the conclusive effort of the battle. Longstreet would make a massive frontal assault upon the Union center while General Ewell would continue to attack Meade's right flank. Longstreet tried hard to dissuade Lee from this strategy, claiming that such a frontal attack across open fields against the well defended Union positions on Cemetery Ridge would be suicidal. He failed.

Lee determined to open the third day of battle at dawn on the morning of July 3rd, but once again his plans went awry. Overnight General Ewell had sent three additional brigades to support General Johnson's division in his early morning attack against the Federal extreme right flank on Culp's Hill. But Meade, anticipating Lee's projected frontal attack, had brought up extra batteries of artillery which would serve the dual purpose of effecting a massive cross-fire over the fields to the front of the Union center and could, if need be, direct their fire against any probable attack on Culp's Hill.

The 29th Pennsylvania forms a line of battle on Culp's Hill..

At 4:30 a.m. the Union artillery positioned along the Baltimore road opened fire on General Johnson's positions. Johnson had no alternative but to advance. As he did so he ran into Union General Geary's division and the rest of the massed divisions of General Slocum's entire 12th Corps. Again and again the Confederate divisions attacked the Union line only to be driven back each time by the massed artillery and musket fire from Culp's Hill. It is said the firestorm was so intense that the trees on Culp's Hill were stripped bare of their foliage. Many of the trees were found after the battle to be imbedded by more than 200 bullets.

The battle for Culp's Hill raged on for more than seven hours until, at 11 a.m., the Confederates were forced to withdraw.

They left the ground in front of the Union trenches covered with a blanket of dead and wounded. It had been an expensive morning for the Confederates that had gained them nothing.

Now it would be Longstreet's turn. Once again he argued forcefully against Lee's planned frontal attack on the Union center. Lee's only concession to Longstreet was to substitute two of his, Longstreet's, divisions for two of General A.P. Hill's; Longstreet, however, was to remain in command. The preparations for the attack took longer to complete than Lee had anticipated. Longstreet, in his reluctance to commit his men to military suicide, did nothing to hurry them. And so it was more than two hours after the battle for Culp's Hill had ended that two Confederate cannon signaled the beginning of the bombardment that was to clear the way for the Confederate advance.

All along a two-mile front 140 Confederate cannon opened fire upon the Union positions as one. These were immediately answered by 80 Federal guns on Cemetery Ridge. The most stupendous artillery battle in American history was under way. In seconds the entire battlefield had disappeared under a dense cloud of gunsmoke and dust through which only the muzzle flashes and the lightning from exploding shell and case shot could be seen. The lethal fragments of the exploding shells tore into the men and horses on both sides of the field; the carnage was unbelievable. For two hours the artillery battle continued without a pause. Then the Union artillery commander ordered a cease-fire in order to cool his guns and to conserve ammunition for the Confederate attack he knew must come.

It was at this point that Major General George E. Pickett rode up to General Longstreet, saluted, and asked: "General. Shall I advance?" General Longstreet, knowing that he was sending untold thousands of men to their deaths, was unable to look Pickett in the eye. With his head lowered he merely nodded in Pickett's direction. Pickett, on his great black war horse, rode away and into history.

When General Pickett reached his men he took up a position at the center of his line and gave the order: "Forward, guide center,

Maj. Gen. George E. Pickett.

march." On that order three Confederate divisions, more than 13,000 officers and men, encouraged by the stirring sounds of the military bands playing the Confederate anthem, moved off in route step toward the Emmitsburg Road and their destiny. Across the open fields with bayonets gleaming in the sunlight and their battle flags and regimental banners fluttering proudly they advanced toward the Union positions on the ridge.

The Union batteries of the Union 2nd Corps on Cemetery Hill double loaded their guns with canister, held their fire, and watched in awe the magnificent pageant that was unfolding before them. Soon the brave gray line had crossed the Emmitsburg road into the open fields in front of the Federal positions. It was at this moment that the entire massed Union artillery on Cemetery Ridge and Little Round Top opened fire upon the hapless Confederate foot soldiers. The effect upon them was, to say the least, devastating.

No words can adequately describe the carnage and systematic killing of the next moments. Great gaps were torn in the Confederate lines as they came first within point-blank range of the Union cannon, and then under a hailstorm of musket fire from the Union trenches on top of the ridge. Longstreet had been right. The attack had turned into a mass suicide, but the advance did not falter for a second. On and on the heroic Confederate line doggedly continued up the slopes of Cemetery Ridge. Of the 13,000 Confederate soldiers that took part in Pickett's Charge only a few hundred reached the Union line here at the Angle to be either killed, captured, or driven back. The copse of trees here to our left has become known as "The High Watermark of the Confederacy." It was the turning point of the Civil War. Never again would Confederate fortunes rise to the heights they had known up until this point in the war. Pickett's Charge was a mortal wound to the Confederacy.

The thousands of Confederate survivors of Pickett's Charge, many of them badly wounded, limped back across the fields towards their own lines on Seminary Ridge. Of the original 13,000 men that took part, more than 7,000 lay dead and wounded upon the killing fields between the two ridges. General Robert E. Lee was waiting for them when they returned. *"This is all my fault,"* he said. And, to his great credit, the General accepted full responsibility for his defeat.

The cost in human lives of the three days of battle was enormous. On the Union side 3,155 dead, 14,529 wounded, and 5,365 missing in action; the Confederates suffered 3,903 dead, 18,735 wounded, and 5,425 missing; the combined number of casualties totaled 51,112. To give you an idea of how staggering that number is this book contains some 80,000 words; a list of the names of the casualties at Gettysburg would fill a book more than half as thick again. The Confederate

Lt. Gen. James Longstreet.

wagon train that carried the wounded southward away from the battlefield was more than 17 miles long. In three days Gettysburg had become a name that would live in history for all time.

Before you leave the battlefield be sure to visit the Cyclorama with its panoramic painting of Pickett's Charge. The painting is the work of Paul Phillippoteaux and is some 356 feet wide by 26 feet high. The Electric Map, too, is worth a visit. The 750 square foot map and accompanying taped narration sets the stage for your tour of the park. And don't miss the Civil War Museum. The historic artifacts, many from the battle of Gettysburg, are arranged into thematic exhibits. The collection was begun within days of the battle itself.

Where to Stay, Things to Do

Attractions

Adams County Winery: Call for hours 717-334-4631.
Catoctin Mt. Zoo: Weekends only 10:00-4:00 p.m.
Gen. Lee's Headquarters: Opens by end of March.
Gettysburg Battle Theater: 8:00 a.m.-8:00 p.m.
Gettysburg Family Fun Center: Weekends.
Hall of Presidents: 9:00 a.m.-5:00 p.m.
Jennie Wade House & Old Town Square: 9:00 a.m.-5:00 p.m.
Lincoln Room Museum: 11:00 a.m.-4:00 p.m.
Lincoln Train Museum: 9:00 a.m.-5:00 p.m.
Mr. Ed's Elephant Museum: 10:00 a.m.-5:00 p.m.
National Apple Museum: Weekends only. 717-677-8728.
National Civil War Wax Museum: 9:00 a.m.-5:00 p.m.
Old Gettysburg Village: Open daily.
Soldier's National Museum: 9:00 a.m.-5:00 p.m.
Battlefield Bus Tours: Baltimore St. Daily, $9.75 & $6.55.
Licensed Battlefield Guides: Park. Daily $20 per car.
Eisenhower Farm Tour: Visitor Ctr. Daily. $3.50.

Annual Events

Gettysburg Spring Bluegrass Festival: 1st full weekend in May. Features some of the country's best stars of bluegrass music. For information call 717-642-8749.

Apple Blossom Festival: 1st weekend in May. Country festival situated in the middle of Adams Country's 20,000 acres of beautiful orchards. For information call 717-334–6274.

Gettysburg Spring Outdoor Antique Show: 3rd Saturday in May; 175 antique dealers display their wares on the sidewalks radiating from historic Lincoln Square. For information call 717-334–6274.

Gettysburg Square-Dance Round-Up: 4th weekend in May. A square-dance festival with nationally known square-dance callers. For information call 717-334-1902.

Memorial Day Parade: Last Monday in May. Parade followed by ceremony in Gettysburg National Cemetery with guest speakers. The placing of fresh flowers on graves by children is a tradition started in 1867. For information call 717-334-6274.

Kustom Kemps of America Car Show: 2nd weekend in June. Held at Oakside Park in Biglerville. For information call 717-637-5229.

New Oxford Flea Market & Antique Show: 3rd Saturday in June. One of the largest and oldest one-day antique shows on the East Coast.

Gettysburg Civil War Heritage Days: Last weekend in June & first week in July. Commemorates the Battle of Gettysburg with living history encampment, band concerts, 4th of July program, Civil War lecture series and a battle re-enactment. For information call 717-334-6274.

Civil War Institute: Last week in June & early July. Held at Gettysburg College. Lectures and tours given by prominent

Civil War scholars. For information call 717-337-6590.

Gettysburg Civil War Collectors Show: lst weekend in July. Presents 250 display tables of original Civil War accoutrements, weapons, documents, books and personal effects. For information call 717-334-6274.

GPBA Civil War Book Fair: lst weekend in July. Over 40 major Civil War book dealers will be selling new, used, out of print and rare books, documents, photographs, and prints. For information: GPBA, Box 1863, Gettysburg, PA 17325.

Gettysburg Firemen's Festival: Week of 4th of July. A week-long festival with special daily activities including rides, midway, entertainment and a fireworks display. For information: 717-334-6274.

Hanover Dutch Festival: Last Saturday in July. Over 200 food and craft vendors, community parade, entertainment and antique car show in downtown Hanover, PA. For information call 717-637-6130.

Littlestown "Good Old Days" Antique Show: 3rd weekend in August. An old fashioned festival offering a flea market, craft displays, antique cars, parade, and hometown cooking in the town park. For information call 717-359-4722.

South Mountain Fair: Last weekend in August. A traditional country fair. For information call 717-677-9625 or 677-7333.

East Berlin Colonial Days: 2nd Saturday in September. Street fair featuring 18th century crafts and demonstrations. For information: 717-259-9000.

Gettysburg Fall Bluegrass Festival: 2nd full weekend after Labor Day. Featuring some of the country's best stars of bluegrass music. For information call 717-642-8749.

Gettysburg Fall Outdoor Antique Show: 3rd Saturday in September. 175 antique dealers display their wares on the sidewalks radiating from historic Lincoln Square. For information call 717-334-6274.

Fairfield Pippenfest: Last Sunday in September. Features apple products, music, crafts and antiques in street fair setting. (Fair weather only). For information call 717-642-5640.

National Apple Harvest Festival: 1st & 2nd weekends in October. Old time festival of apple products, live country music, arts and crafts, antique autos, steam engines, orchard tours, pony rides and plenty of food. For information call 717-334-6274.

Anniversary of Lincoln's Gettysburg Address: November 19th. Commemorates Anniversary with memorial services in the Gettysburg National Cemetery. For information call 717-334-6274.

Remembrance Day: Saturday closest to November 19th. Parade and wreath-laying ceremony held in conjunction with observance of Anniversary of Lincoln's Gettysburg Address. For information call 717-334-6274.

Gettysburg Yuletide Festival: 2nd weekend in December. Highlights include tours of decorated historic homes, live nativity scene, caroling & handbell choirs, holiday dessert tasting, and candlelight walking tour. For information call 717-334-6274.

Hotels

Best Western Gettysburg Hotel 1797: On historic Lincoln Square. 83 rooms appointed with elegant Victorian furnishings. Fireplace and Jacuzzi baths create an atmosphere of refined comfort in 22 suites. Complimentary breakfast, free parking, pool. AAA & AARP discounts. Family rates. Meeting rooms. (800) 528-1234 or (717) 337-2000.

Blue Sky Motel: 4.3 miles north on Rt. 34. A/c, cable TV (HBO/ESPN). Large family rooms, kitchenette suite. Heated pool. Complimentary coffee. Picnic and Children's Play Areas. Fitness Center. Executive secretarial/copy/fax services. Tours arranged from motel. Major credit cards accepted. 717-677- 7736. Reservations (800) 745-8194.

Budgethost-Three Crowns Motor Lodge: 205 Steinwehr Ave. Business Rt. 15, in-town location. Walking distance of all major attractions. Restaurants. National Cemetery, battlefield & Washington DC tours. Pool, phones, CATV, a/c, free coffee. 717-334-3168. For reservations 800-729-6564.

College Motel: 345 Carlisle St. Business Rt. 15; 3 blocks north of Center Square, opposite Gettysburg College. A/c, cable TV, pool, room phones. Battlefield tours arranged. AAA and Mobil recommended. Major credit cards accepted. Family rates. Phone 717-334-6731 or (800) 367-6731.

Colonial Motel: 157 Carlisle St., Business Rt. 15, one block North of Center Square, adjacent to Gettysburg College, a/c, cable TV, room phones. Family rates. Battlefield tours ar- ranged. AAA and Mobil recommended, Major credit cards ac- cepted. Restaurant 1 block. Phone 717-334-3126 or 800-336-3126.

Colton Motel: 232 Steinwehr Ave. Business Rt. 15 in town. Park your car and walk to all major attractions, National Ceme- tery, Visitors Center and a wide selection of restaurants. Bat- tlefield and Washington DC tours arranged from motel. Heated pool, color cable TV, all ground level rooms, kitchenette suite, complimentary morning coffee, phone 717-334-5514.

Comfort Inn Of Gettysburg: New in 1990. Located on Rt. 30 in Gettysburg. 1 mile from junction of Rts 15 & 30. 1 mile east of Lincoln Square. Indoor pool & spa. 26" TV w/ remote, cable, HBO. Battlefield & Washington DC tours from motel. Restau- rant adjacent. AARP discount. Major credit cards accepted. AAA three star. 871 York Road, 717-337-2400.

Criterion Motor Lodge: 337 Carlisle St., 2 1/2 blocks north of Square on Business 15. Convenient downtown location, opposite Gettysburg College. Cable TV, room phones, guest controlled heat and air cond. Battlefield tours arranged. Near all major attractions. Kids stay free. Major credit cards accepted. Phone 717-334-6268.

Days Inn Gettysburg: New in 1989. Features 113 interior corridor rooms with 2 queen beds, cable TV, exercise room. Coin laundry. Meeting & banquet rooms for up to 100 people, Perkins Restaurant adjacent. Mini-golf nearby. Located on Rt. 30 near junction of Routes 30 & 15, 1 mile east of Square. No pets. AAA & AARP. 865 York Rd., 717-334-0030.

Days Inn Westminster: 96 comfortable rooms, Complimentary sideboard breakfast. Outdoor pool. Adjacent to Cranberry Mall and close to Gettysburg, Farm Museum, antique shopping. AAA/AARP. 25 S. Cranberry Rd., Westminster, MD 21157. 4l0-857-0500; 800-336-DAYS.

Econo Lodge: 945 Baltimore Park. Route 97, at National Tower Entrance. Walk to all major attractions, Visitor Center. 2 pools, restaurant, lounge, meeting room, truck parking, non-smoking rooms, room phones, CATV, a/c. Battlefield & Washington DC tours, AAA approved. 7l7-334-67150; reservations 800-446-6900.

Friendship Inn-Penn Eagle Motel: 1 1/2 miles East of Lincoln Square on US Route 30, 1031 York Road, Gettysburg, PA 17325. 717-334-1804. Toll free 800-553-2666. Beautiful a/c rooms, king beds, queen beds, cable TV, HBO movies, room phones, free coffee, credit cards, play area, large pool, sightseeing tours. Restaurant nearby. Mobil Guide approved.

Gettysburg Inn: 1980 Biglerville Rd, Gettysburg, PA 17325. 5 minutes north of Lincoln Square on Route. 34N. Clean quiet rooms, a/c, CATV, tile bath & shower, play area, well landscaped, no pets, free coffee. Battlefield & Washington DC tours, major credit cards accepted. 717-334–2263.

Gettysburg International Youth Hotel: 27 Chambersburg Street in the heart of historic downtown Gettysburg. Ideal for groups and individuals. Library and game rooms. Fully equipped kitchen. Low rates. International Travelers Family Rooms. 717-334-1020.

Heritage Motor Lodge: Located in the heart of the historic area and "Old Gettysburg Village." Within walking distance of leading museums and Gettysburg Tour Center. Restaurants, patio dining, cocktails all within 500 ft. A/c, cable & color TV/HBO, room phones, credit cards, family rooms. 717-334-9281.

Holiday Inn Battlefield: Tour Center next door, walk to all attractions. 100 rooms, many with king beds, steambaths. Teens stay free. Rated AAA three stars. AARP & corporate discounts. 3 meeting rooms accommodate 300. Non-smoking rooms. Pets. Restaurant-lounge. Kid's breakfast 99 cents, dinner $1.99. In the Historic District at PA 97 & Business 15S. 717-334-6211.

Holiday Inn Express: (Formerly Best Western of Gettysburg) New in 1990. Located on Route 30, 1 1/2 miles from junction of Routes 15 & 30. 1 mile east of Lincoln Square. Indoor pool, spa & fitness center. 26" TV w/remote, cable, HBO. Free continental breakfast. Battlefield & Washington DC tours from motel. Restaurant adjacent. AAA three star rated. AARP discount. 869 York Road, 717-337-1400.

Home Sweet Home Motel: 593 Steinwehr Ave. on Business Route 15 South, opposite Visitor Center & Main Entrance to Battlefield. 41 units, guest controlled heat & a/c, color TV, reasonable rates. Walk to all major attractions & restaurants. Battlefield & Washington, DC tours arranged. MC/VISA accepted. Phone 717-334-3916, Gettysburg, PA 17325.

Howard Johnson Lodge: 301 Steinwehr Ave. on Business Route 15 in town. 77 rooms, cocktail lounge, 30-channel TV, HBO, ESPN. Free coffee, kids stay free. AARP discount, AAA approved. Park your car & walk to all major points of interest & better restaurants. Next to National Park Service Electric Map. Sightseeing tours arranged. 717-334-1188 or 800-654-2000.

Bed & Breakfasts

Appleford Inn: Gettysburg's first bed & breakfast. An elegant 1867 mansion featuring 12 guest rooms, all with private baths. Antique-filled parlor, library & sun porch. Enjoy gourmet breakfasts in our Victorian dining room. Fireplaces, a/c, non-smoking. A unique experience for the discriminating traveler. Visa/Mastercard. 218 Carlisle Street. 717-337-1711.

Briarfield Bed & Breakfast: 240 Baltimore Street. Just two blocks from Lincoln Square. Walk to fine restaurants and all major historic attractions. All the comforts of home in this circa 1878 house, including three comfortable guest rooms. 717-334-8725.

Doubleday Inn: The only B&B directly on the battlefield at Stop Number 3 on the park tour. Free Civil War lectures. Library, memorabilia, antiques, country breakfasts, afternoon teas, hors d'oeuvres. A gracious combination of hospitality and history. 104 Doubleday Ave., 717-334-9119.

Farnsworth House Inn: 1810 Original Civil War house. Steeped in history. Museums in garret and cellar. Ghost stories. Gracious Victorian decor. Full breakfast in the garden. Occupied by sharpshooters. Walk to attractions. Afternoon tea in the sunroom. 401 Baltimore St., 717-334-8838.

Keystone Inn: A large Victorian brick house with lots of natural wood. The guest rooms are bright and cheerful. Each room has a reading nook and a writing desk. Choose a breakfast to suit your mood. 231 Hanover Street, 717-337-3888.

Restaurants

General Lee's Family Restaurant: Breakfast lunch and dinner in our casual country dining rooms. Fine family dining at affordable prices. 8 blocks west on US 30., 717-334-2200.

General Pickett's All-U-Can-Eat Buffets: 571 Steinwehr

Ave. Ask about our dinner theater. Seats 200. Group menus. Opens 7 a.m. 717-334-7580.

The Herr Tavern Publick House: Dine in historic 1816 pre-Civil War tavern house. Classical European and American cuisine. Open seven days for lunch and dinner. 717-334-4332.

Gingerbread Man Restaurant: Casual dining in a relaxed atmosphere. Located within walking distance of many major Civil War attractions. 217 Steinwehr Ave. 717-334-1100.

Camping

Always Welcome Traveler Camp Site: Campground with open, grassy sites in historic area. From junction of US 30 & Business Rt. 15: go 1/2 mile on Business Rt. 15, then 1 mile SE on Baltimore St. **Facilities:** 80 sites, 6 full hookups, 80 water & elec. (20 & 30 amp receptacles), 94 no-hookups, 39 pull-throughs, tenting available, flush/marine toilets, hot showers, sewage disposal, laundry, ice, tables, fire rings, wood. **Recreation:** rec. room, pool, playground. Open all year. Facilities fully operational Apr. 1 through Nov. 1. Phone: 717-334-8226. NCHA 10% discount.

Artillery Ridge Campground: Grassy park with open and shaded areas in an historic area. From junction of US 30 & Business Rt. 15: Go 1 1/2 miles S. on Business Rt. 15, then 1 1/4 miles SE on Hwy. 134 **Facilities:** 150 sites, 115 water & elec. (20 & 30 amp receptacles), 35 no-hookups, 46 pull-throughs, a/c allowed ($), heater allowed ($), tenting available, RV storage, flush toilets, hot showers, sewage disposal, laundry, public phone, grocery store, ice, tables, fire rings, wood, church services. **Recreation:** rec. room, pavilion, coin games, swim pool, 2 pedal boat rentals, pond fishing, basket-ball hoop, 18 bike rentals, playground, horse riding trails, horse rental, badminton, sports field, horse-shoes, hiking trails, volleyball, local tours. Open Apr. 1 through Nov. 1. Master Card/Visa accepted. Phone: 717-334-1288.

Drummer Boy Campground: wooded campground in natural

setting. **Facilities**: 300 sites, 70 full hookups, 180 water & elec. (20 & 30 amp receptacles), 50 no-hook-ups, 46 pull-throughs, a/c allowed ($), heater allowed ($), tenting available, group sites for tents/RVs, flush toilets, hot showers, sewage disposal, laundry, public phone, full service store, RV supplies, ice, tables, fire rings, grills, wood, guard. **Recreation**: rec. room, pavilion, coin games swim pool. Lake fishing mini-golf ($), basketball hoop, 12 bike rentals, playground, planned group activities (weekends only), movies, badminton. horseshoes, hiking trails, volleyball, local tours. Open March 26th-November 7th. Member ARCV, PCOA. Discover/Mastercard/Visa accepted. Phone 800-336-DBOY

Gettysburg Campground: stream-side park with shaded and open sites in historic area. From junction of US 30 & Hwy. 116: go 3 miles W. on Hwy. 116. **Facilities**: 278 sites, 90 full hook-ups, 166 water & elect. (20 & 30 amp receptacles), 22 no-hook-ups, seasonal sites, 40 pull-throughs, a/c allowed ($), heater allowed ($), tenting available, group sites for tents/RVs, tent rentals, RV rentals, RV storage, flush toilets, hot showers, sewage disposal, laundry, public phone, grocery store, RV sup-plies, LP gas refill by weight/by meter, ice, fire rings, wood. **Recreation**: rec. hall/rec room, coin games, swim pool, stream fishing, mini-golf ($), 6 bike rentals, playground, 2 shuffleboard courts, planned group activities, movies, badminton, sports field, horseshoes, volleyball, local tours. Open April 1st through Nov. 30. Mastercard/Visa accepted. Member of ARVC; PCOA. Phone: 717-334-3304.

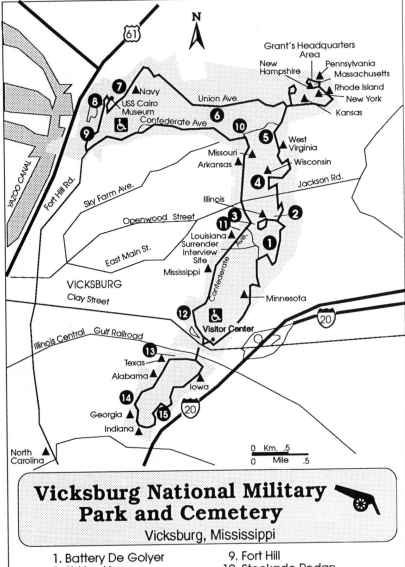

Vicksburg National Military Park and Cemetery

Vicksburg, Mississippi

1. Battery De Golyer
2. Shirley House
3. Third Louisiana Redan
4. Ransom's Gun Path
5. Stockade Redan Attack
6. Thayer's Approach
7. Battery Selfridge
8. National Cemetery
9. Fort Hill
10. Stockade Redan
11. Great Redoubt
12. Second Texas Lunette
13. Railroad Redoubt
14. Fort Garrott
15. Hovey's Approach

Chapter 11

Vicksburg

July 4, 1863

Vicksburg National Military Park is in the northeastern portion of Vicksburg, Mississippi. The park entrance and the Visitor Center are at 3201 Clay Street (US 80), Vicksburg MS 39180, within a mile of Interstate 20. Both Visitor Center and the U.S.S. Cairo Museum are open daily, except for Christmas. Picnicking is allowed only at the U.S.S. Cairo Museum at Tour Stop Number 12. Fires and camping are not allowed. Pets must be on a leash or physically restrained at all times. Phone 601-636-0583.

From Illinois to New Orleans and the Gulf of Mexico the Mississippi River wanders across the countryside for nearly a thousand miles. During the Civil War the river was a vital lifeline for both the Union and Confederate armies. From the beginning of the conflict in 1861 the Confederacy built a great chain of fortifications at strategic points along the riverbank to protect it. The Federal government, however, realized that without the river the Confederate states of Texas, Arkansas, and Louisiana would be cut off from their sources of supply, while the armies from the north would

Gen. Ulysses S. Grant.

have an uninterrupted right of passage of troops and supplies to the South.

By October, 1862, the Union forces had gained control of the river from its source all the way to the heavily fortified Southern town of Vicksburg, and from its mouth northward to Port Hudson. Only a 130-mile stretch of the river between these two cities remained in Confederate hands. In April of 1862, after the fall of New Orleans, the Confederates began fortifying Vicksburg to make it impregnable to an attack from the river to the west and from the land to the east.

Union General U.S. Grant, too, realized the importance of Vicksburg and began to lay his plans to secure "The American Gibraltar" for the Union. On November 4th, 1862, Grant moved southward from Tennessee toward Vicksburg, and so began a classic campaign on a scale that would not be seen again until the Second World War.

When Grant started for Vicksburg, Confederate Lt. General John C. Pemberton there sent urgent messages to Richmond declaring that his situation was desperate. The result was a personal visit from the Confederate President. Jefferson Davis took to the rails and headed west to Vicksburg to inspect its defenses for himself. He was accompanied by General Joseph E. Johnston, the commander of all the Confederate forces in the

West. Johnston was pessimistic and told Davis so. The President told him to do the best he could, and then he returned to Richmond.

But all was not well on the Union side either. In August 1862, an Illinois Democratic Senator, John A. McClernand, now a major general, was commissioned by President Lincoln to raise a private army in the Northwest and launch an attack down the Mississippi River toward Vicksburg. This infuriated General-in-Chief Henry Halleck who disapproved of the plan in general, and of the man in particular. Grant and his subordinate, Major General William T. Sherman, also had little respect for the man whose outspoken contempt for any and all graduates of West Point embarrassed and insulted them. It was Halleck, however, who ruined McClernand's plan, for as fast as McClernand raised his troops, so Halleck sent them to Grant and Sherman waiting in Memphis. The object of the exercise, then, was to move them southward toward Vicksburg before McClernand realized what was going on.

Sherman, with four divisions under his command, moved out from Memphis on December 20th, only days before McClernand arrived. Sherman arrived on the Yazoo river, eight miles to the north of Vicksburg, on December 26th and then moved through the swamps and attacked the ridge north of Vicksburg across the Chickasaw Bayou. Sherman's attack was easily repulsed by the Confederate defenders with heavy losses, and he withdrew his forces back to Milliken's Bend.

It was there at Milliken's Bend, on January 2nd, 1863, that General McClernand finally caught up with him. McClernand, beside himself with rage, showed Sherman the Presidential order placing him, McClernand, in command of the army. Sherman immediately relinquished his command to the one-time Senator from Illinois and, in his own words, *"subsided into the more agreeable office of corps commander."*

Grant, in the meantime had received orders from General Halleck placing him in command of all forces operating in the Southwest. He distributed his army as follows. McClernand's

Army of the Mississippi, much to McClernand's dismay, was split in two: the 13th Corps under the command of McClernand himself and the 15th Corps under Sherman's command. Grant's own army was assigned as follows: the 16th Corps went to General Hurlbut, and the 17th Corps to General McPherson. McClernand was outraged by what he considered his relegation to a subsidiary role in the campaign.

All this had taken time and the land around the Mississippi was, by the time Grant had taken over full command, in the grip of winter; only the most limited of operations were possible. All through the winter Grant kept the men busy, and by the time spring arrived his troops were in excellent physical shape. It was March of 1863 before the swollen waters of the river began to recede and Grant was able to make preparations to implement his plan to move the army south of Vicksburg. At the same time Admiral David Porter was to move northward with his gunboats and heavy transports to ferry Grant and his army across to the east side of the river.

Throughout April Grant's army, led by McClernand, moved south along the west bank of the Mississippi and, by the 29th, they had reached Hard Times where they were met by Porter's fleet. The Confederate army under the command of General Pemberton had done little to stop them.

On April 30th Grant's army began to cross the Mississippi and from then on things moved quickly. First he moved inland toward Jackson and on May 1st defeated the Confederates in the Battle of Port Gibson, then on May 12th at Raymond, then he seized Jackson and, finally, turned westward toward Vicksburg. On May 16th he won the battle of Champion Hill and a day later the battle of Big Black Bridge. By May 18th Union forces w ere approaching the outer defenses of Vicksburg itself.

On the morning of May 19th Grant, certain that the Confederates must by now, after the events of the past two weeks, be thoroughly demoralized and must crumble before an all out attack against the city, decided to move against it at once. He threw his forces, Sherman's division, against what he considered to be the key to the city: the Stockade Redan complex. Sherman was repulsed with heavy casualties. General McPherson tried his hand further to the south with no better results. Grant tried again two days later with simultaneous attacks all along the front. Again his efforts were unsuccessful, and Grant settled down to implement his plan to lay siege to the city and so starve the Confederate defenders into submission.

The city was surrounded by a great Union semi-circle from the river bank to the south of the city, to the other river bank to the north. More than 60,000 feet of trenches were dug from one end of the Union line to the other. Eighty-nine artillery emplacements were built along the line and were equipped with 220 field guns of various shapes and sizes.

As soon as Grant had established his base on the Yazoo River and surrounded the city he sent to General Halleck for reinforcements. These were quickly sent and by June 18th his army had risen in strength to more than 77,000 against Pemberton's 30,000 starving Confederates. Grant set July 6th as the date for the final push into the city.

To begin your tour of the battlefield leave the Visitor Center and drive under the Memorial Arch onto Union Avenue and follow the orange battlefield markers to **Stop Number 1**. Union Avenue follows the line of the Union positions during the siege of the city. Along the way as you tour the park, you will pass more than 1,300 memorials erected to the memory of the various units, Confederate and Union, that fought here at Vicksburg.

Battery De Golyer:
At this point in the tour you are very close to the center of the Union line. The row of cannon you see here is aimed eastward toward the Great Redoubt, a distance of 600 yards. It was here that General James McPherson assaulted the Confederate positions on May 19th and was repulsed. Two days later Grant tried again with a simultaneous attack all along the front with General McPherson's corps at the center, General McClernand's to the left, and General Sherman's to the right.

De Golyer's Battery.

At 10 o'clock on the morning of May 22nd General McPherson's forces rushed forward from here toward the Great Redoubt. The waiting Confederate defenders cut them down with a withering hailstorm of cannon and musket fire. The battle here raged all day long until finally, at eight o'clock that evening, the Union forces withdrew leaving more than 3,000 men dead and wounded on the field.

After the battle of May 22nd, General McPherson positioned 22 cannon here. The emplacement is named after Captain Samuel De Golyer who gave his life directing the battery's fire against the fort. You might like to leave your car in the parking area and visit for a while.

When you are ready to continue you tour, leave the parking area and follow the orange directional markers to **Stop Number 2**.

The Shirley House and Illinois Memorial:
The white house on the corner is the only surviving Civil War

era structure in the park. At the time of the battle it was the home of Mrs. Shirley. She refused to leave her home and soon found herself caught in the crossfire between the two armies. She displayed a white flag in one of the windows and a cease-fire was arranged so that she and her son could be escorted from the house. She lived in a cave at the bottom of a ravine until the battle was over.

The Illinois Memorial, modeled after the Pantheon in Rome, is just a little further on along the road and is the largest monument on the battlefield The memorial is dedicated to the more than 36,000 men from Illinois who fought here at Vicksburg. Their names are inscribed on bronze plaques inside the structure.

Illinois Memorial.

When you are ready to continue, leave the parking area, follow the signs and proceed on along the road to **Stop Number 3.**

The Third Louisiana Redan:

A redan is a triangular shaped fort, the apex of which faces toward the enemy. The Third Louisiana Redan you see before you, along with the Great Redoubt, stood guard over the eastern approaches to the city along the Jackson Road. The Redan was heavily mined by Union Captain Andrew Hickenlooper whose statue now stands at the base of the Redan. Tunnels were dug below the fortifications and explosives were placed beneath the fort. These were exploded on June 25th causing great loss of life and a large crater over which the opposing forces fought for more than 20 hours. The Confederates eventually gained the upper hand and repossessed the lost ground and the crater.

While you are here you might like to park and walk along the pathway marked by the blue plaques to the top of the Redan. Once there you will have a commanding view of the Great Redoubt and the Union positions in front of it.

To continue your tour you will need to return to the Shirley House and then turn left. **Stop Number 4** is a mile from the Third Louisiana Redan near the top of the hill on the right.

Ransom's Gun Path:

The cannoneers of the 2nd Illinois Artillery dismantled two 12-pounder cannon and, with help of the men of General Thomas Ransom's infantry, dragged them down the path until they were only 100 yards from the Confederate defenses. There the two cannon were reassembled and were soon back in action.

When you are ready to continue follow the signs to **Stop Number 5**; it's about a mile further on along the road. On the way, to your left, you will pass the Wisconsin Memorial dedicated to the more than 9,000 men who served here at Vicksburg. The effigy at the top is a six-foot bronze replica of the Eighth Wisconsin mascot: the War Eagle.

The road between the Third Louisiana Redan and The Stockade Redan at Stop Number 5 was, on May 25th, covered with the dead and wounded from the abortive Union attacks of May 21st and 22nd. A truce was called so that the field could be cleared and the dead buried. For more than two hours soldiers of both sides mingled freely together. Some were old friends now separated by the fortunes of war. Some found brothers serving on the opposing side, brothers they thought they would never see again. When the truce was over the men returned again to their respective lines to renew the hostilities.

The Stockade Redan Attack:

This area of the battlefield came under the command of Union General William T. Sherman. His objective was to take the Stockade Redan. You should be able to see it in the distance to the west. Sherman's troops assaulted the Redan from this position all day on May the 19th. Attack after attack was repulsed by the Confederate defenders who inflicted heavy losses upon Sherman's divisions. When you reach the parking area you may wish to leave your car and follow the path until you reach the point from which the stockade can more easily be seen.

As you make your way on along Union Avenue toward Stop Number 6 on the tour you will see the junction of Grant Avenue to your right. If you would like to visit the headquarters sites of Generals Sherman and Grant you should make the turn to the right and then almost immediately turn left to Sherman's headquarters.

After visiting Sherman Circle return to Grant Avenue and turn left then continue on along the road to Grant's field headquarters. Along the way to your left you will see first the Kansas memorial. Beyond the Kansas memorial you see the Rhode Island Memorial, the New York, the Massachusetts, and then the Pennsylvania memorials to the right, and finally the New Hampshire Memorial to the left. On the far side of the circle, beneath the equestrian statue of General Grant, you will see several blue plaques. These markers tell the story of the campaign and siege of Vicksburg.

When you have finished your visit to Grant's headquarters you should return along Grant Avenue until reach Union Avenue and then turn right and follow the battlefield directional markers to Stop Number 6 where you will find the parking area to leave your car and visit for a while.

Thayer's Approach:

This is the position where Union General John M. Thayer and his Federal troops attacked the Confederate fortifications high above. Thayer's attack was unsuccessful but you can see the extent of his advance as marked by the blue plaques on the embankments.

Stop Number 7 on your tour is about a mile and a half along the road from Thayer's Approach so when you are ready, leave the parking area and follow the orange markers until you reach the parking area.

Admiral David Porter was the commander of all naval operations in the South and it was to him that Grant turned, not only for supplies and a way across the river at Bruinsburg, he also relied upon him to maintain the siege from the West by way of the river. Porter was supported by Admiral David Farragut and Flag Officers Davis and Andrew H. Foote. All through the siege the Union ironclads and the Confederate shore batteries pounded away at each other. Porter's fleet was equipped with 10 mortar boats each of which carried a mortar that was capable of hurling a 100-pound shell high into the air and onto the city defenses.

The Battery Selfridge:
On December 12th 1862, while on an expedition with four other ships up the Yazoo River, the gunboat *Cairo* was sunk by a crude Confederate mine. The crew, including its Captain, Lt. Commander T. Selfridge Jr., abandoned ship without loss of life. Selfridge was transferred to duty on the gunboat *Conestoga* until it was removed from Vicksburg to undergo repairs. Rather than leave the action Selfridge volunteered to stay behind and command a land-based Union battery manned by sailors. The Battery Selfridge was located at tour Stop Number 7 where you will find the Navy Memorial, a 200-foot shaft dedicated to the memory of the sailors and their officers who fought here at Vicksburg. Statues of the four fleet commanders surround the base of the memorial.

A little further along the road at the bottom of the hill and to the right is the Cairo Museum where you can see artifacts taken from the gunboat. The ship was raised from the bottom of the Yazoo river in the early 1960s. The museum contains a wealth of interesting information and is well worth a visit.

The National Cemetery:

Stop Number 8 on the tour is the 40-acre National Cemetery wherein lie the remains of more than 17,000 soldiers who died on the battlefields of the Civil War. In terms of Civil War burials it is the largest National Cemetery in the United States. The bodies of Union soldiers from battlefields all over the country were disinterred from their shallow graves and brought here where they were buried with all military honors.

The small rectangular stones mark the resting place of the unidentified soldiers buried here at Vicksburg; there are some 13,000 of them. Along the road through the cemetery you will see plaques inscribed with the poem "Bivouac of the Dead" by Theodore O'Hara. The Confederate soldiers killed at Vicksburg are not buried here.

When you are ready to continue your tour leave the National Cemetery and turn right onto Connecting Avenue, then follow the orange tour markers to **Stop Number 9**; it's a little less than a mile away from the Cemetery.

Fort Hill:

This Confederate fort, known first as Fort Nogales, was established by the Spanish in 1791, and it marks the extreme left flank of the Confederate line. As you can see, it had a commanding view of the river to the West, and of the Confederate line of defense to the East, and because of its obvious strength it was never attacked by Union troops.

Confederate Avenue follows the entire Confederate line of defense. It was manned by some 30,000 men under the overall command of Lt. General Pemberton. His subordinate commanders were Generals John S. Bowen, John H. Forney, M.L. Smith, and Carter L. Stevenson. The area here, around Fort Hill, fell under the command of Confederate General Martin Luther Smith. He faced Union General Sherman on the opposite ridge. The blue markers on the ridges denote the extent of the Union advance against the Confederate positions; the red markers denote the Confederate positions.

As you continue along Confederate Avenue, past the Tennessee Circle, toward Stop Number 10 you should be able to see some areas of the City of Vicksburg off to your right. The City in 1863 was nowhere near as large as it is today. The population then was only about 5,000 people. The Tennessee Circle is located about a mile from Fort Hill on the left.

For 47 days the citizens of Vicksburg withstood the terrible hardships of the city under siege. Many of them left their homes and lived underground in caves dug from the thick clay in the hillside. One unnamed Southern lady describes her experiences in the "City Under Siege":

"The cave was an excavation in the earth the size of a large room, high enough for the largest person to stand perfectly erect, provided with comfortable seats and altogether quite a large and habitable abode.

"The caves were plainly becoming a necessity, as some persons had been killed by fragments of shells. The room that I had so lately slept in had been struck and a large hole made in the ceiling. Terror-stricken, we remained crouched in the cave while shell after shell followed one another in quick succession. My heart stood still as we would hear the reports from the guns and the rushing and fearful sound of the shell as it came toward us. As it neared, the noise became more deafening; the air was full of the rushing sound; my ears were bursting. And as it exploded, the report flashed through my head like an electric shock, leaving me in a quiet state of terror.

"Even the dogs seemed to share in the general fear. They would be seen in the midst of the noise to gallop up the street, and then to return, as if fear had maddened them – then as a shell exploded, they would sit down and howl in the most pitiful manner.

"One evening I heard the most heart-rending screams and moans. I was told a mother had taken a child into a cave about a hundred yards from us and had laid it on its bed. A mortar shell entered the earth about it, crushing in the upper part of the

little sleeping head." (James Murfin, *Battlefields of the Civil War*, Colour Library Books Ltd., Surrey, England, 1988).

When you reach **Stop Number 10**, the Stockade Redan, drive straight ahead into the parking area; it will be in front of you, just before the road curves to the right.

The Stockade Redan:
This stockade was defended by units of General Martin Luther Smith's command. It guarded the Graveyard Road approaches to the city. It was close to 2 p.m. on the afternoon of May 19th when Sherman's divisions attacked the Confederate defenders here at the triangular shaped fortress known as the Stockade Redan. The Union troops fought their way under heavy cannon and rifle fire into the ravine surrounding the redan, and then up the slopes that led to the fort. A few of the Federal soldiers managed to make it as far as the ditch that protects the fort, but they were unable to scale the walls. These men were pinned down for the rest of the day and were only able to make their way back down the slopes to the Union line after darkness had fallen. During the action here on the 19th of May two Union soldiers, one a boy of only 14 years of age, earned the Congressional Medal of Honor for bravery on the field.

Sherman's divisions made a second attack on the redan three days later on May 22nd. Once again the attackers were met by a withering firestorm of cannon and rifle fire, and once again Sherman's troops were repulsed with heavy losses.

If you have the time you should leave your car in the parking area and take a walk. You will find plaques that describe the action and the Union positions located around the area. Perhaps you will be able to get a real feeling for the terrible events that occurred here on May 19th, and on May 22nd, 1863. It was one of the bloodiest actions of the war.

When you have finished your visit at the Stockade Redan, continue on along Confederate Avenue for about a mile until you reach the parking area at **Stop Number 11**. On your way toward the next stop, The Great Redoubt, you will pass the Missouri Memorial on your left, and the Arkansas Memorial to your right. The Missouri Memorial honors the soldiers of that state who fought for both sides, the North and the South. They are depicted here fighting for this very position. As you make your way along the road and up the hill you will soon see the Third Louisiana Redan to your left and the Great Redoubt to your right.

The Great Redoubt:

You will remember that the two great fortresses here at the center of the Confederate line of defense guarded the approaches to the city from the Jackson Road. It was close to this position that Generals Pemberton and Grant met to discuss terms for the surrender of the city. You can visit the interview site if you wish: it's just at the top of the grade to your left. If not, you should continue onward, bearing to your right. From the top of the Redoubt some 600 yards away to the east, you will be able to see the Battery De Golyer. You visited it earlier in the tour, where the 22 guns under the command of Captain De Golyer shelled this entire area.

As you drive on along the Confederate Avenue toward **Stop Number 12** you pass the Mississippi Memorial to your right. The monument is dedicated to the more than 4,600 soldiers of that state who fought here during the siege of Vicksburg.

Just beyond the Mississippi Memorial to the right is a statue of Lt. General John C. Pemberton. After the fall of Vicksburg General Pemberton was without a command; there was nothing available for a general officer of his exalted rank. So, rather than retire from the army altogether, he voluntarily resigned his three-star general's commission and fought throughout the rest of the war as a Lt. Colonel in the Confederate artillery.

The Second Texas Lunette:

Just past the statue of Confederate President Jefferson Davis to your right, you will see, again to your right, the Second Texas Lunette. A lunette is a crescent-shaped fort.

This one guarded the Southern Railroad of Mississippi to the South and the Baldwin Ferry Road. It was this position that came under attack from Union General McClernand. Opposing him here on the Confederate side was General Carter L. Stevenson. You might like to take a little time here to visit the statue of Jefferson Davis and the Lunette. When you have finished your time here, return to your vehicle and continue on along Confederate Avenue. Following the directional markers, turn right and proceed under the overpass, down the hill and then up again to the top of the hill to **Stop Number 13**.

The Railroad Redoubt:

This fort shared responsibility for guarding the Southern Railroad of Mississippi with the Second Texas Lunette. It was the only fort on the entire Confederate line of defense that was penetrated by the Union forces during the siege of the city. During the second Union assault on May 22nd, 1863, the walls of the fort were pierced by Federal cannon fire. The defenders took cover outside and behind the fort as the Federals entered the redoubt. Then, in a determined counter-attack, the Confederates swarmed back into the fort and drove the Union forces out.

You should take a few minutes here to visit the fort and the Texas Memorial. The monument was erected in 1961 and is dedicated to all the Texans who served during the siege. As you make your way along the road toward **Stop Number 14**, you will pass on your right a statue of Confederate General Stephen D. Lee. Lee – he was no relation to Robert E. Lee – was, in 1899, appointed to head the Vicksburg National Military Park Commission. And it was largely due to his efforts the present park here at Vicksburg came into being. He was actively involved in the project until his death 1908.

Fort Garrott:

The Confederate fort here at tour Stop Number 14 is named for Confederate Colonel I.W. Garrott. Garrott was mortally wounded while he was defending the fort. With an infantry

rifle at his shoulder he was hit by a minie ball fired by a
Union sharpshooter on June 17th; just hours before, a courier with news of his promotion to Brigadier General had
arrived at Vicksburg.

You might like take a minute or two to walk the area and
inspect the restored zig-zag trenches the union soldiers used
in their approach to the fort.

The last stop on your tour of the Vicksburg National Military
Park is Number 15. As you continue on along the road you
will be crossing from the Confederate defensive line back to
the Union line of battle and the positions commanded during
the siege of Vicksburg by General John A. McClernand.
Follow the tour directional markers until you reach the
parking area at **Stop Number 15**.

Hovey's Approach:
During the siege of Vicksburg the Union position here was held
by a full division of infantry under the command of General
Alvin P. Hovey. Hovey was a lawyer from Indiana and had
earlier distinguished himself at the battle of Champion Hill.
The trenches you see here were constructed in the classic zig-
zag configuration designed to offer the invading soldiers the
most protection, and minimize casualties, from cannon and rifle
fire as they approached the Confederate fort.

By July 2nd, 1863, Confederate General Pemberton and his
staff had come to the inevitable conclusion that their time was
running out, and that reinforcements from General Johnston
would not arrive in time to save the city. The effective strength
of the Confederate force defending Vicksburg had shrunk to less
than 19,000 against Grant's more than 75,000. They knew that
a determined attack by the Federal forces must be successful,
and so decided it would be better to arrange favorable terms of
surrender for themselves and for the city than to let it to fall to
Union force of arms. So, at 10:30 a.m., on the morning of July
3rd, under a flag of truce, General Bowen, an old friend of
General Grant, left the city with a letter from General Pemberton proposing an armistice to arrange terms of surrender.

On July 4th Grant paroled the Confederate army out of the city. The rank and file were allowed to keep only their personal possessions, the officers were allowed to keep one horse and their side-arms. The siege of Vicksburg was over. As a campaign Vicksburg had been the most effective and the most decisive of the war so far. And as a result, together with Union victory at Gettysburg only the day before on July 3rd, Federal fortunes and moral were flying high; and the Confederacy would never regain the military initiative.

Where to Stay, Things to Do in Vicksburg

Attractions (Including Bed & Breakfast Homes)

Anchuca: (tour and/or bed & breakfast) 1010 First East Street. 601-636-4931. Circa 1830. Opulent, gas-lighted, Greek Revival mansion. Magnificent period antiques and artifacts recreate the grandeur of yesterday.

Belle Fleur: 1123 South Street. 601-638-6311. Circa 1873. Vicksburg's finest example of a five-bay galleried cottage. 30-minute tour.

Cedar Grove Mansion: (tour and/or bed & breakfast) 2300 Washington Street. 601-636-2800. Circa 1840-1858. Greek Revival Mansion overlooking Mississippi River. Four acres of gardens. 30-minute tour.

The Ceres Plantation: (Tour and/or bed & breakfast) 150 Ceres Blvd. (11 miles east of city). 601-631-0547. Circa 1820. Beautiful two-story plantation home. Period antiques and artifacts. Available for parties, receptions, and weekend dining.

The Corners: (tour and/or bed & breakfast) 601 Klein Street. 601-636-7421. Circa 1873. Victorian mansion. Period antiques. May be rented for weddings and receptions. 30 minute tour.

The Duff Green Mansion: (tour and/or bed & breakfast) 1114 First East Street. 601-636-6968. Circa 1856. Hospital for Confederate and Union soldiers. Large ballroom available for private parties and receptions. Can accommodate the handicapped. 30-minute tour.

The Martha Vick House: 1300 Grove Street. 601-638-7036. Circa 1830. The last Vick family home in Vicksburg. Elegant 18th and early 19th century furnishings and a large collection of French paintings.

Mcraven Tour Home: 1445 Harrison Street. 601-636-1663. Featured in *National Geographic Magazine* as "The Time Capsule of the South." Three acres of gardens once used as a Confederate campsite. 1 1/2 hour tour.

Mississippi River Hydro-Jet Tour: City Waterfront. 601-638-5443. Daily March 1st through November 15th. "Jet into history." 40-mile jet boat river tour.

The Old Court House Museum-Eva W. Davis Memorial: 1008 Cherry Street. 601-636-0741. Circa 1858. Has hosted many great Americans. Guided tour.

Toys And Soldiers: A museum and gift shop. 1100 Cherry Street. 601-638-1986. Over 30,000 old and new toy soldiers.

U.S. Army Engineer Waterways Experiment Station: 3909 Halls Ferry Road. 601-634-2502. Largest R&D facility in Corps of Engineers. Nature trail and picnic area.

Vicksburg Historic Tours: Tour leaves daily from Park Inn International. Includes National Military Park, historic Vicksburg and one Southern Mansion. February to mid-November, 9:30 a.m.-1:00 p.m. Reservations advisable. 601-638-8888.

Yesterday's Children Antique Doll Museum: 1104 Washington Street. 601-638-0650. Over 1,000 dolls on display. Gift shop.

Hotels

Hillcrest Motel: 4503 Highway 80 East. 601-638-1491. Swimming pool. Visa/Mastercard.

Beechwood Inn: 4449 Highway 80 East. 601-636-2257. AARP. Visa/Mastercard AE, Discover.

Comfort Inn: 3959 East Clay Street. 601-634-8438. Swimming pool, AARP, AAA. Visa/Mastercard, AE, Discover, Diners Club..

Holiday Inn of Vicksburg: 3330 Clay Street. 601-636-4551. Swimming pool. AARP, major credit cards accepted.

Hampton Inn of Vicksburg: 3330 Clay Street. 601-636-6100. Swimming pool. Visa/Mastercard, AE, Discover, Diners Club.

Days Inn-West: 2 Pemberton Place. 601-634-1622. Swimming pool, AARP. Visa/Mastercard, AE, Discover, Diners Club.

Camping

Vicksburg Battlefield Campground: 4407 & I-20. Frontage Road. 601-636-2025. 80 campsites. No credit cards. Full hook-ups and pull-throughs, laundry, rest rooms, store, motel cabins, covered meeting areas, playground, pool, open year round.

Leisure Living Campground: Route 4, (On Eagle Lake 13 miles north on Hwy. 61, then left on 465 West 15 miles). 601-279-4259. 30 campsites. No credit cards. Full hook-ups and pull-throughs available, lake fishing, store 1/4 mile.

Chapter 12

Chickamauga

September, 1863

The Chickamauga National Battlefield is near Chattanooga, Tennessee at Ft. Oglethorpe in northwest Georgia on
Highway 27. It can easily be reached from either I-24, going
west from Chatanooga toward Nashville, or via I-75, going
southeast from Chatanooga toward Atlanta. It can also be
reached going north toward Chatanooga from Lafayette GA
on Highway 27. The park is open daily from 8 a.m. to 4:45
p.m. during the winter months and from 8 a.m. to 5:45 p.m.
during the summer. There is no charge for admission.
Horses and bicycles can be rented locally and picnicking is
allowed in the park. Phone 423-752-5213.

The battle of Chickamauga
in northwest Georgia was
the climax of the Union's
first invasion of Confederate territory. By September
1863 things were beginning
to look desperate for the
Southern cause. Robert E.
Lee's military domination
of the eastern theater had
ended with his catastrophic
defeat at Gettysburg. He
was now, though not by
choice, fighting the war on
the defensive; struggling
hard, but in vain, to regain
at least some of his former
initiative.

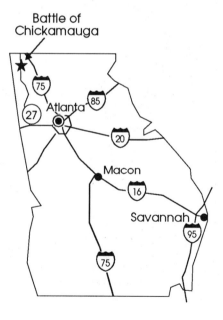

Battle of
Chickamauga

Chickamauga Battlefield
Chickamauga, Walker County, Georgia

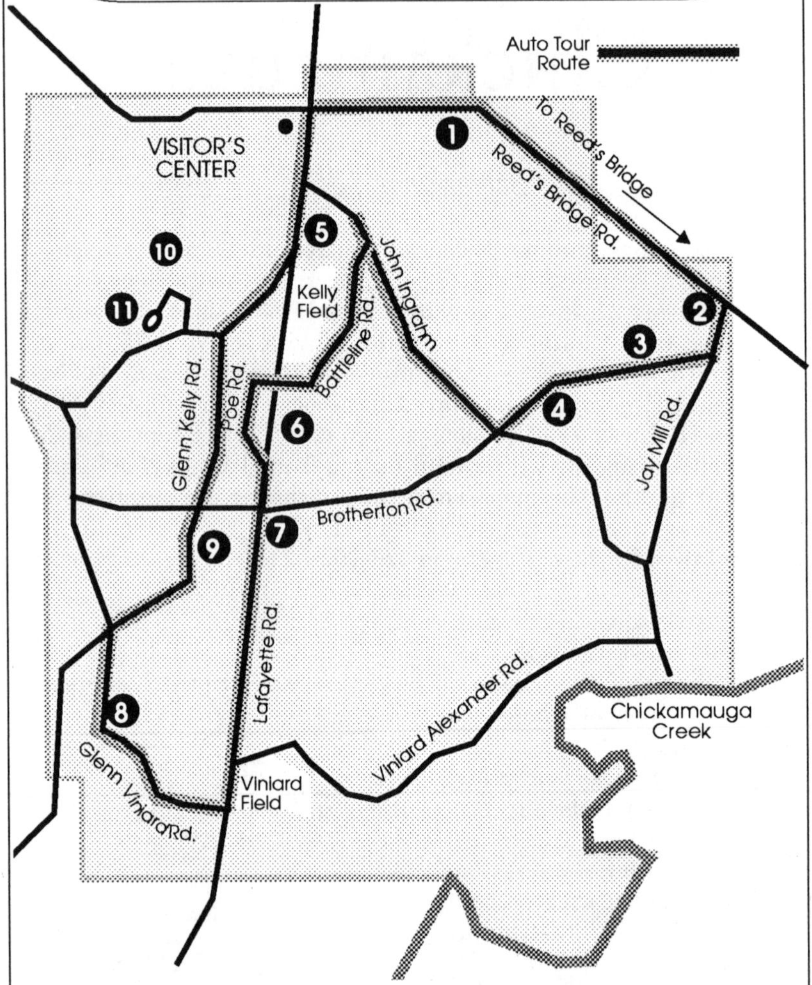

Auto Tour Route

VISITOR'S CENTER

To Reed's Bridge

Reed's Bridge Rd.

John Ingrahm

Kelly Field

Battleline Rd.

Glenn Kelly Rd.

Poe Rd.

Jay Mill Rd.

Brotherton Rd.

Lafayette Rd.

Viniard Alexander Rd.

Chickamauga Creek

Glenn Viniard Rd.

Viniard Field

1. Tenn. Artillery
2. Jay's Mill Site
3. Bragg's Headquarters
4. Winfrey Field
5. Battleline Rd.
6. Mix up in the Union
7. Brotherton House
8. Wilder Tower
9. Rosecran's Headquarters
10. Snodgrass House
11. Snodgrass Hill

Visitor Center, Chickamauga.

In the West, the Confederate garrison at Vicksburg had fallen at last to General Grant, thus freeing him and his Army of the Tennessee to turn their attentions elsewhere. After Generals Rosecrans and Braxton Bragg had fought themselves to a standstill at Stones River it had taken both armies more than six months to recover from the dreadful mauling each had given the other. If the Confederacy was to survive, a major victory was needed, and soon. Now, at last, the Federal Army of the Cumberland was on the move, and the Confederate Army of Tennessee was maneuvering into position close to Lafayette, Georgia, a few miles to the south of Chattanooga, Tennessee. The two great armies were heading inexorably for a cataclysmic confrontation.

They had met before during the closing days of 1862. Confederate General Braxton Bragg had retreated from Murfreesboro on January 2nd, 1863 after the battle of Stones River, claiming a Confederate victory, and by September his 43,000-strong Army of Tennessee was defending the key railhead and river crossing at Chattanooga. Union General William S. Rosecrans, with his

Army of the Cumberland also claiming victory at Stones River, knew that Chattanooga was the key to the invasion. If he could take the city he would throw open the gates to the heart of the Confederacy. Georgia and the South would be his for the taking. Early in September Rosecrans and The Army of the Cumberland, now 60,000 strong, in a series of brilliant maneuvers crossed the Tennessee river well to the west of Chattanooga, forcing the Confederate army to retreat southward. Rosecrans, almost unopposed, occupied the city on September 9th. Bragg then concentrated his forces at Lafayette, Georgia, some 26 miles to the south. Realizing that a major confrontation was inevitable, he called for reinforcements. These came by way of Mississippi and Virginia. Robert E. Lee, concerned that if Bragg should be defeated the South would be left wide open to invasion, sent General James Longstreet with his 1st Corps of 15,000 men to Bragg's aid.

Union intelligence knew at once that Longstreet had disappeared from Virginia. But for some reason they didn't bother to tell Rosecrans who, by now believing Bragg's force to be scattered, had split his own forces into three separate units in order to hunt them down. Bragg's Army of Tennessee, however, was flushed with reinforcements and now numbered more than 66,000. Twice Bragg's commanders managed to lure units of Rosecrans' army into traps, and twice they allowed them to slip away. Bragg was enraged; Rosecrans was more than a little alarmed. Rosecrans recalled his forces and concentrated them at Gordon's Mill just south of Chickamauga Creek. Bragg, frustrated, ordered his army across the creek and into position between the Federals and their base at Chattanooga. By the evening of September 18th both armies were drawn up in two parallel lines, screened from one another by dense woodland. And so the stage was set. More than 124,000 men would soon be engaged here in one of the bloodiest battles of the Civil War.

As you tour the battlefield you will find hundreds of cast-iron tablets located at strategic positions all over the battlefield. These describe the precise movements of every brigade and division that fought here during the two days of September 19th and 20th. To tour the battlefield, leave the Visitor

4th Indiana Battery, on Battle Line Road.

Center and turn left on Highway 27, go to the traffic signals and turn right on Reed's Bridge Road to **Stop 1A** where you will find a monument to the Tennessee Artillery. From there you proceed along the road to **Stop 1B** at the northern end of the battlefield, the site of what was once Jay's Mill and the point where the battle began.

The battlefield at Chickamauga has changed very little over the last century and a half. The open fields, as few of them as there are, were much the same then as they are today, and dense woods still cover most of the area just as they did in 1863. Reed's Bridge Road then was a simple dirt road through the dense woodland.

Stand for a moment or two on the roadside and look across the small field toward the woods. The field was much bigger then. Let your imagination wander back to the morning of September 19, 1863. The time is about 7:30. There's a light ground mist over the forest; the weak sunlight is just beginning to filter through the treetops. The field in front of you is swarming with Confederate horse-soldiers, some on foot tending to their mounts, some still on horseback after returning from an early morning patrol. The whole area is filled with the hustle and bustle of a thousand men preparing to do battle.

Through the woods behind you a full division of General George Thomas's Federal infantry under the command of General John Brannon is making its way quietly through the trees. Their boots make little noise on the soft surface. Only the odd clank of one piece of equipment upon another and the soft whisper of sporadic conversation disturbs the early morning stillness. Then, as they break out of the trees they realize that they've run slap into a division of Confederate cavalry commanded by no less a person than Nathan Bedford Forrest himself.

Both forces are taken by surprise; confusion reigns as troops on both sides rush around in all directions; soldiers on each side falling over one another as they try to take advantage of what little cover there is. There's no time for the Federals to retreat back into the woods and there's no time for Forrest's Confederates to organize and get mounted. Within seconds the air is filled with the crash of gunfire, the screams of wounded men and dying horses, and the yells of officers trying to manufacture order out of chaos. The mist now mingled with gunsmoke adds to the confusion. Suddenly in the midst of the confusion a tall, bearded man appears in the Confederate ranks. He wears a belted, knee-length Confederate coat and carries a cavalry saber in one hand, a pistol in the other, and there's a second pistol stuck in the belt at his waist. Within minutes, by the sheer weight of his personality, General Forrest has restored order to his beleaguered cavalry. His men lie face down in the dew-sodden grass and steadily return the Federals' fire. But, caught in the open as his troops are, the Confederate losses are heavy. In less than an hour Forrest has lost more than a quarter of his command. And so the Battle for Chickamauga had begun.

General Thomas, realizing that Brannon was involved in a major conflict, called in fresh troops. Bragg, headquartered in the woods just to the south of here did the same. Five divisions of Confederate infantry reached the scene of the battle first and charging in from the left of Jay's Mill drove Brannon's force back across the clearing and into the woods. As the morning wore on more troops from both sides were committed to the battle until the conflict was extended from Jay's Mill over a five mile front.

From Jay's Mill turn right onto the Brotherton Road and proceed along it for about a quarter of a mile until you reach **Stop Number 1C**, the site of Bragg's Confederate headquarters.

All day the battle flowed back and forth through these woods as Bragg struck time and again at the Federal divisions, only to be beaten back each time as Rosecrans committed fresh troops in reply. Imagine, if you can, what it must have been like for the troops involved in the struggle; fighting not only each other but the dense woods as well. Amid the confusion most of the commanders had little or no idea where they or the enemy were. The lines overlapped and the fighting, much of it hand-to-hand, became confused.

Monument to 10th Wisconsin Infantry.

As the two great armies clashed again and again all day long on Saturday, the 19th, the battle raged until at last the superior striking power of the Confederate force began to take its toll. Union General Thomas, in a desperate effort to counter the ever-increasing numbers of Confederates attacking his left flank, diverted more and more of his Federal units northward.

This had the adverse effect of opening a gap in the Federal line between his own command and the center of General Rosecrans' line. But Bragg was determined to outflank his adversaries to the north, and so he didn't see the opportunity opening up before him. Fortunately for him, Confederate General Alexander P. Stewart, marching north in command of a division of Simon Buckner's corps, did see it. He turned and broke through the Federal line at the Brotherton house. Confederate General John Bell Hood quickly followed up with two more divisions and smashed his way through at the Viniard Fields. The Confederate forces were now in control of the Lafayette Road and the main lines of communication to Chattanooga. The sheer momentum of the drive threatened to overrun General Rosecrans' Federal field headquarters – located at a place called the Widow Glenn's. Realizing he was now in terrible trouble, General Rosecrans screamed at his men over the roar of the battle that they were to hold the line at all costs. His men responded, and in a frenzy of desperation fought like a pack of cornered wolves.

Once again General Bragg failed to take advantage of the opportunity and before long Rosecrans was able to bring in fresh Federal units to seal the gap in his line; Stewart and Hood had no alternative but to withdraw back across the Lafayette Road

As the day drew to a close, Bragg decided to make one more push against the Federal left, here at Stop 1C, and called in his reserves. Brigadier General Patrick Cleburne relieved the battle-weary Confederates and opened up a mile-wide front extending to the left and right through the woods in front of you.

> Now you can proceed about a half-mile on along the Brotherton Road until you come to the next stop, **Number 1-D**, at Winfrey Fields; pull off the road when you see the sign that indicates the Baldwin Monument.

It was here under a darkening sky that Cleburne's vanguard smashed through the woods and caught the Federals as they were moving back to a safer position. All along the line of woods the Union troops were beaten back under the fury of Cleburne's attack. In near-darkness the two armies collided in fierce hand-to-hand combat. An entire Federal brigade, the 77th Pennsylvania, was surrounded and captured, but so complete was the confusion, and so dark the battlefield, that nearly all the captured Union soldiers were able to slip away under cover of darkness and rejoin their units. In less than an hour it was so dark that the two great armies were fighting almost by instinct with only the muzzle flashes of the enemy fire to guide their aim. Cleburne had no alternative but to end the day and withdraw from the field. General Thomas, too, his men exhausted, pulled back almost a mile to what is now known as Battle Line Road on the wooded edge of Kelly Field; it's marked as **Stop Number 2** on the tour route.

> From here, at the Baldwin Monument, turn right onto Alexander Bridge Road and proceed northward until you see the Stop 2 marker. As you proceed along Alexander Bridge Road you will find a marker that points to a single grave. This is the only identified grave on the entire battlefield. In the grave lie the remains of Private John Ingram of the Georgia Volunteers. All across the battlefield the dead were buried in unmarked, shallow trenches. Private Ingram was a close friend of the Reed family, who buried him and maintained the gravesite.

At the close of Battle on Saturday night, the 19th of September, neither side could claim to have engineered an advantage. Clearly, the Confederate army, if only by weight of numbers, was in better shape than its Federal counterpart. During the night Lt. General James Longstreet arrived from Virginia to reinforce Bragg's already s superior force. Bragg now believed he held the upper hand and, overnight, developed a plan whereby he would hurl his entire army at the Federal lines as soon as it became light enough to see. He gave command of the Confederate right to General Leonidas Polk, and command of the left to James Longstreet.

Throughout the night the Federal army, now compressed into a three-mile front and so on the defensive, toiled – felling trees and building breastworks in the hope that they might be able to hold the enemy forces at bay.

Along the road in front of you, you will see a line of monuments commemorating the beginning of more than a mile of log breastworks built by Union troops during the night of Saturday 19th and early morning Sunday 20th. This is Battle Line Road and it was here that General George H. Thomas dug in on the morning of the second day of battle.

General Polk, commanding the Confederate right, had been ordered by Bragg to attack the Federal positions at dawn. Dawn came and went without a shot being fired. Another hour went by and still Polk did not attack. By now Bragg must have been frantic in his frustration. He sent a messenger to Polk to find out what had gone wrong and urging him to make his move. The story goes that the messenger found Polk seated in a rocking chair reading a local newspaper. The messenger conveyed to Polk Bragg's anxiety about the lateness of the hour and the fact that Polk had yet to mount the expected attack. Polk is said to have replied: *"Do tell General Bragg that my heart is overflowing with anxiety for the attack; over-flowing with anxiety, Suh."* It was not until 9 a.m., some four hours after dawn had broken, that Polk eventually mounted his attack. The delay was to cost him dearly, for General Thomas was able to make good use of the extra time so unexpectedly allotted him. All through the hours of the early morning his men toiled on, building and strengthening the breastworks along the line of the coming battle. Why was Polk so late? To this day, nobody can say for sure. The question remains one of the great mysteries of the Civil War.

When finally Polk did commence his attack he commanded some 16 brigades stretched out along a two-mile front from here at Stop Number 2 through the woods to your left and on across the Alexander Bridge Road.

The Confederate attack began here and slowly spread southward as Polk committed brigade after brigade to charge the enemy breastworks. Bragg's plan was to increase the pressure slowly all along the Federal front. He felt that by so doing he could force the Federal commander to commit reinforcements to strengthen any weak spot that might develop in the line. This would require Thomas to pull those troops in from somewhere else, thus creating a major weakness – or so Bragg believed. If this happened, then Bragg would be able to smash through the Federal lines and drive the enemy from the field. It was a sound plan based upon the fact that Bragg held a decided superiority of numbers. However, things did not go according to plan. First, Polk's assault was made along too narrow a front, and in fact was almost a frontal attack. Second, the Federal breastworks, stronger now from more than four extra hours of construction, proved to be a formidable obstruction. Wave after wave of Confederate infantry charged the barricades only to fall back, decimated by withering Federal fire. Thomas's barricades proved to be impregnable. One of the Confederate brigades in the futile attacks was a unit of Kentuckians commanded by Benjamin H. Helm, president Lincoln's brother-in-law. Helm was killed in the woods behind you while trying to rally what was left of his command after they had been beaten back across the road. In less than an hour of fighting that Sunday morning Bragg lost four of his brigade commanders; three were killed and a fourth was captured by the enemy.

Despite the heavy losses, the superior numbers of the Confederate army began to take effect. Again and again, after each repulsed assault they reformed and renewed their attack. In contrast, and under heavy pressure, Thomas was playing a real-life game of chess. Time after time he moved individual units of his force; first left, then right, then left again as he countered each new Confederate attack. Time and again he called upon Rosecrans to send him reinforcements. Division after division was moved in haste to Thomas's line of battle; so many men were moved to his position that by mid-day he was in command of more than two thirds of the entire Federal army. And still the breastworks held.

Even though his forces were unable to breach the Federal line, Bragg by now held a decided advantage; he had forced Rosecrans and Thomas to commit the bulk of their forces to the defense of one wing. So, while Polk licked his wounds and regrouped his exhausted brigades, Bragg ordered James Longstreet into the fray. But Longstreet, after traveling for most of the night, was not yet ready to do battle, a fact that was to prove critical in the hours ahead.

You should now follow along Battle Line Road until you arrive at **Stop Number 3**.

It was here that John Brannon's Federal division held a camouflaged junction in the Union line. They were the men, you will remember, whose encounter with Confederate General Nathan Bedford Forrest's cavalry on the morning of Saturday the 19th began the conflict. Now they were being held as a reserve unit at the right center of the Federal line. To Brannon's north on Battle Line Road was Major General Joseph Reynolds, to his south was Brigadier General Thomas Wood.

At 10:30 that morning a Federal courier was riding past this position to General Rosecrans with yet another call from General Thomas for reinforcements. As he rode by he looked into the woods, but for some reason he failed to observe Brannon's force. Thinking that Brannon must be out of position, he conveyed that information to Rosecrans. This would have meant that a gap had opened up in the Federal line. That gap would have to be filled, fast. And so Rosecrans, without bothering to check the accuracy of the information, immediately ordered General Wood to close up on Reynolds as fast as possible. Wood, even though he knew Brannon was still holding his position, like the good General he was, carried out Rosecrans' order. He moved his men north and left, leaving a long line of breastworks in front of the Brotherton house undefended. So, in order to fill one gap that didn't exist, Rosecrans had created an even bigger one, one that was almost 500 yards wide. Wood began to move his men out at 11 o'clock, at the same time Confederate General James Longstreet was about to begin a large-scale assault up the Brotherton Road close to the spot at the Brotherton Farm where the Confederates had broken through the Federal lines the previous day.

You can now proceed along the Lafayette Road to **Stop Number 4** and the Brotherton Farm.

The Brotherton Cabin.

You should now be standing beside the log cabin that is the Brotherton House. At the time of the battle this cabin was the home of George Brotherton. He had moved here three years earlier in 1860. Two of his sons served with Bragg's army in the battle. One of them, Tom, when Longstreet called for a scout, is said to have volunteered saying, *"It's a sorry lad that won't fight for his own home."* Tom's sister Adaline, too, was a hero. She returned to the cabin each night of the battle to attend to the wounded, Confederate and Union. What once was the farm stretches away in front of you.

At precisely 11 o'clock that Sunday morning Longstreet with 23,000 men surged out of the woods behind you. His strategy, in contrast to General Polk's brigade-by-brigade assaults earlier in the day, was to smash his way through the Federal line by sheer weight of numbers. He concentrated five full divisions here at the Brotherton Farm in a wedge-shaped formation extending over a half-mile front.

You will remember that Rosecrans had ordered General Wood to move his force to the north in order to fill a gap in the Federal line that did not exist, and to support General Reynolds. Wood was already on the move behind Brannon's position when Longstreet began his assault. When the attack began the Confederate troops streamed through the gap in the Federal line here at the Brotherton Farm and Brannon found himself under attack on three sides at once: the front, flank and rear. Within minutes his men were in full retreat. Wood, still on the move, also was caught in Longstreet's onslaught and his two divisions were soon in full flight as Longstreet turned right and began to clear out the Federal line. Chaos reigned supreme; the sky was hidden beneath great clouds of gunsmoke; the noise became unbearable as the thunder of cannon fire, the crash of musketry, the cries of the wounded and the dying, and the triumphant cheers of the victorious Confederate soldiers rang out across the fields and through the woods as they pursued the now totally disorganized Federal units. The entire Union army, including Rosecrans himself, was driven in headlong flight from the battlefield back toward McFarland's Gap and on to safety in Chattanooga. It was the turning point in the battle: Longstreet's charge is thought by many to have been the most effective battlefield offensive of the Civil War.

Was Longstreet's success due to a lucky chance? Perhaps it was, but Longstreet was a methodical and thorough commander. Had he begun his attack when ordered to do so, Wood's divisions would still have been in place behind the heavily fortified breastworks and the outcome of the charge might have been very different. But Longstreet felt he was not yet fully prepared and so he delayed his assault until everything was in place or, perhaps more to the point even though he didn't know it, until everything on the Federal side was out of place. The outcome of the battle of Chickamauga was no longer in doubt. Longstreet had effectively cut the Federal army in half and was now poised to set about its complete annihilation. But the day was not yet over.

Follow Lafayette Road to the junction of the Glenn-Viniard Road and then turn right and continue on until you reach **Stop Number 6**. The hill in front of you with a tower on the crest is close to the site of The Widow Glenn's Farm.

Wilder Tower, Widow Glenn's Farm.

Following Longstreet's charge, the rest of the Federal right did no better than Rosecrans, Brannon, and Wood. Confederate General Thomas Hindman coordinated his attack to the south of the Brotherton Farm, thus taking the two remaining Federal divisions by surprise and sweeping them aside as the Confederate juggernaught continued its devastating attack. One Confederate brigade, however, under the command of General A.M. Manigault somehow managed to become detached from Hindman's main force and wandered away to the south. Manigault soon found himself looking at the slopes of the hill before you. The crest of the hill, he decided, offered a commanding field of fire over the retreating Union army, but it was occupied by three regiments of Federal infantry, under the command of Colonel John Wilder who had deployed them to cover the Federal retreat. Wilder's men were equipped with the new Spencer repeating rifle and for almost an hour they threw down a devastating hail of fire on the advancing Confederates. Manigault's assault on the hill was repulsed.

Longstreet, always on the lookout, and ever ready to counter any reversal of fortune, spotted the battle raging on the slopes at the Widow Glenn's farm and sent in the last of his reserves. Wilder, on the crest of the hill, too, was well able to assess this new situation and, realizing his position was hopeless, decided to make a strategic withdrawal. His action at the Widow Glenn's, however, had bought General Thomas enough time to form a new line of defense on a ridge just to the north of here at the Snodgrass cabin; George H. Thomas was about to become a legend.

Wilder's success against a vastly superior force was entirely due to the new Spencer repeating rifle. The Spencer was not standard issue in the Union Army at that time and Wilder's men had purchased them with their own money. Their investment had paid off handsomely. The withering firepower of the new weapon from the crest of the hill must have had the same sort of effect as the machine gun years later. Longstreet, so it is said, not knowing the Spencer was in use that day, thought that an entire Federal corps was defending the hill, judging from the steady and continuous racket of fire. The tower you see at the top of the hill was dedicated to Wilder's memory in 1903 by veterans of his command.

The Glenn-Kelly Road:
This is **Stop Number 7** on the battlefield tour and you are now standing on the edge of the fields behind the Brotherton Farm, the scene of Longstreet's Confederate breakthrough. It was just a little way further along this road that Confederate General Bushrod Johnson, spearheading Longstreet's charge, attacked the Federal position of General Woods from the rear, and so triggered the beginning of the end for Rosecrans and his Army of the Cumberland. Rosecrans himself was, at this time, entrenched in his field headquarters on the top of the small hill just 600 yards away to your left.

Following closely behind Johnson, Hindman's division took advantage of the confusion in the Federal ranks and began to roll up the entire Federal right flank; Woods and Brannon's divisions were swept away by a veritable avalanche of Confederate death and destruction. All across the fields in front of you thousands upon thousands of Union infantry turned and fled as

Hindman methodically advanced behind a curtain of cannon and musket fire.

Charles Dana, Abraham Lincoln's Assistant Secretary of War, was observing the action from Rosecrans' field headquarters and described the action as follows: *"I saw our lines break away like leaves before the wind. The headquarters around me disappeared; the whole right of the army had apparently been routed. I was swept away with Rosecrans' staff and was lost among the rabble."* And swept away they were. Rosecrans had no alternative but to follow his fleeing divisions and make his way as best he could back to Chattanooga and safety.

Longstreet regrouped and reformed. He now was poised for one final massive push to destroy the once proud Army of the Cumberland. His jubilant forces prepared to advance on the Federal left and General Thomas's divisions; all that stood between him and his objective were the pitiful remains of Wood's and Brannon's decimated divisions now entrenched on the crest of Snodgrass Hill about a mile away to the northwest of here.

General Thomas, with Rosecrans now driven from the field, assumed command of what was left of the Army of the Cumberland. Quickly assessing his situation, he realized the battle was lost, and that any hopes for saving the army now lay with him. He would, he decided, have to fight a rearguard action in order to buy precious time so that the retreating Union divisions could leave the field and regain the safety of the old Confederate defensive positions in Chattanooga. He realized, too, that Longstreet now posed the greatest threat. Leaving the rest of his command still in the breastworks facing Polk on Battle Line Road, he moved his headquarters, joined Wood and Brannon on the crest of Snodgrass Hill, and prepared to meet the inevitable Confederate onslaught.

Longstreet by now was confident of a total Confederate victory and requested that Bragg send him reinforcements so that he could capitalize on his breakthrough. But Bragg refused, saying that Polk's Confederate brigades had been so severely dealt

The Snodgrass Cabin.

with during their continuous assault on Thomas's breastworks on Battle Line Road they had little fight left in them.

Continue along the Glenn-Kelly Road and follow the tour markers until you reach Snodgrass Hill and **Stop Number 8-A**. The small cabin half way up the hill was built in 1848 and at the time of the battle was owned by George Washington Snodgrass. All through the first day of battle the cabin was a haven for refugees, but as the fighting approached on the second day, Snodgrass and his family had to leave and the cabin became a Federal field hospital. General Thomas pitched his headquarters tents in the fields just to the rear of the cabin; you can find the exact spot at the bottom of the hill; it's marked by a pyramid of cannonballs.

The fighting for Snodgrass Hill began just a little after one o'clock in the afternoon of the 20th. The first assault against the hill came up the slopes from below the cabin and through the trees behind you. General Wood, with three Federal brigades, was first into action and hammered the Confederates back down the hill. And so began the last desperate stand of the now rag-tag right flank of the Army of the Cumberland and its involuntary commander, General George H. Thomas.

As you stand on the crest of Snodgrass Hill, **Stop Number 8**, and look down the slope toward the Brotherton Farm, and toward the west and Horseshoe Ridge it should be easy for you to imagine the drama as it unfolded that fateful afternoon. By 1:30 in the afternoon General Wood was holding a defensive position on the top of the hill, and General Brannon held the right flank on the crest of Horseshoe Ridge, which is an extension of Snodgrass Hill just to the west.

All through the afternoon the never-ending onslaught of Longstreet's divisions up Snodgrass Hill continued. And all through the afternoon General Thomas personally conducted the defense of the hill. A message from one of his staff officers to General Rosecrans read: *"Thomas is standing like a rock!"* Thus a legend was born and George H. Thomas became "The Rock of Chickamauga." The staff officer was none other than James Garfield, who later became the 20th President of the United States.

As the afternoon wore on, inevitably, the persistence of the Confederate offensive and the weight of their vastly superior numbers began to take its toll and Thomas's lines became stretched dangerously thin. Longstreet was now within an ace of achieving a second major breakthrough, enabling him to fall upon the main body of the Army of the Cumberland still fighting gallantly at Battle Line Road. It was at this point that Thomas observed a column of soldiers marching toward his rear from the north. Through the fog of gunsmoke and the clouds of dust he was unable to make out either the color of their uniforms or the regimental flags and pennants that hung loose against their staffs for the lack a breeze to stir them.

General Thomas, his heart in his mouth, waited with baited breath, knowing full well that if this were a Confederate column the day would be lost. He knew that it couldn't possibly be a Federal column; there were none left on the battlefield that could be coming from that direction. But it was a Federal column. Union General Gordon Granger had taken the initiative and, acting without orders, had moved his union reserves from Rossville to join the battle at Thomas's side. General James Steedman was leading the advance.

At 11 o'clock that morning General Granger, headquartered in an open field on the Ringgold Road, almost beside himself with impatience, had climbed with General J.S. Fullerton to the top of a nearby hayrick. General Fullerton describes what happened next.

"We sat there for ten minutes watching and listening. Then Granger jumped up, thrust his glass into its case, and exclaimed with an oath: 'I am going to Thomas, orders or no orders.' I replied: 'It may bring disaster to the army and to you a court-martial.'

'There's nothing in front now but ragtag, bobtail cavalry,' he replied. 'Don't you see Bragg is piling his whole army on Thomas? I am going to his assistance.'

"Thomas was nearly four miles away. The day had now grown very warm, yet the troops moved rapidly over the narrow road, which was covered ankle-deep with dust that rose in suffocating clouds. Completely enveloped in it, the moving column swept along like a desert sandstorm. Two miles from the point of starting, and three-quarters of a mile from the left of the road, the enemy's skirmishers and a section of artillery opened fire upon us from an open wood. This force had worked its way round Thomas's left, and was then partly in his rear. Granger halted to feel them. Soon becoming convinced that it was only a large party of observation, he again started his column moving and pushed rapidly forward.

"A little further on we were met by a staff-officer of General Thomas to discover whether we were friends or enemies; he did not know from whence friends could be coming, and the enemy appeared to be approaching from all directions. All of this shattered Army of the Cumberland left on the field was with Thomas;

but not more than one fourth of army who went into battle at the opening were there. . . .

"Granger quickly sent Aleshire's battery of three-inch rifle guns to Thomas's left to assist in repelling another assault about to be made on the Kelly farm front. Whitaker and Mitchell's brigades under Steedman were wheeled into position and projected against the enemy in the gorge and on the ridge. With ringing cheers they advanced in two lines by double-quick – over open fields, through weeds waist-high, through a little valley and then up the ridge."

At the same time as Granger's reserves were moving into position to the north, Confederate generals Hindman and Bushrod Johnson with an overwhelming force were marching on Thomas's rear along Horseshoe Ridge from the west. Suddenly, General Steedman's vanguard, with Steedman himself carrying the battle flag, came charging up the back slopes of Snodgrass Hill. Taking the approaching Confederate force by surprise, he threw them back in disarray, down the slopes of the ridge. The Confederate breakthrough had been stopped, at least for the moment.

The hour by now was getting late, but Longstreet refused to give up his goal of a total Confederate victory. Calling in the last of his reserve units, he mounted a devastating new offensive against Federal lines along the crest of Snodgrass Hill. Thomas, sensing that the next several hours would be crucial to the retreating union forces, ordered his men to stand fast at all costs. Federal cannon were triple-loaded with canister. Infantry men hunkered down behind the hastily erected breastworks and prepared to "hold this ground or go to heaven from it." The carnage they wrought upon the advancing Confederate battle lines was terrible to behold. Time and again the Federal defenders threw back the decimated Confederate battalions, and time and again Longstreet regrouped and reformed his gallant troops and threw them back up the hill into the jaws of death.

Ammunition on the crest of the hill dwindled to the point where the defenders were reduced to scavenging among the dead for the few remaining cartridges. Brannon's division, its ammunition completely exhausted, fixed bayonets and charged the advancing Confederate lines through a firestorm of minie balls and cannon fire. It was the darkest hour for General Thomas and his thin blue line atop the crest of Snodgrass Hill. Without any hope of reinforcement, he realized that his position was hopeless. And so, taking advantage of a momentary lull in the Confederate onslaught, he determined to make a fighting withdrawal.

By the time the Confederate forces crested the hill the sun had already dipped below the horizon, and "The Rock of Chickamauga" and his gallant force were gone. Thomas had done all he could. He had bought the beleaguered remnants of the Army of the Cumberland, including what was left of the main force that had been fighting all day at Battle Line Road, enough time to pull back and retreat to Chattanooga. The battle of Chickamauga was over. It was a costly but stunning victory for the Confederacy; the threatened Union offensive into Georgia had been stopped.

Bragg had sustained more than 18,000 casualties. Rosecrans had lost more than 16,000 men, 57 pieces of artillery and 24,000 stands of arms. The combined casualties on both sides totaled more than 34,000. The battle for Chickamauga is claimed by many to have been the the Civil War's bloodiest.

Where to Stay, Things to Do

See Chattanooga in the following chapter.

Chapter 13

Chattanooga & Lookout Mountain

November, 1863

The National Battlefield at Point Park is on Lookout Mountain in Chatanooga, Tennessee. It can easily be reached either from the Brown's Ferry exit off I-24 (on the west side of Chatanooga heading east from Nashville), or from the Broad Street exit off I-24 close to the city center (going west from Knoxville and Atlanta). The park is open daily from 8 a.m. to 4:45 p.m. during the winter, and to 5:45 in the summer. There is no charge for admission and picnicking is allowed in the park. Phone 423-752-5213.

After their disastrous defeat at Chickamauga the Army of the Cumberland fell back toward Chattanooga. Confederate General Braxton Bragg now had the opportunity to pursue the beaten and demoralized Federal army and destroy it once and for all. General James Longstreet insisted that they should move upon the beleaguered Federal force without delay. *"We must move now. Every hour is worth ten thousand men,"* entreated Confederate Cavalry General Nathan Bedford For-

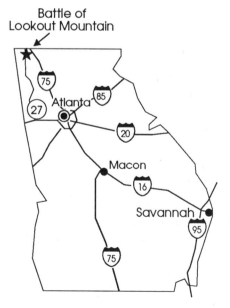

Battle of Lookout Mountain

The view from Lookout Mountain.

rest. Even the tardy Leonidas Polk tried to persuade the Confederate commander to take the initiative. But Bragg was unsure of himself and, complaining that his force was in disarray, he ignored the advice of his generals and refused to take advantage of the situation. Instead of mounting an immediate pursuit he decided to delay the action in the hope that General Rosecrans would abandon Chattanooga and head north. He was to be sadly disappointed, for by the evening of Monday, September 21st the last of General George H. Thomas's corps, the hindmost element of the Federal rearguard, was back in Chattanooga and the entire Army of the Cumberland once again was safely entrenched inside the city's one-time Confederate fortifications.

It was late in the afternoon of September 23rd when the first Confederate brigades under the command of General Polk crested the brow of Missionary Ridge, and later still when Longstreet occupied the heights of Lookout Mountain. Bragg realized that a frontal attack on the city would be suicidal and therefore determined to lay siege in the hope of starving the already supply-short Army of the Cumberland into submission.

Lookout Mountain, with its commanding view of Moccasin Point, was crucial to Bragg's plan. From the top of the mountain Longstreet could halt the Union supply lines from Bridgeport and Stevenson, Alabama, by land, by railroad, and by river. The only route open to Rosecrans was a wagon trail to the north of the city. The already hungry Army of the Cumberland now went onto short rations.

Once again Longstreet, Forrest, and Polk, fearing that Rosecrans might soon be reinforced, tried in vain to persuade Bragg to undertake an invasion of the city from the north. But Bragg was immovable and, as the dissension among his commanders grew and his popularity declined, he settled in to wait for the Federal commander to submit.

Day after day the Union wagon trains trudged back and forth along a 60-mile route over the Cumberland Plateau with a meager supply of food from Stevenson. As the days wore on the Four Horsemen of the Apocalypse – famine, pestilence, disease, and fire – ran rampant among the once-proud Army of the Cumberland. It seemed at first inevitable that Bragg must win the contest. But time was not on his side. Rosecrans and his beleaguered force had not been forgotten. Already the events that would decide the outcome of the contest at Chattanooga had begun to unfold.

President Lincoln, on hearing of Rosecrans' defeat at Chickamauga and of his by now impossible situation at Chattanooga, decided to send reinforcements from the Army of the Potomac. Two corps, the 11th and 12th under the commands of Major Generals Oliver O. Howard and Henry W. Slocum, were placed under the overall command of Major General Joseph Hooker. Then General U.S. Grant was ordered to send all available troops to Rosecrans' aid. Grant in turn ordered General Sherman in Mississippi to speed via river to Memphis and from there by railroad to Chattanooga. While all this was going on Lincoln was meeting with his cabinet to ponder Rosecrans' plight. It was decided to combine all three western armies, the Cumberland, the Tennessee, and the Ohio, under the overall command of General Grant. All this took time. Meanwhile,

The Incline Railway up Lookout Mountain.

Rosecrans and his army starved.

Grant reached Chattanooga on October 23rd. Having already replaced Rosecrans with Thomas as commander of the Army of the Cumberland, his first job was to break the siege and supply the starving army. To do this he decided that he must capture the river crossing at Brown's Ferry on the western side of Moccasin Point, well beyond the range of the Confederate guns on Lookout Mountain. The operation was carried out under cover of darkness in the early morning of the 27th by some 1,200 men in a flotilla of 50 pontoon boats. The attack was a complete surprise. General Hooker arrived in Lookout Valley the next day from Bridgeport and reinforced the occupation of Brown's Ferry. Supplies began pouring in to Chattanooga, lifting the moral and the enthusiasm of the Federal armies. The stage was now set for the battle of Chattanooga.

Today, few fortifications remain in and around the city. Missionary Ridge technically falls under the umbrella of the National Parks organization but there is little of interest to the visitor left on the ridge, with the exception of the outstanding view of the city. Nothing remains in the city other than one small park on the far side of the city. The real interest lies, as indeed it did in 1863, on Lookout Mountain. The action that began to develop on the evening of November 23rd, 1863 can best be described from there.

There are several ways to approach the mountain, and it might be a good idea to try them all, for each one is interesting. The most obvious, route is the Incline Railway from St. Elmo to the top of the mountain. Claimed to be the World's Most Amazing Mile, the railway climbs almost vertically, more than 2,000 feet to a tiny station just below Point Park. A second approach can be made by way of the Scenic Highway just off Interstate 24 at Brown's Ferry. Take this route and your tour of Lookout Mountain begins about half way up the mountain at the Cravens House. It was here at the one-time Confederate headquarters that some of the fiercest fighting on the mountain took place.

The Cravens House is the oldest surviving structure on Lookout Mountain. It was the home of local businessman Robert Cravens and his family. When Braxton Bragg's Confederate army occupied the mountain General E.C. Walthall established his headquarters in the Cravens House. For more than a month the General and his staff lived side-by-side with the Cravens family. Then, on the morning of November 24th, Union General Joseph Hooker with a force of more than 10,000 men stormed the slopes of the mountain. Walthall's position was a strong one, but his brigade was heavily outnumbered and by early afternoon the Cravens House belonged to Hooker.

The Cravens family returned to the mountain after the war and, finding little of the original house remaining, decided to rebuild it. Robert Cravens died in 1866. His wife lived in the house until her death in 1896. The house was restored to its Civil War condition in 1950 by The Chattanooga Chapter of the Association for the Preservation of Tennessee Antiquities. Today the house and grounds are part of the National Park System.

The entrance to Point Park on the peak of Lookout Mountain is interesting in itself. It was constructed in 1905 by the U.S. Corps of Engineers and is in fact the largest replica of the corps' insignia in the world. As your explore the tiny park you will be able to appreciate the formidable task the Union forces under General Hooker faced as they stormed the top of the mountain. There are three Confederate batteries still

The gate at Point Park.

in place on Point Park. They are but a very small representation of the siege line that encircled Chattanooga almost
entirely. The first is a battery of two Parrott Rifles, named
for their inventor, Robert Parrott of New York. These two
guns weigh about 1,750 pounds each and feature rifled
barrels that gave them great accuracy. Their maximum
range was about two miles.

The second battery, Garrity's Alabama, points due north
and overlooks the valley and Moccasin Point below. The
battery consists of two 12-pound Napoleon howitzers, the
standard cannon used by both sides during the Civil War.
They were effective only up to about 1,700 yards and they
could not be depressed – tilted – so were of little use during
the conflict on the slopes of the mountain below.

The third battery, Corput's, is located on the far western
overlook of Point Park, with an outstanding view of the
Federal lines of communication by road, rail and river from
Stevenson and Bridgeport, Alabama.

It was from the rocky outcrop, just below the gun emplacement, that General Longstreet watched the action as it took place in the valley below. Longstreet, however, unable to get along with Bragg, left the mountain on November 5th and went to Knoxville to engage Union General Burnside. So he was long gone when the action took place here in what was to become known as "The Battle Above the Clouds."

The battle began on November 23rd. Union Generals Wood and Sheridan rushed the Confederate posi-

Battery overlooking Chattanooga on Lookout Mountain.

tions on Orchard Knob and quickly captured them. The following day, the 24th, the peak of Lookout mountain was obscured from the Union forces in Chattanooga by a heavy fog. All day the fighting on the mountain could be heard by Grant and his staff as they waited anxiously for news of the battle. As darkness fell and the sounds of battle subsided Grant was little wiser than he had been at the start of the day.

The next day, the 25th, however, dawned bright and clear and as the sun's first rays hit the peak of the mountain a mighty shout went up from the assembled Union armies in the valley below. Floating proudly on the early morning breeze, high above the mountain top, was the Stars and Stripes – the battle standard of the 8th Kentucky Volunteers. Missionary Ridge fell the same day. Chattanooga and the Lookout Valley belonged once again to the Union. The gateway to the South had been flung open wide. Sherman soon would begin his March through Georgia to Atlanta and on to Savannah. The battles for Chattanooga and Lookout Mountain were a deathblow for the Confederacy.

Between the two batteries here on the peak of Lookout Mountain, Corput's and Garrity's, you will find a small pathway that leads for several hundred feet down the side of the mountain to Umbrella Rock and Ochs' Museum. The tiny museum located high above the Tennessee River was named in honor of Adolph Ochs, a one-time resident of Chattanooga and publisher of the *New York Times*. The exhibits inside the museum include several original Civil War period uniforms, many pieces of the bric-a-brac so important to the daily life of the soldier, and dozens of original photographs, letters, and drawings that depict the story of the battle for Chattanooga and Lookout Mountain.

The center of Point Park is dominated by the 90-foot-tall New York Peace Memorial, the top of which features two soldiers, one Confederate and one Union, shaking hands beneath a single flag. The monument, constructed of Tennessee marble and pink Massachusetts granite, signifies the concept of peace and brotherly love. Point Park can easily be reached either from the Brown's Ferry exit off I-24 going east from Nashville on the west side of Chattanooga, or going west from Knoxville and Atlanta by taking the Broad Street exit close to the city center. The park is open daily from 8 a.m. to 4:45 p.m. during the winter and from 8 a.m. to 5:45 during the summer There is no charge for admission and picnicking is allowed in the park.

Where to Stay, Things to Do

Attractions

Hunter Museum of Art: 10 Bluff View. Paintings, sculpture, glass, drawings; permanent collection of major American artists; changing exhibits. Gift shop-(Daily exc. Mon.; closed most holidays). Donation. Phone 423-267-0968.

Houston Museum of Decorative Arts: 201 High St. Glass, porcelain, pottery, music boxes, dolls, collection of pitchers, country-style furniture. (Daily exc. Mon.; closed holidays). Donation. Phone 423-267-7176.

National Knife Museum: 7201 Shallowford Rd. Permanent display of knives of every age and description; also changing exhibits. (Daily exc. Sun; closed holidays). Phone 423-892-5007.

TVA Energy Center: 1101 Market St. Learning center shows how TVA produces energy and consumers utilize it; hands-on exhibits and interactive computer games. (Daily exc. Sun). Phone 423-751-7599. Free.

Tennessee Aquarium: 101 W Second St., on the banks of the Tennessee River. First major freshwater life center in the country, focusing primarily on the natural habitats and wildlife of the Tennessee River and related ecosystems. Within this 130,000 sq.-ft. complex are more than 4,000 living specimens. The Aquarium re-creates riverine habitats in 7 major freshwater tanks and 2 terrestrial environments and is organized into 5 major galleries: Appalachian Cove Forest re-creates the mountain source of the Tennessee River; Tennessee River Gallery examines the river at midstream and compares the "original" river with the river as it now exists; Discovery Falls is a series of interactive displays and small tanks; Mississippi Delta explores the river as it slows to meet the sea; and Rivers of the World explores 6 of the world's great river systems. Highlight of the Aquarium is the 60-ft.-high central canyon, designed to give visitors a sense of immersion into the river. (Daily; closed

Thanksgiving, Dec. 25). Phone 423-265-0695.

University of Tennessee at Chattanooga (1886): (7,800 students) 423 McCallie Ave. Fine Arts Center has Arena stage entertainment and special events. Tours of campus by appointment. Phone 423-755-4363.

Tennessee Valley Railroad: 4119 Cromwell Rd. South's largest operating historic railroad, with steam locomotives, diesels, passenger coaches of various types. Trains leave hourly for six-mile ride, including tunnel. Audiovisual show displays; gift shop; dining room. (June-Labor Day, daily; Mar.-May & Sept.-Nov., weekends only). Phone 423-894-8028.

Chattanooga Choo-Choo: Terminal Station, 1400 Market St. Converted 1909 train station with hotel and restaurants. Formal gardens, fountains, pools, turn-of-the-century shops, gaslights, trolley ride (fee), model railroad (fee), 48 Victorian sleeping cars. Phone 423-266-5000.

Lookout Mountain Incline Railway: Lower station at 3917 St. Elmo Ave. World's steepest passenger incline railway climbs Lookout Mountain to 2,100-foot altitude; near top, grade is at 72 degree angle; passengers ride glass-roofed cars. Smoky Mountains (200 miles away) can be seen from upper station observation deck. Round trip approx. 30 minutes. (Daily; closed Dec. 25). Phone 423-821-4224.

Point Park: Lookout Mt. View of Chattanooga and Moccasin Bend from observatory. Monuments, plaques, museum tell story of battle. Visitor Center. Part of Chickamauga and Chattanooga National Military Park. (Daily; closed Dec. 25). Phone 423-821-7786.

Cravens House (1866): On Lookout Mt. Oldest surviving structure on mountain, restored with period furnishings. Original house (1856), center of the "Battle Above the Clouds," was largely destroyed; present structure was erected on the original foundations in 1866. (Apr.-Nov. daily). Phone 423-821-6161.

Ruby Falls: Caverns on Lookout Mt. Under the battlefield are twin caves with onyx formations, giant stalactites, stalagmites. Ruby Falls, 1,120 feet below the surface, drop 145 feet. View of the city from the tower above the entrance building. Guided tours (daily; closed Dec. 25). Phone 423-821-2544.

Rock City Gardens: On Lookout Mt. Fourteen acres of mountain top trails and vistas. Fairyland Caverns and Mother Goose village, rock formations, swinging bridge, observation point. Restaurant; shops. (Daily; closed Dec. 25). Phone 404-820-2531.

Confederama Hall of History: 3742 Tennessee Ave. at the foot of Lookout Mt. Automated, three-dimensional display recreates Civil War battle of Lookout Mt. Miniature soldiers, flashing lights, smoking cannons and cracking rifles. Also here are dioramas of the area history prior to the Civil War. (Daily; closed Thanksgiving). Phone 423-821-2812.

Annual Events

Riverbend Festival: Musical events, Children's activities, racing, fireworks display. Mid-June. Phone 423-265-4112.

Autumn Leaf Special: All day reserved seat steam strain ride 130 miles through mountains to Oneida, TN. Air-conditioned and adjustable window coaches, diner, snack bar and souvenir shop on board. Two weekends in October. Contact Tennessee Valley Railroad Museum. 4119 Cromwell Road, Chattanooga, TN 37421. Phone 423-894-8028.

Fall Color Cruise & Folk Festival: Riverboat trips, arts & crafts, entertainment. Last two weekends in October. Phone 423-892-0223.

Theatrical & Musical Productions: Tivoli Theater, 709 Broad Street. Events, plays, concerts, opera; 423-757-5050. Little Theater, 267-8534. Memorial Auditorium, 756-5042. Chattanooga Symphony and Opera Ass., 267-8583. Backstage Playhouse, 629-1565.

Hotels

Chanticleer Inn: 1300 Mockingbird Lane, Lookout Mt., GA 30750, 404-820-2015. 16 rooms, crib free, TV, cable, pool. free continental breakfast, cafe nearby, check-out 11 a.m., meeting room, picnic tables, grill, accept credit cards.

Comfort Inn: 7717 Lee Hwy., 423-894-5454. 64 rooms. Under 18 free, crib free, TV, cable, pool, free coffee in lobby, free continental breakfast, cafe nearby, check-out 11 a.m., free airport transportation, accepts credit cards.

Days Inn Airport: 7014 Shallowford Road, 423-855-0011. 132 rooms, under 16 free, crib free, TV, cable, pool, cafe, check-out 11 a.m., accepts credit cards.

Days Inn Rivergate: 901 Carter St., 423-266-7331. 135 rooms, under 18 free, crib free, TV, cable, pool, cafe, room service, bar, check-out noon, accepts credit cards.

Econo Lodge: 1417 St. Thomas, 423-894-1417. 89 rooms, under 18 free, TV, cable, pool. free continental breakfast, cafe nearby, check-out 11 a.m., accepts credit cards.

Friendship Inn: 7725 Lee Hwy., 423-899-2288. 80 rooms, under 18 free, TV, cable, pool, free coffee in lobby, cafe, check-out 11 a.m., accepts credit cards.

Hampton Inn: 7013 Shallowford Road, 423-855-0095. 126 rooms, under 18 free, crib fee, TV, cable, pool. free coffee in lobby, free continental breakfast, cafe adjacent, check-out 11 a.m., meeting rooms, exercise equipment, accepts credit cards.

Holiday Inn Tiftonia: 3800 Cummins Hwy. at I-24, 423-821-3531. 163 rooms, under 19 free, crib fee, TV, cable, pool, cafe, check-out 11 a.m., meeting rooms, exercise equipment, accepts credit cards.

King's Lodge: 2400 West Side Dr., 423-698-8944. 139 rooms, under 12 free, TV, cable, pool, cafe, check-out 11 a.m., accepts credit cards.

Quality Inn & Convention Center: 1400 Mack Smith Road, 423-894-0440. 237 rooms, under 18 free, crib fee, TV, cable, pool, cafe, check-out noon, meeting rooms, free airport transportation, accepts credit cards.

Red Roof Inn: 7014 Shallowford Rd., 423-899-0143. 112 rooms, under 18 free, crib fee, TV, cable, pool. free coffee, cafe adjacent, check-out noon, accepts credit cards.

Super 8: 20 Birmingham Hwy., 423-821-8880. 74 rooms, crib fee, TV, cable, free coffee in lobby, cafe adjacent, check-out 11 a.m., accepts credit cards.

Best Western South: 6710 Ringgold Rd., 423-894-6820. 138 rooms, under 18 free, crib fee, TV, cable, pool, cafe, check-out 11 a.m., meeting rooms, free airport transportation, accepts credit cards.

Holiday Inn Chattanooga Choo-Choo: 1400 Market Street, 423-266-5000. 360 rooms, crib fee, TV, cable, 3 pools, free coffee, cafe, meeting rooms, free airport transportation, accepts credit cards.

Comfort Hotel River Center: 407 Chestnut, 423-756-5150. 205 rooms, under 18 free, cable TV, pool, cafe, check-out noon, meeting rooms, free airport transportation, accepts credit cards.

Marriott: 2 Carter Plaza, 423-756-0002. 343 rooms, under 12 free, crib fee, cable TV, pool, cafe adjacent, check-out 11 a.m., meeting rooms, exercise equipment, accepts credit cards.

Radisson Read House: M.L. King & Broad St., 651-266-4121. 243 rooms, 10-story, under 18 free, crib fee, TV, cable, pool, cafe, meeting rooms, accept credit cards.

Restaurants

Fifth Quarter: 5501 Brainerd Rd., 423-899-0181. Children's meals, specializes in prime rib & fresh seafood. Accepts credit cards.

Mt Vernon: 3509 Broad Street, 423-266-6591. Children's meals, specializes fresh seafood & desserts. Accepts credit cards.

Narrowbridge: 1420 Jenkins, 423-855-5000. Children's meals, specializes in steak, fresh seafood & own baking. Accepts credit cards.

Perry's: 1206 Market St., 423-267-0007. Specializes in prime rib & fresh seafood. Accepts credit cards.

Vine Street Market: 414 Vine Street., 423-267-0162. Children's meals, specializes in desserts. Accepts credit cards.

Chapter 14

Conclusion

And so the war dragged on. The Union Armies of the Cumberland, the Ohio, and the Tennessee wintered in the shelter of Chattanooga, and by May of 1864 were ready to begin the march through Georgia to Atlanta and then on to the sea. The Confederate Army of Tennessee, now under the command of General Joseph E. Johnston, awaited the Federals at Rocky Face Ridge in Georgia, just to the south of Chattanooga. From there, through one battle after another, the Confederate army was driven slowly southward toward Atlanta, which fell to General Sherman on August 31st, 1864. The battle of Atlanta was followed by the famous march to Savannah and the sea. Sherman marched into Savannah on December 21st. From there he turned his attention northward.

In the theater in the north the Army of Northern Virginia struggled in vain to hold off the ever-advancing Union forces under the command of General-in-Chief, U.S. Grant.

On May 5th 1864 the Battle of the Wilderness resulted in a stalemate. Then, on May 11th, just to the north of Richmond at Yellow Tavern, Lee lost his "eyes and ears." General Jeb Stuart was killed in a cavalry engagement. It was a serious set-back for the beleaguered Army of Northern Virginia.

Grant continued his inexorable advance toward the Confederate capitol. The two armies clashed first at North Anna on May 23rd, and then again at Totopotomy on May 30th. This was followed by the battle of Cold Harbor near Mechanicsville on June 3rd. The fighting there continued until June 12th and ended in yet another stalemate. But the end was in sight. Lee's army was badly depleted by the mounting numbers of casualties suffered during the previous two months. Richmond was now in great danger of falling into enemy hands.

Lee realized that his one hope was to take up a strong defensive position between Grant's army and the Confederate capitol. He decided that any Union attempt to capture Richmond must fail if he could hold a line at Petersburg, Virginia. The Confederate position at Petersburg was indeed a strong one. Repeated attempts to capture it were staved off, with the Union forces suffering heavy casualties. General Grant was forced to lay siege to the city. After his success at Vicksburg it was a strategy that Grant knew well.

All through June and most of July the Union forces dug in. Then, on July 30th, more than 8,000 pounds of explosives in a 500-foot long tunnel beneath the Confederate fortifications were exploded, obliterating the Confederate fortifications for more than 150 yards on either side of the crater. The Confederate defenders recovered, and from then until March of 1865 the battle around Petersburg and Richmond deteriorated into trench warfare.

The New Year of 1865 brought only a sense of desperation to the now beleaguered Confederacy. It was obvious that there was no help coming from Britain and France. Sherman was in Savannah, the West was in the hands of General Thomas, and Grant was continuing to press his siege of Petersburg. It was obvious that the war could not continue for very much longer.

By April 3rd Grant decided the time had come to put an end to the siege and ordered a concerted attack against both Petersburg and Richmond. By nightfall the Confederate Army of Northern Virginia was in full retreat; Lee's once proud army had been reduced to an effective strength of no more than 30,000 officers and men. They were hungry, exhausted, and their morale was sinking rapidly.

On April 7th, 1865, General Lee and his now tiny army crossed to the northern bank of the Appomattox river. The Union forces pursued and harassed them until, with his army trapped and in the poorest of condition, General Lee had no alternative but to surrender to Grant at Appomattox Courthouse on Sunday April 9th, 1865.

General Grant immediately sent food and supplies to the defeated Confederate army. Five days later Confederate General Joseph Johnston surrendered to General Sherman at Raleigh, North Carolina, and on May 26th General Kirby Smith surrendered to General Edward Canby. The American Civil War had ended. Reconstruction was about to begin.

Chapter 15

Soldiering in the Civil War

Infantry:
The majority of Civil War soldiers of both sides served in the infantry. These were the people who inflicted and suffered the most casualties – the people who won or lost the battles. They were formed in line of battle, for the most part, as two ranks, one behind the other, to afford the maximum fire power. At the front of such a formation would be the advance guard – skirmishers – a widespread screen of soldiers who protected the main body of the army and gave warning of the advancing enemy.

The troops were organized into fighting units. The smallest of these was a company, about 60 men. Ten companies made up a regiment. The basic infantry unit was the brigade. Brigades usually numbered some 2,000 to 3,500 men, and would be made up of five to eight regiments. The next largest unit was the division, made up of three or more brigades. The corps comprised two or more divisions.

The basic weapon of the infantryman on both sides was the muzzle-loading rifled musket. It was a little more than five feet long, weighed about nine pounds, and fired a large caliber bullet called a minie-ball. The minie ball varied in caliber from .54 to .69. The rifled musket at a range of 200 yards was absolutely lethal, and was deadly accurate up to a thousand yards. Pistols and swords were carried by the officers.

Artillery:
All Civil War artillery could be effective only when the cannon-

eer could see his target, and even though the cannon of the period could shoot much farther, its effective or accurate range was only about 1,500 yards. There were two basic types of Civil War cannon: the bronze smoothbore, and the iron rifled gun bearing the name of its maker – the Blakely, the Parrott, the Whitworth, the Armstrong and so on. The rifled gun had an increased range and greater accuracy than its bronze counterpart. Both types of cannon fired solid iron shot, or explosive shells of two types: a hollow iron container filled with black powder that exploded by way of an impact device or a timed fuse; and the case shot, a hollow shell filled with explosives and a lethal payload of metal balls, timed to explode in the air above or in front of the target.

The devastating, anti-personnel canister, too, could be fired by either type of gun. The canister was a soft metal can full of sawdust and large caliber iron balls that would burst open upon leaving the muzzle of the cannon, very much like a giant shotgun shell. At close range the effect of canister was always deadly.

Each type of projectile was fitted with a charge of gunpowder in the form of a powder bag. When double-loading canister, the cannoneer was supposed to knock the powder bag from the second load to ensure the barrel of the weapon wouldn't burst under the strain of a double load of explosive. Often, though, the gunners got carried away by the urgency of the moment, and the great weapons would bound high into the air under recoil of an overloaded explosive charge. A full compliment of nine cannoneers could operate their gun at a rate of fire from two to three rounds per minute.

The light artillery cannon was an extremely mobile weapon. It could quickly be transported from one area of a battlefield to another by use of a two-wheeled limber that was pulled by a team of six horses and three drivers. The horses were harnessed in three pairs. The limber also carried a single ammunition box, and the three drivers rode the three horses on the left-hand side of the team, one behind the other. Each cannon was supported by a caisson: a four-wheeled carriage that carried three more ammunition boxes; it, too, was pulled by a team of six horses and three drivers.

A typical Confederate artillery battery would be outfitted with four six-pounder guns and two 12-pounder field howitzers. The average Union battery consisted of four guns, all of the same caliber.

Cavalry:

The romantic concept of the dashing cavalryman charging into battle, the reins between his teeth, a pistol in one hand and sword in the other is, for the most-part, an inaccurate one. The cavalry acted mostly as the intelligence, the eyes and ears, of the army. When it became necessary for them to fight they would dismount and fight just like infantrymen. Every fourth man would hold the horses back behind the firing line while his comrades engaged the enemy. The basic weapon of the cavalry-man was officially the single-shot carbine. More often than not, however, the most popular weapon of the saddle was a sawed-off 12-gauge shotgun loaded with buckshot. The effect of such a weapon at close range was devastating. The cavalry of the Civil War on both sides produced some of the most romantic charac-ters of the period. On the Confederate side there were Nathan Bedford Forrest and Jeb Stuart, and on the Union side George Armstrong Custer, to name but a few.

For most of the enlisted men, and for the officers, too, whether they were a part of the infantry, artillery, or cavalry, there was nothing romantic about the Civil War or what they did. They were, after all, expected to fight and die in the fields for cause and country, and more than 620,000 of them did just that.

Reenacting:
A New Kind of War

Introduction

Reenacting the battles of the Civil War is becoming a popular hobby. Just as they did all those years ago, men and women from all walks of life are setting forth to fight for cause and country: laborers, doctors, dentists, lawyers, company executives and postal clerks leave behind their briefcases, tools and homes and head for the killing fields. This time, however, they are doing it for different reasons. And today's Civil War soldiers are just as serious about what they're doing as were their forbears back in 1861. Oh, they'll tell you they're doing it for fun, and perhaps they believe it, but it takes a dedicated individual to spend several days several times a year out in all weathers being ordered about in an uncomfortable facsimile of a uniform that was little more than an instrument of torture when worn for real.

These men and women live for a few days by the same military code as did the armies of the Civil War. They carry the same weapons, though most are only replicas – the real thing being far too valuable to risk – and belong to units that bear the famous, honored names of the past. And those regiments mean just as much to the modern-day reenactor as they did to those who fought and died for them.

The dedicated reenactor loves what he does. He has feelings that cannot properly be described; you'll simply have to try it to understand. There's nothing quite like the chill in the air on a crisp, clear early morning in fall when a campground on one of the great fields of glory begins to stir. Or the excitement as the troops are called into line of battle, simulated or not. And, to those who know, the charge is just as real, just as thrilling, just as awesome as it must have been all those years ago. The blue-white smoke over the battle line is just as thick, the gunfire just as loud, and the yelling just as enthusiastic. To stand and watch as the gun crews work feverishly at their great weapons, trying for all they're worth to achieve a rate of fire that was second nature to the artillery man of long ago, is to get entirely caught up in the moment. Yes, reenacting is addictive. Do it once, even just to watch, and you're hooked.

Having said that, there are a couple of ways you can become involved and enjoy reenacting. You can watch the action or you can join in, on one side or the other.

To watch the action requires little more than a basic knowledge of the Civil War and the events played out during those terrible years. The reenactment of any given battle is rarely historically accurate. Lack of numbers and an inability of those involved to understand the mind-set of one who might have spent a couple of years, or more, experiencing conditions and hardships that no one could even imagine today, are the principle reasons for this. But, where the reenactment is to be played out and how many attend also significantly impacts the authenticity of the event. For instance, at the first reenactments of the Battle of Tunnel Hill in north Georgia there were several hundred Confederate soldiers complete with two batteries of artillery and commanded by a full complement of officers from a general down. This significant force was pitted against no more than a couple of dozen Union soldiers with a single three-inch ordnance rifle – a tiny contingent commanded by a captain. Most of the smaller reenactments are like this, and if you add the inevitable boyish enthusiasm and the desire for "a good day out," it's no wonder the event turns out to be a little inaccurate, to say the least. Still, it's fun to watch, and there's no doubt that spectators do become caught up in the moment, many of them leaving the event determined to take a more active part in the next one.

And that brings us to those who do the real work at a reenactment, the participants themselves. These people are usually die-hard Civil War buffs. Many are amateur historians; some are professional historians; some just like to get out there and play; all are enthusiasts. And you have to be very enthusiastic

indeed to spend $10,000 on a reproduction canon and all its ac-
couterments, another several hundred dollars on an artillery
captain's uniform, and heaven only knows what on the means to
transport it all around the country.

Most reenactors, however, cannot afford such luxury. Just like
the average soldier 135 years ago, they are infantrymen, the
backbone of the army. Their uniforms and weapons are authentic, though reproduction, down to the underwear, and they go to
war with a will that would rival that of the first volunteers of
1861, be it only for a weekend or so.

Then there is the civilian reenactor: the doctors, nurses, photographers, and the like. These people also play important parts,
just as their ancestors did way back when. Their dress, too, is
authentic. They man the field hospitals and look after the
wounded and the dying in much the same way as did the field
surgeons and staff all those years ago. True, the wounds are
rarely more serious than a simple bump on the head, but the enthusiasm inside and outside the tents is real enough.

Most reenactments are accompanied by a tented village, a trade
fair, if you will, where you can purchase all sorts of Civil War
memorabilia, from books to photographs, from reproduction
uniforms to fine dresses, flags, unit histories, buttons, spent
bullets, cheap souvenirs and a plethora of other bits and pieces.
These villages, the tented shops and refreshment stands, are
run by the modern day version of the sutler. The sutler was a
merchant who sold goods and supplies directly to the troops.
They followed the armies from battlefield to battlefield, riding a
covered wagon crammed full with everything a soldier might
need to maintain his existence. They would stay on the road, following the army for months on end, leaving only to replenish
their stocks. Some were rogues, but most were honest business-
men fulfilling a need. The same is true of the modern sutler.
You'll find authentic antiques for sale alongside reproductions
being passed off as authentic. Be careful.

Then there are the photographers, those who follow in the footsteps of men like Matthew Brady. They dress the part and tote

reproduction wooden cameras that sometimes house modern 35mm equipment. These people record the action, make portraits of the soldiers, and generally add a little extra authenticity to the event. You'll see one or two at every reenactment.

And then there are the social events that usually accompany a reenactment: balls, dances and dinners. Here the participants go all out. The ladies wear elegant ball gowns of the period; the men wear dress uniforms. To attend one of these events is to step back in time. These people talk, or try to, just as they might have 135 years ago; they affect the manners and accents of the mid-19th century, and they thoroughly enjoy themselves.

How Do You Get Started?

To watch, all you have to do is turn up in plenty of time, pick a good spot, and settle down. Bring some food and plenty to drink – soft drinks only. You may even want to arrive a little early, a couple of hours or so, and watch the units marching and drilling, perhaps breaking camp, or maneuvering into position. You'll probably have to pay to watch. Entrance fees run from a couple of dollars on up. Don't worry. Your small investment will be repaid many times over.

To become a reenactor you only have to ask. Most units are short on numbers, though long on enthusiasm, and will welcome you with open arms. Attend a reenactment and you're sure to find a unit that will take you on. If not, you can make inquiries in your home town. The local historical society is the best place to start. If you don't have a historical society you can try the library. Be aware, though, that even though these are basically weekend soldiers they will expect you to make a commitment. You'll be required to turn up regularly, learn the history of the Civil War in general, and that of the unit you are joining in depth. You'll start out as a private soldier, be taught all about the weapons and tactics of the times, and you'll drill and march just as rookie soldiers would have in 1861. The men that run these units and do the training are just as effective as were their peers of 130 years ago, perhaps even more so. You'll be expected to kit yourself out, at no little expense, and turn out in all weathers. You'll go to camp, train hard, and you'll fight. You'll get caught up in the action, which will seem real beyond belief. You'll get dirty like never before, and you'll return home at the end of the day tired, even worn out, but fulfilled.

Authenticity

Most reenactments are small affairs, often hosted by a local historical society or Civil War unit. Here, perhaps a couple of hundred men and women get together for a weekend. In most cases it's no more than a gathering where the participants get into character and live the life for a couple of days; it might even include the reenactment of some small, insignificant skirmish. Then there are the large national events where units from all across the country participate. Here the reenactors, sometimes as many as 10,000, refight a major battle. Events such as these will draw spectators from around the world. Small or large, local or national, authenticity is the watchword. Nothing that will detract from the overall illusion of perfection will be allowed. Even press photographers are asked to wear appropriate gear or stand outside the line of sight.

Modern items – cameras, etc. – may be used but should be covered by something of the period. Even in camp, out of sight of spectators, at least until they're allowed in on the morning of the reenactment, you'll be expected to maintain the illusion. This means modern sleeping bags, frowned on in some circles, should be covered by a period blanket, and removed from sight when the spectators arrive. Drinks should be kept in period containers – canteens and bottles, not aluminum cans.

But there's more to living the period than just wearing and carrying the gear. Doing without all the trappings of life in the 1990s – food, clothing, conveniences – will teach you more about the history of the period than you could ever learn from a book. And you'll be expected to affect the grace and mannerisms of a time long gone.

Authenticity also provides a deep sense of belonging, a way of casting off the worries and stress of modern day life, at least for a couple of days. Far away from the asphalt roads, modern buildings, fast cars, heavy trucks, telephones and computers, you'll find things proceed at a much slower, more relaxed pace. The company is friendly and outgoing, the conversation lively, and the atmosphere exciting.

Uniforms

You'll be expected to purchase an authentic period uniform in keeping with those worn by the particular unit you're joining. Check with the powers that be before you spend any money. They'll provide a basic list of what you'll need.

In the early days of the Civil War, especially in the south, the uniforms worn by volunteer units often bordered on the eccentric. They were rarely practical, but designed more to attract the opposite sex and new recruits than for everyday life on the march. Uniforms of the period just prior to the outbreak of the war were influenced by those of earlier times – bright colors and lots of gold braid were the order of the day. So were the hats. At first, these came in every shape and size, even turbans. Some uniforms had their origins in Napoleonic France, some in the British army of a century before. Confusion on the field reigned supreme. Friendly fire was responsible for large numbers of casualties. Even the flags looked the same. Slowly, however, after the first great battles had been won and lost, things began to change. The bright colors were discarded and more standard modes of dress were adopted.

Confederate Uniforms. By the spring of 1862 the standard Confederate army uniform consisted of a gray jacket or frock coat with light blue or gray trousers. In practice, however, few Southern units (never call them Rebels) ever looked alike. Grays varied, not only from unit to unit, but from individual to individual. Some were light, some were dark, some were not gray at all. Confederate soldiers, perhaps from necessity, included more civilian items of dress in their uniforms than did their Union counter-parts, especially where headgear was concerned.

Trousers were made of heavy wool, fine in winter when the weather was dry, but torture in hot or wet weather. They were worn loose, with plenty of room for long underwear and to move, bend or squat. They never had the sharp creases we've come to expect in modern uniforms. Jackets were also loose-fitting. The shell jacket must have been uncomfortable, especially if it didn't fit properly, and most of them didn't. The frock coat was often heavy and restrictive, but warm in winter; uncomfortably so in summer. Your prospective unit will dictate which style you should buy.

Hats were as much a personal statement as a part of the uni-form. Two styles were popular: the familiar kepi or the more practical slouch hat. The slouch or plantation hat was more popular because its wide brim kept out the sun and rain. You'll probably be allowed to wear whichever style suits you best.

In the early days of your reenacting military career it's probably best to borrow your uniform and weapon. It wouldn't be wise to invest a lot of money in clothing and equipment, only to realize you're unsuited to the pastime. Spare uniforms, loaners, are kept on hand by most units for just such a purpose.

Union Uniforms. Most Union troops wore light blue woolen pants, although some did wear dark blue pants. The regulation jacket was a dark blue, knee-length, woolen frock coat, but some units did wear a waist-length shell jacket. What you will wear will depend very much on your chosen unit. Be sure to check be-fore you buy; some outfits will not allow anything that isn't authentic to that particular unit.

The uniform shirt might have been any of a number of colors ranging from dark to light blue, gray or white.

During the early days of the war, the kepi was the most popular style of hat for the Union soldier. Toward the end, however, mostly because the kepi didn't give much protection from the elements, many adopted the wide-brim slouch hat, which gave more protection from the sun and rain. There were several styles of slouch hat, but the most popular was undoubtedly the one named for General William Hardee. The Hardee was a black hat with a wide brim turned up on one side and fastened in position with a brass pin, usually in the form of an eagle.

Other styles, the wheel hat, several styles of straw hat, and even panamas were the legacy of the Mexican war and were worn by one and all well into the 1860s.

And then there were the hat decorations. We've all seen them in movies: the golden cords adorned with golden acorns worn on cavalry officer's hats. But there were so many more unit badges, corps badges, regimental numbers and company letters, all worn by the foot soldier; the bugle was worn by mounted infantry. What will adorn your chosen hat will depend upon the unit to which you belong.

Shirts. Most shirts, on both sides, were pullovers. They were made mostly from flannel or muslin, and those worn by Union troops were often dark blue and, in warm weather, were worn over a muslin shirt instead of the heavy woolen jacket. Shirt pockets were rare.

Boots – Confederate and Union. In the early days of the war, boots on both sides were plentiful. They were tough and strongly made from hide leather. The most common style worn by soldiers in both armies was the "Jefferson bootie," so named for the Confederate president who approved its use by Federal troops when he was the United States Secretary of War. It was a heavy, square-toed boot that covered the ankle. Union versions were made with the smooth side of the leather out, Confederate models with the smooth side in.

Soldiers in the cavalry, and mounted infantry units, were allowed to wear high-topped boots with the pants tucked into the tops. Other than that, only officers were allowed to wear such boots.

There's been a lot made of the fact that, especially during the later stages of the war, many Confederate solders were reduced to marching and fighting in bare feet. Well, that's true, but not always out of necessity. Soldiers in the ranks on both sides often went barefoot by choice in the summer months, just as they did in civilian life.

Socks. These, believe it or not, were not so very different from those worn today. There's not much you can do with the design of a sock. They were made mostly of heavy wool, were hand-knitted by the ladies waiting at home, and were much darned and patched in the field. They were washed, mended, and worn until they literally fell off the feet. Many were knitted by the soldiers themselves. Socks, especially in winter when leather shoes became water-logged, not only kept the feet warm, but also protected them from chaffing, and thus helped prevent blisters.

Underwear. There was little difference between what was worn in the Union and Confederate armies. During the 19th century, soldiers, and civilians for that matter, wore more underwear than we do today. The longjohns of the movies were just that, movie props. They didn't become common until the later part of the 19th century, well after the Civil War had ended.

The underwear of the Civil War era, officer and common soldier alike, was an earlier version of the longjohns: a two-piece affair with long sleeves and legs that covered the body almost entirely – this as much out of a strong sense of modesty as a desire to keep warm. White and red were the popular colors, although the red quickly turned to pink with wear and washing. So, what will you wear? It's best, of course, that you wear something warm: longjohns or thermals, or both. If so, be sure you keep them covered and out of sight.

Weapons

Firearms. The most popular weapon, then and now, on both sides, was the Springfield rifle musket, Model 1861, simply called by the soldiers that carried it, the Springfield.

The Springfield was a little more than five feet long and weighed in at just over nine pounds. It was a .58 caliber – just a little more than a half-inch – weapon with an effective range for a regular soldier of about 500 yards, although sharp-shooters could kill a man at twice that range.

The 1853 Enfield was also popular with soldiers on both sides. Made in England with a caliber of .577, it was more accurate than the Springfield and, in the right hands, deadly at well over 1000 yards. The Enfield was imported by both sides in vast numbers.

Both of these weapons were three-banded. Shorter weapons, carbines and the like, were two-banded.

Carbines or musketoons were much shorter, and less accurate, than the infantry long-rifles and were used mostly by cavalry units and mounted infantry.

As to the famed repeating rifles, these didn't become widely available until 1863, and then only to solders who could afford to purchase them themselves – as did the members of the famous John Wilder's mounted infantry units that caused so much havoc among Longstreet's soldiers at Chickamauga. It's doubtful that your unit will allow such weapons.

All reenactor units insist that every rifle musket have three bands; this as much for safety as authenticity.

A word of warning: if you're lucky enough to own an antique musket, don't use it while reenacting. Not only because it's a valuable piece and might get damaged, but because time may well have weakened the barrel and working parts. An exploding rifle is a terrible thing to behold, and the damage it does is devastating.

How about pistols? Even though you may have seen Civil War era portraits of young bloods brandishing or wearing large pistols, unless you're an officer, they are not appropriate. Swords, too, are reserved for officers, except for members of cavalry units who are allowed to wear a cavalry saber.

You should also be aware that if you're under 16 you probably won't be allowed to carry a rifle; if you're between the ages of 16 and 18 you'll be allowed to carry a rifle, but you won't be allowed to fire it. These rules are applied, mostly for insurance reasons, but also for safety.

Gunpowder. Black powder, gunpowder, is rated by the size of its grain from fg (1f) to ffffg (4f). The coarsest, 1f, is used for cannons; the finest, 4f, is used as the primer for flintlock weapons. Revolvers, single shot pistols and rifles under .45 caliber use 3f powder. Larger weapons, rifle muskets of .577 and .58 caliber as were common in both armies during the Civil War, use 2f powder. So, 2f is what you should use, too.

There are several commercial brands of gunpowder. Of these, *Goex* and *Pyrodex* are the best known. *Pyrodex* is not recommended for reenacting. It's a black powder substitute used mostly for live ammunition. It requires magnum caps, burns slowly, and, without the compression of a bullet in the barrel, it makes little noise when fired as a blank. On the other hand, *Goex* is a true black powder, burns much cleaner than *Pyrodex*, and makes a satisfying BANG! when fired blank.

Both types of gunpowder can be bought at most sporting goods stores. It comes in convenient one-pound cans, but should always be stored in a steel container, preferably an army surplus ammunition box, in a cool place where the kids can't get hold of it. Gunpowder seems to have a magnetic attraction for boys of all ages. Back in my youth, I used to dismantle fireworks to get a supply of the stuff. Very dangerous, very stupid.

Paper Cartridges. You can buy these ready-made at some of the larger events, but most reenactors prefer to roll their own; during the winter, many units have cartridge rolling parties. These are often social events, and can be a lot of fun. If you want to try your hand, it's quite easy. All you need is a supply of 2f black powder, a short piece of half-inch wooden dowel, slightly tapered at the end, some old newspaper or some pre-cut cartridge papers – these can often be bought at local reenactments – and some strong thread. If you decide to cut your own cartridge papers, take a sheet of newspaper and cut trapezoids from it: 4¼ inches along the base, 5¼ inches along one side, three inches along the other, then make a slanting cut that joins the ends of the two sides together. Roll the paper around the dowel and leave about a quarter-inch over the tapered end. You'll tie off the longer end of the trapezoid. Place the dowel with its roll of paper still around it in something that will hold it upright while you tie off the end of the paper. Use your thread to tightly tie the tip of the paper. Now slide the dowel out of the resulting tube and pour a measured amount of black powder into the opening: the recommended measure is 60 grains of 2f black powder, and it's best that you don't exceed this. You can, if you like, place a small ball of cotton wool where the ball would normally go, but it's not necessary. If you do, you can use the dowel to tamp the wool into the bottom of the cartridge before you apply the charge. After you've charged the cartridge, pinch the paper in toward the center of the cartridge, fold it flat, tightly against the powder, first one way to make a crease, and then the other. Finally, fold the flattened tail of the cartridge back so that it lies toward the tie-off tail end.

If you don't want to go to all that trouble, you can always buy ready-made paper rolls sold in boxes of 100 or more at many of the larger events. All you have to do is fill them with the required amount of black powder, close the ends, and you're ready to go; simple, but a little more expensive than the do-it-yourself paper cartridge.

Bayonets. The Civil War era bayonet was an unwieldy weapon, 18 inches or so in length, triangular, with dull edges and a sharp point. It turned an already over-long rifle into something that was hard to handle at best, and downright dangerous at worst. Bayonets were carried by all soldiers on both sides throughout the war. They were fixed over the end of the barrel via a socket that locked over the front sight. Though fearsome to behold by an enemy on the receiving end of a charge, they were not an effective weapon, and rarely used with any real effect, except in the movies, of course. Even Chamberlain's famous charge downhill at the Battle of Gettysburg produced fewer than 100 casualties. Although, when it was used effectively, the resulting wound was often fatal, not so much from the severity of the injury as from the inevitable infection that was almost always its aftermath.

The bayonet was, however, even from its inception long before the Civil War, one of the first real psychological weapons of war. One can only imagine the horrifying spectacle a raging, screaming soldier, brandishing one of these awful looking weapons, must have presented as he bore down at full speed, fully intent on ramming the thing deep into you. It's no wonder, then, that most soldiers, when on the receiving end of a bayonet charge, simply turned and ran.

But the mighty bayonet served many more purposes. Around camp it was ideal for hanging a coffee pot above the fire, holding a chunk of meat or chicken above the flames, and so on.

Care and Maintenance of Weapons and Equipment. It's not wise to wash woolen items too often. Wool has natural water-repellent properties that will be destroyed by constant washing. When you do wash your woolen items you should do so by hand, only in cold water, and then they should be hung out to dry, preferably in sunshine, on a clothesline; never use a washer and dryer. If you do, the uniform that emerges will not fit even GI Joe. You can, however, have your uniform dry-cleaned. If you do, make sure that the items are returned to you un-ironed. Wool becomes shiny if ironed without a cloth between it and the iron, and then again, Civil War uniforms never had a crease down the trousers or on the sleeves of the jacket; that was a later invention.

Brass items were often allowed to tarnish. Steel was oiled to prevent rust.

Your rifle, the most expensive part of your investment, should be cleaned thoroughly after each event. Black powder leaves a great deal of residue in the barrel. During the Civil War, this was such a problem that, after firing only a few rounds, it became more and more difficult, eventually impossible, to ram the bullet down the barrel.

To clean your rifle you'll need to remove the barrel from the weapon, then pour warm, soapy water down the barrel to loosen the residue. Once this has been done you can use a wad and cleaning rod to remove what's left. Don't pour water down the barrel while it's still attached to the stock. If you do, water will inevitably creep into the crevices between stock and works, thus causing rust; water's not good for the wood either.

Among many other items you'll find on sale at most of the larger events will be a variety of cleaning tools. One you should buy is a bristle, a small round brush that attaches to the end of the ramrod or cleaning rod. It does a great job of cleaning the inside of the barrel. Just make sure you get one that's the right size for your particular weapon. The worm and bullet pull are also useful tools. Both attach to the end of the ramrod or cleaning rod. The worm is used to remove the remains of unburned powder and paper from the barrel, the pull to remove an unfired ball.

Finally, when you feel the weapon is clean, reassemble the barrel to the stock, and then wipe it down with an oily rag. This will prevent rust and help to repel any water you might contact during your next time out in the field.

Equipment

The Knapsack. These, and haversacks, were issued to both sides at the beginning of the war, and were carried throughout the conflict by soldiers on the Union side. Confederate soldiers, however, rarely carried them after the first year of the war.

They came in many different styles. What you carry will depend largely on the unit you join.

Mess Kits. Soldiers on both sides carried a mess kit. This consisted of a tin cup, tin plate, knife, fork and spoon. There was little difference between Union and Confederate issue. The cup was large, often with at least a two-pint capacity; the plate, some eight inches in diameter, after only limited use was always dented and beaten up; your irons – knife, fork and spoon – should, of course, be of the period. Mess kits can be found for sale at most large, and some small, events.

The Canteen. This was THE essential part of the Civil War soldier's equipment. He could get by for days, if he had to, and that was often the case, with little or no food. But the long, forced marches through the choking dust raised by thousands of marching feet meant that a soldier was always thirsty and had to drink often.

Canteens of several different styles were issued to troops on both sides, but almost all were made to the same basic design. They were round, had a spout closed off with a cork that was held by a small chain. Some had woolen covers of one color or another and, although no one knows for sure, it's thought that these were blue for the union side and gray for the Confederate side; some covers were brown. Some canteens were made of wood and will leak if allowed to dry out. They soon seal themselves, however, when refilled.

Canteen straps are traditionally very long. This causes problems when you're moving quickly. New recruits to reenacting are tempted to hold the canteen in place by putting their belt over the straps, thus securing the canteen close to their side. Don't do this. Not only will it label you as a rookie, you'll have to take off the belt every time you want to drink, and this can be something of a problem at the height of battle, even a simulated battle.

What Shall I Purchase First?

This is a fair question, and the answer is that you should buy those items that are the most difficult to borrow: rifle and boots. When you have these two essential pieces you should put together the basic necessary equipment: uniform jacket, hat, pants, belt, suspenders, socks, shirt, canteen, knapsack, cartridge box, and a bayonet and scabbard. Give it a few weeks, at least, before you begin to buy on a grand scale. Once you've decided you're in for the long haul, however, you should make efforts to obtain as much equipment as you can as soon as possible.

Your boots will be the most important part of your uniform. Just as the Civil War soldier of old did, so you will you do your share of marching and drilling. Buy an ill-fitting pair of boots and you'll surely regret it. Always try them on before you make your purchase. You'll spend most of your reenacting time in them, even asleep. Make sure there's plenty of room for socks; you'll need at least a couple of pairs in cold weather.

Where Can I Find Weapons & Equipment?

The following is a list of sellers and manufacturers from whom you can purchase your every need. Most of them will deal direct through the mail and have catalogs to support their businesses. It's recommended that you find a supplier, or suppliers, from among these names. They are all known for their fair dealings, and the authenticity of their products. Almost all are small businesses. Their owners are enthusiasts, and will go out of their way to help with answers to your questions. On the other hand, you should be wary of the many retail stores dealing in souvenirs; their prices are high, and the quality of their merchandise is often shoddy.

Uniforms

Tim Allen, 1429 Becket Road, Eldersburg, MD 21784. 410-549-5145. Confederate and civilian hats.

Lynn Ball, 702 N. Spruce Avenue, Goldsboro, NC 27534. Hats.

Ray Bass, Route 2, Box 4R, Newton Grove, NC 28366. 919-594-0070. Shirts, underwear, shoes and suspenders.

Bolivar Boutique, Route 1, Box 407, Walkerton, IN 46574. 219-586-3586. Ladies' period clothing and accessories. Free catalog.

Isaac Cantrell & Co, 933 Westedge Drive, Tipp City, OH 45371. 513-667-3379. Uniforms.

County Cloth, Inc., 13797-C Georgetown Street NW, Paris, OH 44669. 216-862-3307. Fax 216-862-3604. Top quality goods. Confederate and Union fabrics, patterns and pre-cut uniform kits. Catalog $5.

Crescent City Sutler, 127810 Highway 57N, Evansville, IN 47711. 812-938-4217. Male and female clothing, military and civilian. Also equipment and other supplies. Catalog $3.

Dirty Bill's Sutlery, 7574 Middleburg Road, Detour, MD 21757. 401-775-1865. Hats, military and civilian. SASE for brochure.

D.L. Roder, Clothier, 3607 Highway 48 North, Nunnelly, TN 37137. 931-729-5597. Uniforms.

Fugawee Corp., 3127 Corrib Drive, Tallahassee, FL 32308. 800-749-0387. Fax 904-893-5742. Jefferson bootees; comfort guaranteed; available in all sizes from 5E through 14EEE. Catalog $3.

Gettysburg Sutler, 424 R. East Middle Street, Gettysburg, PA 17325. 717-337-9669. Top quality, museum-grade reproductions: male, female and children, military and civilian.

Goldberg Textile Co., 2495 South Alden Street, Salt Lake City, UT 84106. 801-476-2343. Uniforms and uniform kits.

Grand Illusions, 108A East Main Street, Newark, DE 19711. 302-366-0300. Full-service outfitter of period clothing for men and women. They supplied the uniform and civilian clothing for the movie *Gettysburg*. Catalog $3.

His Lady and the Soldier Sutlery, 851 Kaypat Drive, Hope, MI 48628. 517-435-3518. Small goods – jewelry and accessories – for male and female reenactors. Catalog $2.

L&H Hats, 179 Melville Street, Dundas, ON L9H 2A9, Canada. 905-627-7492. Civilian and military hats, male and female.

Missouri Boot and Shoe Co., 951 Burr Crossing Road, Neosho, MO 64850. 417-451-6100. Top quality reproduction boots and shoes. Catalog $2.

Petticoat Junction, 307 Lakeside Avenue, Angola, NY 14006. 716-549-4998. Period clothing for men, military uniforms and civilian. SASE for catalog.

Salt Springs Sutler, 5645 Gulf Drive #1, New Port Richy, FL 34652. Period military uniforms, ladies' clothing, eyeglasses. Catalog free.

Greg Starbuck, 1581 General Booth Boulevard, #107, Virginia Beach, VA 23454. 804-583-2012. Kepis.

Suckerboys Clothing, 825 11th Street, Chaleston, IL 61920. Period clothing, male and female.

Uniforms of Antiquity, PO Box 613B, Mena, AR 71953. Military uniforms and kits.

Uriah Cap and Clothier, 220 Old Route 30, PO Box 93, McKnightstown, PA 17343. 717-337-3929. Handmade period headgear.

Winchester Sutler, 270C Shadow Brook Lane, Winchester, VA 22603. 703-888-3595. Fax 703-888-4632. Military and civilian period clothing. Catalog $4.

Weapons & Equipment

Border States Leatherworks, Route 4, 14 Appleblossom Lane, Springdale, AR 72764. 717-259-9081. Leather goods and weapons. Catalog $2.

Cartridges Unlimited, 3253 Nebraska Street, St. Louis, MO 63118. 314-664-4332. Black powder, cartridges and percussion caps. Catalog $3.50.

The Cavalry Shop, PO Box 12122, Richmond, VA 23241. Cavalry equipment, artillery gear, uniforms, etc.

Dixie Gun Works, Gunpowder Lane, Union City, TN 38261. 901-885-0700. Black powder supplies. Catalog $4.

Dixie Leatherworks, PO Box 8221, Paducah, KY 42002. Period leather goods, haversacks, etc. Catalog $2.

Drummer Boy, Christian Hill Road, RR 4, Box 7198, Milford, PA 18337. 717-296-7611. Firearms, tinware, insignia, buttons, leather goods and uniforms. Catalog $1.

Fairoaks Sutler, Route 2, Box 1100, Spotsylvania, VA 22553. 703-972-7744. Wide range of equipment. SASE for catalog.

Fall Creek Sutlery, PO Box 92, Whitestown, IN 46075. 317-482-1861. Fax 317-769-5335. E-mail afj5577@aol.com. Civil War era weapons, uniforms, shoes & boots, leather goods, tents, etc. Large catalog $3.

Fort Branch Supply, PO Box 222, Hamilton, NC 27840. 919-798-2671. Period military equipment, including wooden canteens.

Jarnigan, PO Box 1860, Corinth, MS 38834. 601-287-4977. Full-service supplies for reenactors.

Owens Accouterments, 1639 Belvedere Boulevard, Silver Springs, MD 20902. 310-681-7462. Manufacturer of museum-grade haversack, scabbards, and other leather goods.

Rapidan River Canteen Co., 16205 Trainham Road, Beaver Dam, VA 23015. 804-449-6431. Confederate wooden canteens.

Regimental Quartermaster, PO Box 553, Hatboro, PA 19040. 215-672-6891. Reproduction weapons, uniforms and equipment. Catalog $2.

S&S Firearms, 74-11 Myrtle Avenue, Glanedale, NY 11385. 718-479-1100. Fax 718-497-1105. Antique and reproduction firearms, gun parts, and other equipment for reenactors. Catalog $3.

Spencer Firearms, Inc., 5 S. Main Street, Sullivan, IL 61951. 217-728-7128.

Tentsmiths, PO Box 496, North Conway, NH 03860. 603-447-2344. Fax 603-447-2344. Period tenting. Catalog $2.

Reenacting For Men

Rank

If you're not an officer or noncommissioned officer (corporal of sergeant) you will, obviously, be a member of the ranks. How do you rise from this lowly status? Just as in the real military world, you have to earn your promotion within your own particular unit.

There are some exceptions to this, although often the recipients of these unearned ranks are not well thought of, nor do they receive the respect they think they should. Horse owners often award themselves officer status in the cavalry, dress for effect, and spend much of their time ordering around members of the infantry, over which they have no authority.

The one real exception where assumed rank is acceptable is in the artillery. A canon is a very expensive piece of equipment. A reproduction three-inch ordnance rifle, for example, can cost upwards of $10,000; the caisson and other equipment can cost as much again; a 12 pounder bronze Napoleon can cost $25,000. It's no wonder, then, that the owner of such a piece should be a lieutenant or captain of artillery. His dedication to reenacting, not to mention his investment, deserves no less. The owner of a canon and all its accouterments will also be the one who will re-cruit his gun crew, and will rank them according to position on the gun and skill in operating the weapon. He and his crew, however, will be expected to fall under the command of the offi-cer, usually a colonel or general, that's in overall command of the field, Union or Confederate.

You will be expected to show proper respect to all who rank above you, including civilian reenactors. Often officials of the times – state governors, congressmen, senators, cabinet mem-bers, even Presidents Lincoln or Davis – are portrayed by reen-actors. Should you encounter such individuals, you will be expected to come to attention, present arms, salute, just as you would in a real situation.

You will also be expected to pay your respects to lady reenac-tors: act with deference and courtesy.

Civilian Roles

Some reenactors prefer a less organized role in the field. These might include, but are not limited to, doctors, photographers, preachers, blacksmiths, sutlers, and so on. Unfortunately, the cost of the authentic equipment needed to support these roles is often prohibitive. Even so, these reenactors are essential to the overall ambiance of the event and there should be a place for one and all. If you do decide upon a civilian role, you should al-ways check with the organizers of each event to make sure you will be accepted in your chosen capacity, and that they will set aside a location from which you can operate.

One more thing, if you do decide to play a civilian role, you should know as much about it as possible. The chances are you will be bombarded with questions from both military reenactors and the spectators, so you'd better be knowledgeable and ready to answer.

Reenacting For Women

Women played many important roles in the conflict between the states. Most played supporting roles: seamstresses, letter writers, cooks, laundresses, and so on. Most nurses of the times, however, were men. Today, at reenactments, you'll see women everywhere, except on the battlefield, dressed in period costume. Most are spectators, wives of reenactors that enjoy playing a part just as much as their erstwhile partners on the field. These ladies also play an important role at the dress balls that are becoming more and more part of the larger events. These are happy events where the men wear dress uniforms and the ladies their finest gowns.

Rules of the Game

As already mentioned, your first responsibility is to learn and become familiar with the etiquette and manners of the period. Then, from the moment you step into uniform and onto the field, until you leave it again, stay in character. You'll adopt the demeanor, customs, speech patterns and social behavior that reflect the times. In short, you should become the person you are trying to portray, at least for the weekend.

At first, it will seem strange to be addressed by your fellow reenactors in the speech patterns of a by-gone era. You might even be tempted to laugh. Don't. This is serious business.

Always obey orders given by your superior officers, just as you would be expected to if you were a member of a modern military unit.

Safety and consideration for yourself, your fellow reenactors, and for the private property upon which most events take place, should always be first in your thoughts and actions. Reenacting can be dangerous. After all, even though live ammunition is never used, the weapons involved still can inflict serious wounds: bayonets, blank rounds, etc.

Never engage in hand-to-hand fighting, unless it's fully scripted and supervised.

When under fire, stay with your unit at all times.

If you do get hurt, or feel sick, go down and don't hesitate to call for assistance. You should understand, however, that such a call will immediately stop all the action.

Never move in front of, or get too close to, artillery units. Reenactors' cannon are usually charged with a one-pound load of black powder; the resulting blast at close range can do a great deal of damage. A ramrod placed across the mouth of a cannon means there's a live round in the barrel; a ramrod upright against a wheel of the cannon means the weapon is loaded and ready to fire.

When loading your own rifle, never use a ramrod. Black powder leaves a thick, sticky residue that can cause your ramrod to become stuck in the barrel. Also, it has been known, in the heat of the action, for a ramrod to be accidentally fired from the weapon; the result can be deadly.

It also goes without saying that bayonets should never be fixed on the field. In fact, they should be tied safely in their scabbards where they can do no harm.

It was not unusual for Civil War regiments to lose a third, even 50%, of their number during a battlefield engagement. This is usually also the case at reenactments. Don't be afraid to take a hit now and again. You can die on the field, or simply fall wounded. If you do, you can make all the noise you want. Wounded men of the day screamed in agony, called for their loved ones, and yelled for help; you can do the same. Don't overact, though, and don't fool around. Remember, you will often be reliving actual historical events, and you should respect the memory of the men who really did die.

When you take a hit, you should fall forward. This will prevent you from falling into someone behind you, or from falling on a rock or something you can't see that might do you harm. When on the ground, protect your weapon by lying on it, and lie still.

Sunglasses, or modern eyeglasses for that matter, should not be worn at reenactments. If you must wear eyeglasses, you should try to find an old pair of the period and have your prescription lenses fitted to them. Sometimes, at the larger opthamologists, you can find reproduction frames. Ovals were most common during the period, but it was not unusual to find hexagonals. If you can't find something that works, you might want to try contacts.

Sunstroke and heat exhaustion can sometimes become a problem at reenactments. The days are long and hot, the uniforms hot, heavy and uncomfortable, and you might need to spend several hours on your feet. Keep your canteen full and drink plenty of water. Keep the top of your head covered and, especially, your neck; wear a wide-brimmed hat or a bandanna.

During the winter, cold can be a problem, too. Wool uniforms are great insulators, but only to a point. Thermal underwear should be worn under the uniform; period gloves, if you can find them, will keep your hands warm, but an old pair of woolen socks will do just as well; never wear modern gloves. As to keeping your feet warm, try wearing a plastic bag between two pairs of socks.

Finally, always look to your own safety and that of others.

Bibliography

Catton, Bruce, *Mr. Lincoln's Army* 1951; *Glory Road* 1962; *A Stillness at Appomattox* 1953; *Gettysburg* 1974, Doubleday & Co, Inc, New York; *The Civil War* American Heritage Press, New York, 1971; *Grant Moves South* Little, Brown & Co, New York 1960.

Commager, Henry Steele (Ed) *The Blue and the Gray: The Story of the Civil War as told by the Participants* The Bobbs-Merrill Co Inc.

Davis, William C. (Ed) *The Image of War: 1861-1865* (6 vols) Doubleday & Company, Inc, New York 1984.

Grant, Ulysses S. *Personal Memoirs of U.S. Grant* L. Webster & Co, New York, 1894.

Humble, Richard *The Illustrated History of the American Civil War* Multimedia Publications (UK) Ltd, London, 1986.

Long, A.L. (Ed) *Memoirs of Robert E. Lee* The Blue & Gray Press, Inc., New Jersey, 1983.

Macdonald, John *Great Battle of the Civil War* Macmillan Publishing Company, New York, 1988.

Murfin V. James *Battlefields of the Civil War* Colour Library Books Ltd., (UK) Surrey, England, 1988.

Rossiter, Johnson *Campfires & Battlefields* The Civil War Press, New York, 1967.

Time Life Books *The Civil War* (27 vols), Alexandria, VA, 1988.